THE FUTURE FACE OF TERRORISM

The Future Face of Terrorism

Dr. S.K. Awasthi

MD Publications Pvt Ltd
New Delhi
www.mdppl.com

Published by :

MD Publications Pvt Ltd
"MD House", 11, Darya Ganj,
New Delhi - 110 002
Phone : +91-11-41563325 (Customer Service)
+91-11-41562846 (Editorial)
E-mail (orders): order@mdppl.com
Website: www.mdppl.com

ISBN: 978-81-7533-205-8

Published and Printed by Mr. Pranav Gupta on behalf of **MD Publications Pvt Ltd** at Times Press, New Delhi.

PREFACE

In our modern world, discomforting truths are usually discarded in favour of fictions. One such fiction is the idea that terrorists are disenfranchised dissidents who independently generate the wealth and resources necessary for their heinous acts.

The face of terrorism is changing. While the motivations remain the same, we are now facing new and unfamiliar weapons. The intelligence systems, tactics, security procedures and equipment that were once expected to protect people, systems, and nations, are powerless against this new, and very devastating weapon. Moreover, the methods of counter-terrorism that our world's specialists have honed over the years are ineffectual against this enemy. Because, this enemy does not attack us with truckloads of explosives, with briefcases of sarin gas or dynamite strapped to the bodies of fanatics. This enemy attacks us with ones and zeros; at a place we are most vulnerable, the point at which the physical and virtual worlds converge. Let us first define these two domains.

In the past, terrorists have been ruthless opportunists, using a bloody, but relatively narrow, range of weapons to further clear, political ends. The next 15 years may well be the age of super terrorism, when they gain access to weapons of mass destruction and show a new willingness to use them. Tomorrow's most dangerous terrorists will be motivated not by political ideology, but by fierce ethnic and religious hatreds. Their goal will not be political control, but the utter destruction of their chosen enemies. Nuclear, biological, and chemical weapons are ideal for their purpose.

The face of global terrorism is changing so rapidly and dramatically that counter-terrorism experts and security agencies are finding it almost impossible to keep track of the growth and spread of terrorist networks. Today's jihadi is home-grown, autonomous, and computer-savvy and is willing to give up the comforts of middle-class home to become a suicide bomber.

The Al Qaeda, which represents global jihad, is witnessing a makeover today, transforming itself into myriads of cells safely sheltered in unsuspecting societies, staffed by young men who would otherwise find place in sedate community newspapers as benign volunteers.

I am very grateful to Mr. Pranav Gupta, Director of MD Publications Pvt Ltd, New Delhi, for his cooperation and support for this book.

Dr. S.K. Awasthi

Contents

Preface *v*

1. Future Face of Terrorism: An Introduction 1
2. The New Face of Terrorism 15
3. The Changing Face of Terrorism 33
4. The New Terrorism and their Origins 65
5. International Efforts against New Terrorism 91
6. Defeating New Terrorist 127
7. The Effects of War and Terrorism on Children 149
8. Terrorism and the New Security Strategy 177
9. Tomorrow's Terrorist and their Expertise 225
10. The Truth about Terrorism 249
11. Future of Suicide Terrorism 297
12. Future of Terrorism 321

Bibliography 357

Index 361

1

Future Face of Terrorism
An Introduction

In the past, terrorists have been ruthless opportunists, using a bloody, but relatively narrow, range of weapons to further clear, political ends. The next 15 years may well be the age of super terrorism, when they gain access to weapons of mass destruction and show a new willingness to use them. Tomorrow's most dangerous terrorists will be motivated not by political ideology, but by fierce ethnic and religious hatreds. Their goal will not be political control, but the utter destruction of their chosen enemies. Nuclear, biological, and chemical weapons are ideal for their purpose. They will increasingly be joined by another variety of terrorist—criminals with the goal of maximizing profit, minimizing risk, and protecting their enterprises by intimidating or co-opting government officials.

We have already seen their brand of terrorism in Colombia and holy war "criminal terrorism" has not yet been fully accepted as a legitimate target for the antiterrorist community. We use counterterrorist forces against "narcoterrorists," for example, but still believe we are diverting specialized resources to aid the "war on drugs." Before the 1990s are over, we will be forced to recognize that it is the method, not the motive, which makes a terrorist. Alongside all of these developments, the traditional brand of terrorism—seeking political power through the violent intimidation of noncombatants—will continue to grow at the global rate of about 15% per year.

Instability bred by the proliferation of the more violent religious and ethnic terrorist groups, coupled with an almost exponential growth in "mini-states" in the former Soviet Union and Eastern Europe, could produce a two-to three-fold increase in international terrorist incidents by the turn of the century. Technology in particular has made terrorism more attractive to dissident groups and rogue states. In the high-tech global village that the world is fast becoming, modern telecommunications provides near real-time coverage of terrorist attacks, whether in Beirut, Buenos Aires, Khartoum, or New York. As terrorism expert Brian Jenkins has noted, terrorism is theater and terrorists can now play to a global audience. As we move into the twenty-first century, new and even more powerful communications links will give terrorism still greater power and appeal.

Super-terrorism

The most ominous trend in terrorism is also a matter to technology. With the end of the Cold War, weapons of mass destruction have slipped from their traditional controls. If nuclear, biological, or chemical weapons are not yet available to terrorist organizations and the states that support them, they soon will be. The proliferation of mass-destruction technologies and of groups that actively seek to inflict mass casualties has forever changed the face of terrorism. This confluence of means and will is a benchmark development that has qualitatively changed the nature of the terrorist challenge. According to members of both the Futurist and Terrorist Advisory Boards, assembled by Forecasting International, an improvised nuclear, biological, or chemical attack on the United States is increasingly probable — perhaps within the next five years.

Though North Korea's weapons program represents a

pressing concern, the former Soviet Union and its one-time satellite states present the greater risk. In North Korea, such weapons remain under the firm control of a strong central government, whose willingness to distribute them is a troubling possibility but is not yet clear. In many former communist states, control over many of these weapons has been so badly weakened that it may not matter what their central government intends. Throughout the former East Bloc, scientists, technicians, and military personnel have families to feed, but suddenly lack jobs to pay their way. Many have firsthand knowledge of biological, chemical, and nuclear weapons. Therefore, many states and terrorist groups are hungry for their expertise and able to pay handsomely for it.

The weapons themselves may also be an immediate danger. While state strategic nuclear weapons remain too well guarded to be stolen or sold, tactical weapons lie scattered across what is left of the Soviet Union. Controls over these weapons are reportedly lax, and there is little hope that they will remain where Soviet troops left them. A single artillery round could provide enough material for a crude but effective nuclear device, particularly if it were designed for contamination rather than for use as a conventional nuclear weapon. Chemical and biological weapons are even easier to acquire. Neurotoxins are closely related to many pesticides. Anyone capable of making common agricultural chemicals can make these poisons. As early as 1972, American authorities broke an ultra-right-wing terrorist organization and discovered a weapons cache that included 80 pounds of botulin toxin, a deadly food poison.

Today, genetic engineering is sophisticated enough to produce even more virulent, custom-tailored pathogens. With such technology within the reach of many would-be terrorists, this is one form of proliferation that no one can even hope to prevent. Easy access to biological, chemical, and nuclear technologies will bring many new players to the game of mass destruction; they may not even be limited to states and traditional terrorist groups. Organized crime, fanatical single-issue groups, and even individuals will all be able to acquire weapons once limited to regional and world powers. Using chemical or nuclear-type weapons effectively would be easy, too. For example, if the World Trade Center bombers had packed their van with cobalt-60 or iodine-131 (both commonly available in medical and industrial laboratories), they might well have rendered New York's financial district uninhabitable for generations.

Pulmonary anthrax kills 99% of the victims it infects, and only a few grams would be needed to kill virtually everyone in a major government office complex. If released in a subway tunnel, the convection currents created by the passing trains would carry the spores throughout the system, to be inhaled by thousands of commuters. Clinging to people's clothing, the anthrax spores would also be spread through offices, public buildings, and suburban homes. Thousands would die. It would be days before we even know we had been attacked, and it would be virtually impossible to assign blame. Those weapons will be used, and not only because once possessed they represent an overwhelming temptation, but because — in the United States particularly — the public pays attention only to the spectacular. A year after the World Trade Center bombing, the blast was little more than a dim memory, to be revived only briefly when the perpetrators were brought to trial.

Future terrorists will find that they need ever more spectacular horrors to overcome people's capacity to absorb and forget what previously would have seemed intolerable. In the past, other concerns would have restrained terrorists from using weapons of mass destruction. Politically motivated terrorists require popular support to function. That support is seldom as committed or ruthless as the violent core of a terrorist movement, and the true extremists must temper their actions so as to avoid alienating the sympathies of those they hope to recruit, as well as those who provide money and logistical support. But for many of those now embarking on terrorist careers, those restraints do not apply.

Ethno Religious Terrorism

Since the end of the Cold War, many forces have combined to unleash terrorist causes that either are new or had been buried under the crushing weight of the Soviet security apparatus. Where most old-line terrorist organizations served political causes, in the early twenty-first century they will be joined by a growing number of terrorist groups that are motivated by religious fervor or ethnic hatred. This is a dangerous development. With many traditional terrorist groups, we could assume that their targets and tactics would be constrained by the need to retain political sympathies. We appear to be entering an era in which few, if any, restraints will remain.

Religious and ethnically motivated terrorists are more willing than most to pursue their aims by whatever means necessary. Unlike politically motivated terrorists, religious fanatics do not shrink from mass murder because they are struggling against what they perceive as "the forces of darkness" or are striving to preserve such quasi-mystical concepts as "the purity of the race." Mass casualties are not to be shunned, because they demonstrate the cataclysmic nature of divine retribution.

If innocents suffer, God will sort them out. The late Hussien Mussawi, leader of the Shiite Muslim group Hezbollah, once commented, "We are not fighting so that the enemy recognizes us and offers us something. We are fighting to wipe out the enemy." Radical Islam not only attacks moderate Arab regimes, but has spread beyond the Middle East. It now has significant followings in Muslim communities in Africa, Asia, Europe, and the Americas.

Ethnically motivated terrorists are driven by forces almost as powerful — a visceral, tribal fealty with a mystical and almost religious overlay. These terrorists are defending their family and community, the memory of their ancestors, their cultural heritage, and the identity of their people, any of whom have suffered and died simply because they were Armenians, Bosnians, Basques, Irish, Quiche, Ibo, or Kurds. They believe that their enemies seek the subjugation or annihilation of their people. It is the ethno terrorist's sacred duty to prevent this evil, not only for the sake of the living and future generations, but out of reverence for the dead.

Given such powerful motives, ethno religious extremists are the terrorists most likely to kill indiscriminately and to embrace weapons of mass destruction. Thus, Hezbollah, the Basque ETA, and the Tamil Tigers rank among the world's most professional and deadly terrorist groups.

Many ethnic groups, liberated by the collapse of communism, are now free to act on their ancient hatreds. Their animosities threaten to engulf the patchwork of states and independent republics that have emerged from the ruins of the Soviet empire. Only now are we beginning to learn their names, histories, and agendas. Because such groups were of little interest to the traditional intelligence collector, Western security services know little about their ethnic allies or their depth of support, either on their home turf or in other countries.

Economic Terrorism

Terrorist operations that target a nation's economy can be extremely effective. Radical Egyptian Islamists attacking foreign terrorists have all but destroyed Egypt's lucrative tourist trade, dealing a serious blow to the nation's economy. The discovery of two cyanide-tainted grapes almost destroyed the export market for Chilean produce. Even Mother Nature can be enlisted in the terrorist cause. One potential weapon could be the Mediterranean fruit fly, a voracious agricultural pest that feeds on some 250 varieties of fruits, plants, and nuts. A malevolent Johnny Appleseed could single-handedly devastate the economies of whole regions. California produce, for example, earns the state $18.1 billion annually.

Recent reports of a sophisticated counterfeiting operation in Lebanon's Bekka Valley underscores how counterfeiting may be used as a more unconventional weapon. Using state-of-the-art equipment, American $100 bills are being churned out by terrorists. They are of such high quality that even experienced bank officials were fooled. If terrorists were to flood a country with high-quality counterfeit currency, economic confidence and faith in the government could take a nosedive, particularly if such an operation were combined with other forms of economic warfare and more-conventional forms of terrorism.

Other operations could target a nation's infrastructure. Our increasing dependence on the information superhighway could provide terrorists a new spectrum of targets. Several nations are believed to be developing computer viruses to disrupt military command and control systems, as well as other vital computer-dependent components of a nation's infrastructure. A massive disruption of East Coast telephone service in 1992, coupled with the airlines' dependence on it, forced flights scheduled to land in New York and other eastern cities to divert and major airports to close down. The failure was attributed to the system's dependence on telephone networks, which were handling an unusually high volume of holiday traffic. We must expect that rogue states and terrorist groups are exploring techniques to induce such failures by attacking the critical nodes of interdependent communications systems. International banking systems would also be particularly lucrative targets for both terrorists and criminal elements. Doubtless, such groups are exploring ways to penetrate and alter account information, as well as to manipulate electronic fund transfers. Stock exchanges would similarly be at risk.

In the future, we may expect some industries and governments to engage in systematic campaigns to destroy their economic competitors, as well as to advance their political position. Spreading false rumors and engaging in forms of psychological warfare will become increasingly common, as will more-direct measures that could include product contamination, intimidation, and terrorist operations. State-sponsored operations, such as the bombing of Greenpeace's ship, Rainbow Warrior, by a French sabotage team, are less likely in the future. Governments inclined toward such activities are more likely to develop "arrangements" with organized crime, which will carry out operations for money or favours.

We can expect increased criminal terrorism and criminal alliances. Improbable opportunistic alliances of criminal gangs have achieved a global reach. Highly sophisticated Nigerian drug barons are linked to Jamaican posses that, in turn, use California-based gangs such as the Bloods and the Crips for distribution and enforcement purposes. The Italian and Russian mafias, as well as organized crime in the United States, are developing operational linkages and will probably diversify into new enterprises ranging from trafficking in weapons of mass destruction to manipulation of stock market and international banking systems. Criminal enterprises along the lines of the Bank of Commerce and Credit International (BCCI) will become increasingly common. The BCCI operation not only engaged in massive money laundering and defrauding of its shareholders, but also served as a financial conduit to some of the world's most-dangerous terrorist groups.

We can also expect a growing nexus between criminal multinational and established political parties, perhaps along similar lines as the relationship that has existed in Italy for the past 40 years and that recently brought down the ruling Christian Democratic Party and some of Italy's most-prominent political figures. A similar system of opportunistic alliances is emerging in the republics of the former Soviet Union, where local and ethnic mafias have gotten a lock on the emerging private sector by allying with elements in the security service and party apparatus. Single-issue groups will also evolve in the years to come. For example, the militant wing of the antiabortion movement is likely to split.

The larger and less dangerous faction will confine its activities to largely high-profile, but essentially legal, forms of protest. The other, driven by religious imperative, will turn to violence as traditional means of protest prove ineffective. Two assumptions guide this belief. One is that Roe v. Wade will not be overturned. The other is that the current administration in Washington will investigate and prosecute crimes of the violent fringe far more aggressively than its recent predecessors. In this, it will win support from the public, which appears increasingly alienated by the strong-arm tactics of militant antiabortion groups. These factors will drive antiabortion extremists underground, where isolation will further distort their view of reality. Frustration and rejection will almost surely spur them to new violence. Environmental extremists and radical animal-rights advocates are less likely to escalate their violence than the radical antiabortionists. Rather, they will develop more-sophisticated ways to harass and sabotage their ideological enemies. Their goal will be the highest possible psychological impact — not destruction for its own sake.

As a Strategic Weapon

Terrorism has seldom threatened the core interests of the United States. Yet, it has had more of an impact than most policy makers care to admit. Much of Europe and the Middle East believe that the 1983 bombing of the U.S.

embassy and Marine barracks in Beirut drove the United States out of Lebanon — graphic testimony to the power of two truck bombs and the will of their suicidal drivers. (In truth, to the extent that they choose to think about it, many Americans are probably under the same impression.) The successful seizure of the U.S. embassy in Tehran and the 444-day ordeal of its staff dramatically raised the prestige of Islamic militants and the Khomeini revolution. It was also widely credited for the defeat of President Carter's bid for a second term — no mean feat for a clutch of student radicals.

Whether or not these beliefs are correct is beside the point. As in so many aspects of politics and war, perception is key. As long as terrorists believe they can strike at the United States and its interests effectively and with almost total impunity, they will continue to do so. Further, terrorist states will shape their foreign policy in the belief that the West's interests need not be taken into account. For many years, the United States has promised "swift and effective" retribution for terrorist acts, but it has seldom delivered. In the eyes of terrorists around the world, the United States has become a "paper tiger."

And because most allies of the United States have been no more effective in combating terrorism, many terrorists find the price of hitting Western targets, including U.S. ones, eminently affordable. In the "new world disorder," terrorism remains a very attractive option for the weak and the desperate — and for governments who wish to maximize their leverage while concealing their hand. In the Third World, particularly Africa, the Western democracies will increasingly be targeted for their perceived failure to stem their slide into chaos. The West will also be held responsible for many natural and political calamities. Already, the United States has been accused of creating the AIDS virus as a weapon to decimate blacks, a canard that has found acceptance abroad and even within the African-American community.

In general, state-sponsored terrorist incidents should continue their recent decline, largely because Western democracies are better able to identify the sponsors and to retaliate. But there is a downside. Those operations that are carried out will represent the core interests of the sponsoring state and thus may be pursued with more resources and greater zeal. As a consequence, they are more likely to be terrorist "spectaculars" on the scale of the bombing of Pan Am Flight 103 or the "Munich massacre" of Israeli Olympic athletes. To conceal their sources of support, terrorist operations will use increasingly sophisticated tradecraft. Rogue states will also look to their nationals living in the immigrant ghettos of the United States and Western Europe to establish support networks and, on occasion, serve as cannon fodder. Because many are illegal immigrants, they leave no paper trail. This places security services at an additional disadvantage.

In some cases, it may remain uncertain whether a catastrophe was a terrorist operation or merely an unfortunate accident. This was the likely intent of the Libyans who bombed Pan Am Flight 103. Investigators believe the explosion was timed to occur over the ocean, where the recovery of wreckage for forensic analysis would have been difficult or impossible. In that case, the crash might well have been written off as a tragic accident. One form of state-sponsored terrorism that will certainly continue is the assassination and intimidation of political dissidents living in exile abroad. Such operations will continue to increase because no world power has taken serious action to punish the offending states. Instead, host countries almost invariably have allowed murderous regimes to operate on their soil, as long as their own citizens are not targeted. As long as most governments seek to placate and accommodate the terrorists, it will remain open season on political refugees.

Defending Against Terrorism

Governments generally respond to increased terrorism by beefing up the security of government installations, key components of the nation's infrastructure, and other lucrative targets. This pressures the terrorists to seek softer targets that effectively coerce the government to meet their demands. Operations that generate large civilian casualties fit these parameters and are anywhere large numbers of people gather. Choice targets include sports arenas, shopping malls, houses of worship, and movie theaters. Targets such as the World Trade Center not only provide the requisite casualties but, because of their symbolic nature, provide more bang for the buck. In order to maximize their odds for success, terrorist groups will likely consider mounting multiple, simultaneous operations with the aim of overtaxing a government's ability to respond, as well as demonstrating their professionalism and reach.

Despite all this, terrorism will remain a back-burner issue for Western leaders as long as the violence strikes in distant lands and has little impact on their fortunes or those of their constituents. Until a country's citizens believe that terrorism poses a significant threat, traditional economic and political concerns will remain paramount. The industrialized nations will be too busy jockeying for access to markets and resources to be concerned with the less immediate problems. In a world dominated by economic and political interests, most of the industrialized West will deal with terrorism one incident at a time, playing it by ear. Many developed states will seek accommodation with terrorists and their sponsors, as long as they can find a "fig leaf" to minimize potential embarrassment. France and Germany have done business this way for many years.

Both to secure immunity and for commercial advantage, Paris and Bonn have tacit agreements with some of the world's most-lethal terrorist groups and their state supporters. France has reportedly formalized some of these arrangements in writing. Terrorists in the early years of the twenty-first century will reflect the causes that excite passion and move people to violence. During this period of tumult and transition, terrorism and other forms of low-intensity conflict will increase until a new stasis or "world order" is established. Religious and ethnically motivated terrorists, who exhibit few constraints now, will have within their grasp the potential to create the Armageddon they seek. It is this confluence of will and means that has forever changed the face of terrorism. As a consequence, we will face future dangers that would have seemed wildly improbable only a few years ago, and we must prepare to defend ourselves against them.

2

The New Face of Terrorism

Terrorism has been around for some time. There have been over 6,500 documented incidents since 1980 resulting in more than 5,000 dead and 12,000 injured. While terrorism may take many forms, the one that concerns businesses the most is the terrorist bomb. When United States' companies first decided to develop contingency plans for extended unplanned outages in the mid 1970s, the compelling reasons were natural disasters and the resulting power outages that usually accompanied them. The basis of their concern and the reason for taking action was to protect the heart of all businesses; the data center. There were not enough computers integrated into businesses in 1965 when the first great Northeast Power Outage occurred to stimulate much activity in contingency planning. However, a second similar event in 1974 served as a wake-up call to many companies as they witnessed their business operations come to a screeching halt as evidenced by the fatal silence of their power-starved computer rooms.

Business recovery planning and awareness have matured substantially in most companies since that time. An entire new industry has been created to provide for the new and more complex recovery requirements of American businesses. It is not difficult today to find alternate recovery sites, consultants, software, education and publications dedicated entirely to products and services for contingency-minded companies. The business recovery industry has evolved to include the wherewithal to provide for total business recovery; including end-user recovery and a wide variety of resumption services. For all these advances in requirements and capabilities and for all the maturity and sophistication that has characterized business contingency planning in recent times, the specter of terrorism as a meaningful and realistic threat has begun to pose some new and very unique problems.

Customers in the United Kingdom cite "bombings" as the number one threat to their businesses and the primary reason they engage in contingency planning. The statistics bear that out. Of the 467 most recently documented international disasters (excluding the United States), 6 percent were caused by bombing. Until the incident at the World Trade Center in February 1993, this category did not even appear in the statistics for the United States in a significant way. After the World Trade Center incident, "bombing /sabotage" jumped to 8% of all causes of declared disasters, the fourth most frequent cause behind power (29%), storm (11%) and flood damage (10%).

A large proportion of the international terrorist incidents (approximately 2,500 or 38%) have been directed at the United States. These incidents include hostage-taking and terrorist bombing, among others. Most of these acts, however, have occurred against U.S. properties overseas. The State Department, nevertheless, was so concerned about these incidents and threats that the Act to Combat International Terrorism (Public Law 98-533) was passed in 1984. This law, known as the Rewards Program for Terrorism Information, provides up to 2 million dollars for information that prevents or resolves acts of terrorism.

The bombing at the World Trade Center signaled a significant change in the tactics of international terrorists. It should have provided a serious warning about the potential dangers of the calculated detonation of an explosive device in a large office building. It is not clear, however, that the pure and simple impacts of such a demonstration of violence were fully appreciated and acted upon. The most likely reason for this, perhaps, is that the most significant business impact of the Trade Center bombing was denial of access. Once that problem was resolved, many companies had little difficulty in resuming normal business. The April 19, 1995 bombing of the Alfred P. Murrah Federal Building in Oklahoma City, on the other hand, was a very different incident. It was similar only in the fact that the explosion was caused by a terrorist bomb. Almost every other aspect of Oklahoma City differed from the World Trade Center incident.

First, the World Trade Center bombing was a true disaster but the Oklahoma City bombing was an American tragedy. The loss of life was appalling and the impact on the community was devastating. An enormous feeling of loss and sorrow reached out from TV screens all across the nation and touched every viewer, every night, in their living rooms. Shocked Americans everywhere counted the bodies and mourned the children, too stunned to believe it and far too angry to even begin to understand the long-term ramifications of this utterly senseless act. There has been nothing in our history to compare this to; no example of what to do, what to say or how to behave. There was no guidance to help people understand that which had no explanation. But yet somehow, the people, the community and the businesses are expected to eventually put this catastrophe behind them and move on. And one way or another they will.

The World Trade Center bombing was the work of international terrorists; Oklahoma City was a home-grown event. Some people viewed the Oklahoma City bombing as a stab in the back from an unexpected quarter. There are those whose emotions felt betrayed that Americans committed this ruthless act; who would have somehow understood better if the plot was hatched by radicals from foreign shores. The pragmatists, however, see this as an escalation in the threat probability; a greater risk of future terrorist bombings from yet another source. The World Trade Center bombing in New York City was intended to make a political statement in the starkest terms. Choosing to do this in the media capital of the world was neither an accident nor a surprise. Terrorists wage psychological warfare and frighten and intimidate by the threat of action as well as the action itself.

This usually results in attacks on highly visible, high profile targets. It is this technique that the terrorist employs to gain the most widespread publicity. Oklahoma City changed all of that. These fanatics chose an obscure target, perhaps deciding that its obscurity made it that much more vulnerable. And they decided to make it a particularly savage attack; apparently to assure the notoriety that might otherwise be absent in Oklahoma City. The message is clear; there is no place, however removed from the mainstream that is invulnerable to a terrorist bomb. Those that have considered themselves and their businesses secure from this threat because their location is remote or removed from the beaten track should heed the warning of Oklahoma City; no place, however removed, is safe. This event has significantly raised the stakes!

Finally, there is a substantial difference to the business impact between the World Trade Center and Oklahoma City. There was a disruption of one day, a Friday, on February 26, 1993 when the WTC was bombed. Most of the 900 businesses were ill-prepared as they found it necessary to return to their offices (under the watchful eye of a Port Authority Police escort) to recover critical records and files. Thankfully, in this case, most companies were able to resume normal business because they were able to locate and retrieve data and equipment. We were even able to witness, through the miracle of live television coverage, many businesses disaster recovery contingency plans in action. Unfortunately, some of these plans consisted of nothing more than an old coffee cart piled up with personal computers, floppy disks and peripherals as they were wheeled continuously out of the lobby of the World Trade Center throughout the weekend.

There would be no such luxury in Oklahoma City. Destruction on this scale leaves no margin for error or forgives any omission in a disaster recovery plan. Everything in the building was destroyed and anything needed for business resumption, especially data, had better have been backed up someplace else. This is just one small example of the differences between an Oklahoma City-type disaster and those that we have been coping with the last few years. Contingency planners should be re-evaluating their plans with Oklahoma City in mind, especially since the probabilities of a repeat event in the future just jumped off the scale.

What areas of contingency planning need to be re-examined in light of this increased threat? To start with, it is essential to review the equipment replacement provisions of the plan. Older equipment particularly that which may be difficult if not impossible to replace must be identified. The used equipment market, leasing companies or brokers may be able to locate the required types and quantities. The contingency planner must then evaluate the cost case and either acquires the replacement gear or recommend an upgrade to more modern and therefore more readily available equipment.

Those companies that store backup tapes in that huge fireproof vault in the basement should rethink that approach in light of the nature of the Murrah Federal Building disaster. Everything in the lower levels was covered by over 25 tons of debris and, if not completely destroyed, could not have been accessed for an extended period of time assuming there was a vault that was not crushed. Even the practice of keeping the latest backups on site while sending prior versions to an off-site vault should be reconsidered. (This practice is a holdover from the days when head crashes were a more common occurrence and data center managers wanted the backup tapes within easy reach for a quick recall). Recovery plans should also consider the use of an alternate site for office workers. Buildings damaged as severely as the Murrah Federal Building will never be repaired and reoccupied. Both temporary and permanent replacement quarters need to considered in any plan.

Alternate site vendors do provide office and end-user office space but in a case like this, it is probably a better bet to make arrangements for another facility reasonably close to the damaged site. Had this disaster struck a building with a large computing center, the business impacts might have been cataclysmic. Presuming that there was an alternate site recovery plan for the data center, it was clear that many of the personnel would have been unwilling or unable to travel there for recovery purposes. Whether an alternate site recovery plan is in place with an outside supplier or with another data center within the same enterprise, a successful recovery would have been unlikely if it depended on people from the afflicted site. Therefore, prudent recovery planning and subsequent exercises should be designed to achieve business recovery and continuity without the onsite presence of the client's recovery specialists.

Contingency planning managers are not the only corporate personnel who are compelled to re-think their plans. Security managers are also challenged by the higher threat of the probability of bombings in the United States punctuated by the Oklahoma City occurrence. They, more than most, realize that there were over 1900 bombings in the U.S. in 1992 (according to statistics from the Bureau of Alcohol, Tobacco and Firearms), compared to under 600 bombings in 1982. They also know, based on those same statistics, that bombings have increased every year since 1981 and there is no reason to expect that this trend will not continue. Compounding this bleak outlook is the considered opinion of most security experts that it is nearly impossible to prevent a bombing conducted by a determined, highly motivated and well backed radical group or individual.

It is questionable whether current structures can be made "bomb-proof" with retro-fit building modifications. It is also highly doubtful that the architecture and design of many future buildings will be strengthened to better withstand a bomb. It is simply too expensive and would result in unsightly and unfriendly structures. Weight bearing vertical columns, however, will most likely be made round in the future (instead of square) because square columns are more susceptible to the pressure of the explosion's shock wave. So what can be done to mitigate this risk today? There are a few actions that can be taken.

As a result of the 1983 destruction of the U.S. Marine Barracks in Beirut by a truck bomb, the United States government began developing a high-tech sensor called EGIS. Today, EGIS is on guard at 18 airports and screens cars boarding the new Chunnel rail service (between England and France). It can detect minute fragments of residues used to make explosives. This may be an answer for highly sensitive installations. There is also a software system on the market today called Bomb CAD. This program will assess the vulnerability of a structure to explosive blasts by simulating the detonation of devices at various design points.

Finally, most security experts conclude that there is no substitute for vigilant and resourceful security personnel. It could be argued that an attempt could have been anticipated on April 19 (on April 19, 1992, FBI agents raided the homestead of Randall Weaver in Ruby Ridge, Idaho and shot and killed his wife and son; on April 19, 1993, the

Branch Davidian compound in Waco, Texas was assaulted by ATF agents) since this anniversary date is meaningful to some anti-government groups. However the federal government occupies over 8,000 office buildings in the U.S., so the precise one could have hardly been predicted.

Security can be improved in most buildings by simply keeping vehicles away from near proximity to the structure. Any bomb large enough to damage a building would necessarily have to be carried in a car or truck. If these vehicles are kept away from buildings, damage would be minimized. The truck that carried the explosives in the Oklahoma City incident was allowed to get within 15 feet of the building by using a pull-in lane. This was close enough to rupture enough vertical support columns to start the "progressive collapse" of the upper floors. Keeping vehicles away from buildings (as well as preventing them from parking under buildings) is the most significant action that security managers can take to significantly reduce the risk of a building collapse should an explosive device be detonated.

It also makes sense, according to the experts, to examine all letters and parcels coming into a building for explosives. The "Unabomber" appears to have been awakened by recent events and has become active once again. Yet another threat to be wary of and take precautions to prevent these policies, if strictly enforced, may discourage terrorists from even attempting to bomb buildings that exhibit a careful, firm and comprehensive security posture. As with all disasters, there are many lessons to be learned from Oklahoma City. Once the horror of the attack fades into the memories and people all over America begin to move on with their lives, perhaps some good could be gleaned from this event. Maybe, in the aftermath, the mixture of emotion and determination to prevent future disasters of this kind will result in real and tangible solutions and actions. Hopefully, the lessons learned from this tragedy will have a more profound and lasting impact than the "lessons not learned" from the disasters that preceded it.

Responding To Terrorism

The number and lethality of international terrorist incidents directed against U.S. interests increased last year. The Riyadh and Al Khobar bombings in Saudi Arabia resulted in the largest number of U.S. fatalities at the hands of international terrorists since the December 1988 downing of Pan Am 103 over Lockerbie, Scotland. Terrorist violence represents a serious threat to U.S. personnel, facilities, and interests around the world. Terrorism remains a complex phenomenon spawned by a mix of factors and motivations. Loosely organized groups of radical Islamics, such as those that carried out the bombing of the World Trade Center, pose a growing challenge. Established entrenched ethnic, nationalist, and religiously motivated terrorist movements continue to operate and have been joined by groups that espouse new causes and ideologies. Despite the collapse of the Soviet Union and international communism, leftist ideologically-based terrorists continue to operate. State sponsors of terrorism, particularly Iran, pose a significant continuing threat. Other state sponsors such as Syria, Libya, Iraq, and Sudan, although more cautious, provide safe haven and other forms of support to a variety of terrorist movements.

The world is in a period of transition and flux as it moves from the relative stability of the bipolar model to a new political order which has yet to be defined. The disintegration of the Soviet Union and the collapse of the East European communist regimes produced a power vacuum that has enabled nationalist, ethnic, and religious forces long thought dormant to reassert themselves and contribute to the volatility of the post-Cold War era. Violent militant Islamic elements, often with the help of state sponsors, now operate worldwide and have a demonstrated global reach.

Local and regional conflicts, famine, economic disparity, mass movements of refugees, brutal and corrupt regimes, and the increasing porosity of national borders contribute to instability — fueling a frustration and desperation that increasingly finds expression in acts of terrorism. Ready access to information and information technologies, coupled with the ability to communicate globally via the Internet, fax, and other media, provides terrorists new tools for targeting, fundraising, propaganda dissemination, and operational communication. Just as the established political order is in a state of fundamental flux and transition, so is terrorism and the challenge it presents to the United States, its friends, and its allies.

A Phenomenon in Transition

The terrorist threat has changed markedly in recent years, due primarily to five factors: the disintegration of the Soviet Union; changing terrorist motivations; the proliferation of technologies of mass destruction; increased access to information and information technologies; and the accelerated centralization of vital components of the national infrastructure, which has increased their vulnerability to terrorist attack. DoD expects that the majority of terrorism directed against U.S. targets will be tied to ethnic and religious conflicts. It will be primarily urban in nature, often occurring in capital cities. Terrorism for the foreseeable future will remain a weapon of choice for governments, groups, and other parties to conflict.

Traditionally, terrorist movements that affected U.S. security interests were politically motivated, and even the most brutal groups usually refrained from mass casualty operations for fear of alienating their political constituencies and potential recruits. Today, religiously motivated terrorism is increasingly ascendant. Religious zealots, when members of a terrorist group or cult, usually exhibit few such constraints and actively seek to maximize carnage. An additional threat comes from religious cults that view the coming millennium in apocalyptic terms and seek through violence to hasten Armageddon. DoD anticipates that as the year 2000 approaches, such movements will become increasingly prevalent, prominent, and lethal.

The proliferation of weapons of mass destruction and the availability of individuals schooled in their design and construction represent another development that impacts fundamentally on the nature of terrorism. The fragmentation of the former Soviet Union and the lack of adequate controls on biological, chemical, and nuclear technologies have resulted in a flood of buyers eager to purchase lethal material from an expanding black market or from rogue states. Added to this volatile mix are scientists and technicians prepared to sell their skills to the highest bidder.

An emerging and significant threat is represented by improvised biological, chemical, and nuclear devices that exploit technologies that once were the sole preserve of world and regional powers. The potential to decimate large population centers and wreak havoc on an unprecedented scale has devolved from nation states to groups and even individuals. The possibility of a biological Unabomber and all that implies is a fast approaching reality. Proliferation enables those who were traditionally at the margins to play a major role on the world stage. Improvised weapons of mass destruction will likely prove to be the great equalizers of tomorrow, providing the means for the disaffected and deranged to directly impact on the core interests of world powers.

Future Terrorism

Religious zealotry creates the will to carry out mass casualty terrorist attacks; proliferation provides the means.

It is this nexus of will and means that has forever changed the face of terrorism. Traditional forms of terrorism like car bombs, assassinations, suicide bombers, and aircraft downings will undoubtedly continue, but their impact will diminish as the public becomes increasingly inured to such operations. In a world of competing headlines, terrorists will find it necessary to escalate the carnage in order to maintain their ability to intimidate and terrorize. As a result, increased experimentation with improvised biological, chemical, and nuclear devices may be expected as a means to rivet public attention and thereby advance the terrorist agenda. Paradoxically, progress has made key elements of the national infrastructure increasingly vulnerable. These elements include telecommunications, energy distribution, banking and securities, transportation, military/defense, water supply, emergency services, and public health.

As countries modernize, they become increasingly dependent on sophisticated technologies, with computers both running and linking vital, once disparate systems into a national infrastructure. Because of its complexity and interdependence, infrastructure presents unique targeting opportunities to a technologically sophisticated adversary. Complex national infrastructures are vulnerable because they all have critical nodes or choke points that, if properly attacked, will result in significant disruption or destruction. The attack may be computer generated or rely on more conventional assaults employing truck bombs, dynamite, or cable cutting to unleash a chain of events in which a service grid, pipeline, or air traffic control system collapses in a cascading effect.

Major power failures that black out large parts of the country, systemic problems with the air traffic control system, and breaks in highly vulnerable gas and oil pipeline systems are covered in detail by the press, discussed on radio talk shows, and dissected and analyzed on the Internet. Terrorists, as part of the attentive public, are increasingly aware that the national infrastructure represents a high value and vulnerable target. Technological advances may have the unintended consequence of increasing system vulnerabilities. For example, fiber optic cables enable phone companies to use a single line to carry tens of thousands of conversations that not many years ago would have required thousands of separate copper cables.

The results have been greater efficiency, better service, and lower costs; however, there is a downside. Progress has heightened infrastructure efficiency, but the resultant reduction in redundancy has produced vulnerabilities that make U.S. infrastructure an increasingly attractive terrorist target. International banking and finance, transportation, the electric grid, the gas pipeline system, computer links and services, and more than 90 percent of all DoD communications are dependent on the telephone system. Major disruptions in service can be caused by an errant backhoe operator or an enterprising terrorist.

Combating Terrorism

DoD divides its response to terrorism into two categories. Antiterrorism refers to defensive measures used to reduce the vulnerability of individuals and property to terrorist acts. Counterterrorism refers to offensive measures taken to prevent, deter, and respond to terrorism. Both fall under the rubric of Combating Terrorism. Force Protection is the umbrella security program involving the coordinated efforts of key U.S. departments and agencies designed to protect military and civilian personnel, their family members, and U.S. property from terrorist acts.

In response to the recent tragedies in Saudi Arabia, the Joint Staff established a Deputy Directorate for Combating Terrorism under the Director of Operations, Joint Staff. The Directorate is charged with the mission of supporting the Chairman and the Joint Chiefs of Staff in meeting the nation's security challenges as they relate to combating terrorism now and into the next century.

DoD also has been a leader in recognizing the vulnerability of the national infrastructure. To obtain a better understanding of the nature and extent of the problem, the Under Secretary of Defense for Policy on March 9, 1995, established the Infrastructure Policy Directorate. Its primary responsibilities relate to infrastructure warfare and information assurance. The Directorate has briefed senior government and cabinet officials and is conducting an in-depth examination of key infrastructure elements to determine how they interrelate and how best to protect them from attack. A series of working groups have been established to ensure continuity of effort.

To meet the challenge, the Deputy Secretary of Defense in August 1996 established the Critical Infrastructure Protection Working Group (CIPWG) to support actions directed in Executive Order 13010, Critical Infrastructure Protection, which was signed by the President on July 15, 1996. The CIPWG addresses issues related to threats and vulnerabilities of the defense infrastructure and information systems, develops recommendations for assurance technologies and procedures, and examines roles for DoD in infrastructure protection and assurance.

Antiterrorism

In recognition of the changing nature of the terrorist threat, DoD on August 27, 1996, established the Antiterrorism Coordinating Committee (ATCC). The committee meets monthly, as well as on an as needed basis. Its purpose is to identify issues that affect force protection, exchange ideas and information, and develop policy recommendations. It also serves a valuable function by providing a synergism that enhances the effectiveness of DoD's antiterrorism planning. The Assistant Secretary of Defense for Special Operations and Low-Intensity Conflict and the Joint Staff Director for Operations co-chair the ATCC Senior Steering Group. Meetings are attended by representatives from the Services; the Joint Staff; the Office of the Assistant Secretary of Defense for Command, Control, Communications and Intelligence; the Defense Security Assistance Agency; the Defense Intelligence Agency (DIA); and other DoD elements as required.

To further the exchange of knowledge and experience, for the past seven years DoD has sponsored the Annual Worldwide Antiterrorism Conference. These conferences not only draw on the expertise of the U.S. antiterrorism community but on an international array of security, intelligence, and law enforcement specialists who offer new insights, perspectives, and recommendations for action. Each conference focuses on a particular theme and specific force protection issues. The 1996 theme was changing the terrorism mindset. Conference participants explored ways to make antiterrorism increasingly proactive rather than primarily defensive and reactive. They devoted considerable effort to the critical examination of terrorist attacks and the lessons learned. A conference report forwarded to Secretary Perry contains detailed recommendations for consideration and implementation.

To better prepare for the terrorist threats of the future and how they might impact on U.S. security interests, DoD in 1994 prepared a major study entitled, Terror-2000: The Future Face of Terrorism. The aim was to forecast the nature of the future terrorist threat, projecting significantly beyond the traditional one year timeframe. The study drew on the expertise and experience of American and foreign terrorism experts in an effort to anticipate changes in terrorist targeting, tactics, strategies, and capabilities. Many of the core predictions have come to pass and others appear increasingly likely. Central to the study were recommendations on how best to meet the future terrorist threat.

In response to the November 1995 bombing in Riyadh, Saudi Arabia, Secretary Perry established the Antiterrorism Task Force. The task force was directed to develop a plan of action to eliminate complacency and significantly enhance the security of DoD and DoD-associated facilities and personnel worldwide.

The task force forwarded 22 major initiatives and recommendations to Secretary Perry, who approved an implementation plan on July 15, 1996. The more recent Downing Report, which examined the June 1996 bombing of Khobar Towers, produced a second set of recommendations. These have fundamentally changed the way DoD does business with regard to antiterrorism.

As a result of these two tragedies, a number of initiatives have been implemented. On September 16, 1996, Secretary Perry issued a revised Directive 2000.12, entitled DoD Combating Terrorism Program. This directive mandated Department-wide combating terrorism standards. In recognition that intelligence is the first line of defense, steps are being taken to improve its collection and use, and to get the intelligence product into the hands of the local commanders. DIA is engaged in an aggressive long-term collection and analytic effort designed to provide the type of information that can aid local commanders detect, deter, and prevent terrorist attack. Close working relationships between DIA and other members of the national intelligence community are being made even stronger, and intelligence exchanges with U.S. friends and allies have been increased. Other members of the national intelligence community are being made even stronger, and intelligence exchanges with U.S. friends and allies have been increased.

To better protect the public and U.S. military forces from the consequences of a chemical or biological terrorist attack, the Commandant of the Marine Corps established a Chemical/Biological Incident Response Force (CBIRF).

Formed in April 1996, the CBIRF is uniquely qualified to perform consequence management in an environment contaminated by chemical or biological agents.

In addition to DoD's accelerated focus on combating terrorism activities, steps are being taken to improve overall force protection. These include giving local commanders operational control over force protection; strengthening cooperation with host nations; raising funding levels of force protection programs, particularly in the area of antiterrorism; making the Chairman of the Joint Chiefs of Staff the focal point for force protection activities, including initiatives to standardize antiterrorism and force protection training for deploying forces; and realigning certain force protection responsibilities from the Department of State to the Department of Defense. In addition, antiterrorism will be made a special interest item for inspectors general throughout the Department, and the Defense Federal Acquisitions Regulations will be changed to ensure antiterrorism readiness of DoD contractors.

Counterterrorism refers to DoD's offensive combating terrorism capabilities. These capabilities provide means to deter, defeat, and respond vigorously to all terrorist attacks against U.S. interests, wherever they may occur. Resources allocated to these sensitive activities have been significantly increased, and efforts are underway to maximize readiness so that U.S. counterterrorism forces are trained and equipped to meet any challenge posed by future forms of terrorism. U.S. counterterrorism forces receive the most advanced and diverse training available and continually exercise to maintain proficiency and to develop new skills. They regularly train with their foreign counterparts to maximize coordination and effectiveness. They also engage with counterpart organizations in a variety of exchange programs which not only hone their skills but also contribute to the development of mutual confidence and trust.

The war against terrorism will be a protracted conflict. It is war in which there are no front lines and in which terrorism's practitioners have intentionally blurred the distinction between combatants and noncombatants. Terrorism differs from traditional combat because it specifically targets the innocent and, as a result, is particularly repugnant. Because each terrorist group and the challenge it represents are unique, DoD must work with the interagency counterterrorism community to develop a flexible response that is a mix of political, economic, military, and psycho-social capabilities, tailored to meet a broad range of challenges and threats.

Terrorism is more than the bomb and the gun. It is a struggle that ultimately is fought in the political arena and, as such, is also a war of ideas and ideologies. Combating terrorism requires patience, courage, imagination, and restraint. Perspective is essential. Overreaction and bombast play into terrorist hands. Good intelligence, a professional security force, and a measured response are necessary. Most important for any democracy in its struggle against terrorism is a public that is informed and engaged, and understands the nature of the threat, its potential cost, and why the fight against terrorism is its fight too. It is how well the United States meets this challenge that will determine the winners, the losers, and the price paid by each.

3

The Changing Face of Terrorism

Public memory is short and we usually forget events as time passes. But are we going to forget the Mumbai terror attacks? What was there in 26/11 attack which has left an imprint in our minds? It is the method which the terrorists adopted which succeeded in creating an impact. And that was exactly what the terrorists wanted, shake us from within, make the event unique and get international coverage. They targeted the places where cream of the society, the diplomats and foreign nationals were staying. Their modus operandi was totally different.

They were not concerned with the common man on the road, in a busy marketplace, shrine or a railway station. This time they wanted to spread terror among those who thought they will be least affected with such an incident. The selection of locations like Taj Mahal Palace & Tower, The Oberoi Trident and Leopold Café were well thought out. The terrorists also wanted to convey another message loud and clear that they targeted the Jews when they attacked Nariman House.The mayhem started by 10 terrorists and the war they fought against our security forces has forced us to stop and think. There were many areas where we went wrong. Firstly we never imagined this kind of situation. When the terror attack actually happened, it took us by surprise. The image of gun toting some 20 something terrorists creating havoc in the commercial capital of India, explained much about the security system.

Who will answer some pertinent questions like why the Navy and the Coast Guard didn't get alert when they got information from RAW that there is a possibility of terror attack through sea route. When the terrorists started the carnage in Mumbai what was needed was prompt action. But instead we had the police first associating it with a gang war and more serious blunder was when the NSG Commandos reached the spot after 10 hours.

Enough time provided to the terrorists to chalk out their plan. To top it all live media coverage of the operations gave away vital clues to the terrorists. The worst nightmare the country saw didn't finish quickly. Coupled with this there were lapses on part of the government and the lax security system. The NSG Commandos arrived at the terror scene not in helicopters but in government buses. Is this how terrorism of this magnitude needs to be tackled?

Statistics reveal that there are only 2221 weapons for strength of 180000 policemen in Maharashtra. The alarming fact is that most of the police personnel have not opened fire for years. Now compare this with the terrorists who arrived here with ammunition fit for an army. They waged a battle for 60 hours and kept the NSG, the Marine Commandos, RAF and the police on their toes. How equipped was the police force in comparison? The bullet proof vests which the police officials were wearing may have been defective. Does it explain why the country lost its top officials? What happened on November 26 and continued till November 29 damaged the brand image of Mumbai. It also affected each one of us. We may not be a Mumbaikar but we could associate ourselves with the pain. It came as a jolt to us when we saw Mumbai bleeding. At the same time it left us wondering how safe we are in such situations.

We need to think seriously now and plug the loopholes in the system. Right now we are taking part in the blame game but what is important at this juncture is to find out how we faced it and how we plan to prepare for future. Is it by deploying best of forces for the protection of long list of VIPs and VVIPs or is it by creating Federal Investigating Agency whose investigation in terror incidents will not be hampered by bureaucratic delay. We need to ask ourselves some questions- Why after a week of the terror attacks in Mumbai RDX was found at Chatrapati Shivaji Terminus. Why no one cared to do a thorough search of the busy railway station after this gruesome incident. Why don't we fight terrorism on a war front and why we consider it as just another incident?

Face of Middle Eastern Terrorism

Terrorism is a cancer that has plagued the Middle East for decades. It is now metastasizing into new and more deadly forms that pose grave challenges to the United States and the West. Middle Eastern terrorists are striking outside their home region, boldly attacking high-profile targets, and killing in a more indiscriminate manner. Last year the U.S., which had never suffered a major terrorist attack on its soil by Middle Eastern terrorists, was rocked by the bombing of the World Trade Center in New York City, which killed six Americans and wounded over 1,000. This was the highest casualty toll ever recorded for a single terrorist incident. A subsequent bombing campaign against targets in New York City was stopped in its tracks in June 1993 by the Federal Bureau of Investigation.

The World Trade Center bombing embodies several ominous trends in Middle Eastern terrorism. It epitomizes the drift toward large-scale, indiscriminate violence. It also underscores the degree to which radical Islamic extremists have supplanted radical nationalists, such as the Palestine

Liberation Organization, as the chief Middle Eastern terrorist threat to the U.S. Moreover, radical Islamic groups are inciting Sunni (orthodox) Muslims to support revolutionary terrorism in Egypt and Algeria, just as radical Shia Muslims were incited by the Iranian revolution. Finally, the Sudanese connection of several of the bombers demonstrates how Sudan has become the "new Lebanon" — a host for a wide variety of terrorist groups and an important bridge between Shia Iranian radicals and the new wave of Sunni Arab radicals.

The United States cannot afford to ignore the wake-up calls presented by the World Trade Center bombing and the foiled Iraqi- sponsored assassination attempt against former President George Bush during his April 1993 visit to Kuwait. The taboo against international terrorist attacks inside the country and against important national symbols has been broken. Washington must lead a concerted international effort to make such terrorist attacks more difficult, more costly to the perpetrators, and more risky for the states that back them.

The Worldwide Spread

The U.S. is by no means the only country to feel the wrath of Middle Eastern terrorists in recent months. In July, 117 people were killed in a series of four bombings in nine days that swept Argentina, Panama, and Britain. Most, if not all, of this carnage is believed to be the handiwork of the world's most deadly terrorist organization — Hezbollah (Party of God), an Iranian-sponsored and Syrian-backed terrorist group based in Lebanon that perpetrated the October 1983 bombing of the U.S. Marine barracks in Beirut. In August, radical Islamic terrorists seeking to overthrow the Algerian government killed two Chinese and five French citizens in Algeria, as part of a terrorist campaign against foreigners that has claimed 60 lives since September 1993.

Yet, the U.S. and its citizens have been the world's foremost targets of international terrorism in recent years. The FBI estimates that 32 percent of terrorist attacks worldwide from 1982 to 1992 were targeted against Americans or American property. (FBI Terrorist Research and Analytical Center, "Terrorism in the United States: 1982-1992" (Washington D.C., 1993), p. 11.) Middle Eastern terrorism remains the greatest terrorist threat to the United States. Although some 20 percent of all international terrorist incidents from 1982 to 1992 have been traced to Middle Eastern quarrels, these incidents have accounted for about 35 percent of terrorist-related fatalities. (Testimony of terrorism expert Brian Jenkins before the House Foreign Affairs Committee, Subcommittee on International Security, International Organizations and Human Rights, March 12,1993.) Middle Eastern terrorist incidents repeatedly have drawn the U.S. into international crises. State-sponsored terrorist attacks against Americans have triggered U.S. military retaliation against Iran, Iraq, and Libya.

Iran has been the foremost state sponsor of terrorism since the 1979 Iranian revolution. But terrorist attacks against Western targets dropped off after the 1989 election of President Ali Akbar Hashemi Rafsanjani, who was more interested in rebuilding Iran with Western help than in exporting revolution. Now that Rafsanjani is steadily losing ground to more radical leaders in a bitter internal power struggle, there could be an escalation of Iranian-sponsored terrorism. Indeed, this may already have started to happen with Hezbollah's July bombing campaign.

Despite the growing danger, the Clinton Administration has failed to mount a credible effort to stem the tide of terrorism. Although it pays lip service to counterterrorism, the Administration unwisely remains wedded to a State Department reorganization plan that would downgrade the Office of Counterterrorism and signal friends and foes that fighting terrorism is not a high priority. To more fully protect American citizens from the scourge of Middle Eastern terrorism, the Obama Administration should:

- Make counterterrorism a top priority in American foreign policy.

  The Administration should shelve its plan to downgrade the status of the State Department's Office of Counterterrorism and make terrorism a top permanent agenda item at the annual G-7 summits.

- Tackle international terrorism as a form of low-intensity warfare.

  Treating it as a purely criminal matter does not effectively address the issue of state-supported terrorism.

- Punish state sponsors of terrorism on as many fronts as possible.

  Raise the diplomatic, economic, political, and military costs of state terrorism to the point where they exceed the expected benefits.

- Mobilize reluctant allies to maximize pressure on terrorist states and groups.

  Washington increasingly should apply public pressure on allied governments, particularly in Europe, that appease terrorist states.

- Maintain the option to retaliate unilaterally for terrorist attacks with decisive military force.

  The use or threat of force is an essential deterrent to state- supported terrorism.

- Stand firmly behind states threatened by Middle Eastern terrorism.

  Algeria, Egypt, Israel, and Turkey require firm U.S. support and close cooperation against international terrorism.

- Upgrade counterterrorism intelligence.

  The FBI, CIA, and other intelligence agencies need to expand their sources of human intelligence on international terrorism and consult closely with allies and other concerned states.
- Reform immigration laws to improve internal security.

  Deportation proceedings should be streamlined, political asylum requests should be screened more quickly and decisively and visas should be denied to members of groups that use, support, or advocate terrorism. Federal criminal penalties for visa and passport forgeries should be toughened.
- Work to restore order in anarchic areas where international terrorist groups thrive.

  The U.S. should back efforts by the governments of Lebanon and Afghanistan to roll back the influence of Islamic radicals and dismantle terrorist training camps.
- The Upsurge in Radical Islamic Terrorism Outside the Middle East

Middle Easterners are the prime suspects in a series of four terrorist attacks against far-flung Western targets in July. On July 18 a car bomb destroyed a Jewish community center in Buenos Aires, killing 96 people and wounding more than 200. The next day a bomb destroyed a commuter plane in Panama, killing 21, most of them Jewish businessmen. A car bomb exploded outside the Israeli Embassy in Lebanon on July 27, wounding 13 people. The next day another car bomb demolished the London offices of a Jewish charity organization. A previously unknown group calling itself Ansarallah (Partisans of God) claimed responsibility for the Buenos Aires and Panama bombings.

American intelligence specialists believe that the group is a subsidiary of Hezbollah, the Lebanon-based radical Shiite terrorist organization. Sheik Sobhi Toufeili, the leader of Hezbollah's most militant faction, is suspected of being the leader of the group. There has been speculation that the attacks were meant to derail the Arab-Israeli peace negotiations, because the bombings straddled Jordanian King Hussein's July trip to Washington to sign a non-belligerency accord with Israel. A more likely explanation, however, is that this spate of terrorism was a spillover of the intensifying fighting between Israel and Hezbollah in southern Lebanon. Hezbollah undoubtedly was smarting over Israel's capture of one of its leaders, Mustafa Dirani, in Lebanon on May 21.

The radical Islamic terrorists also may have been angry over Israel's June 2 air strike that killed some 45 of its cadres in Lebanon. Israeli and American intelligence officials are said to have little doubt that Iran also was behind the July 18 Buenos Aires bombing. Up to 20 Iranian Revolutionary Guards, who train and equip Hezbollah forces, apparently were killed in the June 2 air strike. Iran was implicated in a similar terrorist operation in Argentina that took the lives of 29 people in March 1992. Hezbollah claimed responsibility for that bombing, which destroyed the Israeli Embassy in Buenos Aires, possibly retaliating for an earlier Israeli attack that killed its military chief. Electronic intelligence intercepts and an extensive forensic investigation revealed that Iranian officials had helped acquire the plastic explosives used in that 1992 bombing.

Iran also has been implicated in the July 18 Buenos Aires bombing by an Iranian defector questioned by Argentine criminal investigators. The string of bombings in July greatly concerns U.S. counterterrorism officials. They are worried about the ability of Hezbollah terrorists to mount a sustained, coordinated, and well- organized terrorist campaign against targets all over the globe. (The car bomb used against the Israeli Embassy in London was delivered by a woman, a fact that has led some experts to doubt involvement of Hezbollah in that particular attack, because the organization previously has condemned the use of women in terrorist actions. Nevertheless, the possibility that a secular terrorist group carried out that attack does not necessarily let Iran off the hook, because Tehran has used secular groups such as the Popular Front for the Liberation of Palestine - General Command.) The attacks apparently were planned well in advance and utilized local support networks for reconnaissance and preparation. The July 19 mid-air bombing of a Panamanian commuter plane is especially troubling because it may be the first suicide terrorist attack on an airliner.

The Mystery of the World Trade Center Bombing

The February 26, 1993, bombing of the World Trade Center was a curious terrorist operation. On the one hand it was well-planned and professional; the terrorists were able secretly to construct and deploy a massive truck bomb. On the other hand, it was a surprisingly amateurish operation. The four terrorists convicted of the attack took unnecessary risks, such as giving a correct name and address when renting a vehicle for delivering the bomb. So far, no foreign state has been found responsible for the World Trade Center attack. But there are disturbing shreds of circumstantial evidence that point to possible Iranian or Iraqi involvement. Sheik Omar Abdul Rahman, the radical Egyptian cleric who inspired and possibly directed the bombers, long has been on the Iranian payroll, according to Vincent Cannistraro, the former head of CIA counterterrorism operations.

Sheik Omar regularly was given large sums of money by Iran's intelligence service, using Iran's delegation to the United Nations as a conduit. U.S. government investigators discovered that about $100,000 was transferred to the suspects before the bombing from banks in foreign countries, including Iran, but it is not known if this was payment for the attack or for other activities such as propaganda or recruitment. Other signs point toward Iraq.

For instance, the attack took place during the second anniversary of the ground offensive against Iraq in Operation Desert Storm. Terrorist attacks launched on anniversaries historically have been a common means of seeking vengeance in the Middle East.

Another troubling circumstance is that Ramzi Yousef, who apparently set the plot in motion, entered the U.S. in 1992 on an Iraqi passport on a trip that began in Iraq. Moreover, Abdul Yasin, an Iraqi suspect who cooperated with the FBI and was released from jail, later flew back to Iraq and is now believed to be living in Baghdad. Many New York law enforcement officials reportedly believe that Iraq was involved, although they can not prove it. Iraq also would seem to have more to gain from such a terrorist operation than Iran. Saddam would have had a strong incentive to punish the U.S. for its role in Desert Storm. Iraq also may have wanted to provoke a confrontation between the U.S. and its arch-rival Iran by casting suspicion on Tehran for the bombing.

This would strengthen Iraq's perceived value in the Middle East as a bulwark against revolutionary Iran, an argument Iraqi diplomats have made in attempts to persuade members of the United Nations Security Council to lift the U.N.-mandated sanctions against Iraq. (Iraq also had sponsored a similarly deceptive terrorist operation in June 1982, when it ordered the Abu Nidal Organization, a renegade Palestinian terrorist group, to shoot the Israeli Ambassador to Britain, an act which provoked Israel to punish the Palestine Liberation Organization (PLO) by invading Lebanon to destroy its base camps. The payoff for Iraq was that the Israelis dealt Iraq's rival Syria a sharp military setback in the course of the Lebanon War, and precluded Syria from joining its ally Iran in its 1980-1988 war with Iraq.)

A final disquieting consideration was the nature of the World Trade Center bomb itself. Not only was the bomb huge, loaded with 1,200 pounds of explosives, but it was customized with compressed hydrogen to magnify the blast and sodium cyanide to create a poisonous cloud after the explosion. A bomb that big and sophisticated has never before been detonated by a terrorist group that did not have state sponsorship or long-standing experience in building explosive devices.

The Radical Islamic Terrorists

The World Trade Center bombers are a new breed of terrorist. Unlike the tightly disciplined cells that dominated terrorism in the past, they functioned in a loosely organized ad hoc manner. Three of the six charged with the bombing were dedicated followers of Sheik Omar Abdul Rahman, the fiery spiritual leader of the Islamic Group, a radical fundamentalist movement that has waged a terrorist campaign to overthrow the Egyptian government.

At least three of the six bombers had fought in the war in Afghanistan against Soviet and Afghan communists. The Sheik also made at least three visits there since 1980 and two of his sons reportedly fought there. Thousands of Muslims from roughly 40 countries flocked to Afghanistan following the 1979 Soviet invasion. Radicalized veterans from the Afghan war — called by some journalists the "University of Jihad"(Holy War) — have returned home and have become the spearheads of radical Islamic movements in Algeria, Azerbaijan, Bosnia, Egypt, Sudan, and many other places around the world. Hundreds of these "Afghanis" are being trained by Iranian Revolutionary Guards in Sudanese training camps.

Radical Islamic movements have mushroomed not only in the Muslim world, but also among Muslim immigrants in the West. The World Trade Center bombers were all either recent immigrants or illegal aliens. Although they may have been drawn to America by economic opportunities and political freedoms, these terrorists rejected America's values and what they considered to be its degenerate culture of materialism and secularism. Rejecting assimilation into the resented society of their host country, they were susceptible to incitement by Sheik Omar. What they did mirrors what happened in several other terrorism cases, such as Hezbollah's 1985-1986 bombing campaign in France and its bombings in Buenos Aires in 1992 and 1994. In all three cases, small portions of local immigrant communities provided support for the terrorist operations.

Ironically, many radical Islamic movements outlawed in their own countries have found sanctuary in Western countries. So long as they are in the West, they cannot be arrested by the police back home. Like Sheik Omar, leaders of these radical movements lambaste their host countries while taking advantage of their open political systems to travel freely, organize politically, raise funds, recruit new members, support underground opposition movements in their home countries, and sometimes to direct terrorist activities. Germany long has been a base for Islamic extremists. The U.S. has become a safe haven for Hezbollah, the Islamic Group, Algerian fundamentalists, and Palestinian fundamentalists. Israeli officials claim that Hamas (Islamic Resistance Movement), the radical Palestinian Islamic group that is using terrorism to undermine the nascent Palestinian-Israeli peace, actually is directed from a headquarters in the United States.

The support networks that these terrorist groups are forming inside the U.S. for fundraising, recruitment, and propaganda activities could become the nucleus for terrorist attacks on American soil. These potential terrorists are dangerous because, unlike hit teams dispatched from the Middle East, they are now blending into Western societies where they have established personal and communal roots. U.S. counterterrorism officials worry that "sleeper cells" already established inside the U.S. could lie dormant for many years until activated for specific terrorist actions. (The FBI discovered a sleeper cell of the Abu Nidal organization inside the U.S. in 1986 and arrested four Palestinian members in April 1993 after one member of the group murdered his daughter.)

Moreover, the decentralized structure of many of the radical Islamic movements makes it difficult for host governments to detect, defend against, or apprehend terrorists lurking within these movements. The loosely linked informal webs of Islamic militants, often organized in small groups around a charismatic cleric, are harder to track and infiltrate than the more rigidly organized Palestinian terrorist groups that have been a major threat for decades. The Palestinian groups had a more straightforward organization and often were corrupt and therefore susceptible to bribery. They also were easier to penetrate because infighting between rival organizations led them to provide information on each other.

The new breed of radical Islamic terrorist is more intractable, less likely to betray other terrorists, and more unpredictable. In contrast to long-established Palestinian terrorist groups who had more predictable targets and objectives, Islamic radicals have more unclear motives and a wider variety of targets. They not only attack Israel, secular governments in Muslim countries, and states that support the secular regimes they oppose, they also target reporters with whom they disagree, intellectuals they despise (such as Salman Rushdie, the author of The Satanic Verses), and Western cultural institutions such as the American University in Beirut.

Most Palestinian terrorist groups refrained from assaulting Americans or launching attacks on American soil. The reason: they wanted to influence American public opinion to change U.S. foreign policy and to drive a wedge between Israel and America. They made the cold-blooded political calculation that killing Americans would hurt, rather than help their political cause. This self-imposed restraint often is not as strong among Islamic militants. This new breed of terrorist is hostile not only to American policies, but to many American values. For example, they reject secular law and democracy and the separation of church and state. They view American culture as a threat to Islamic piety and revile what they perceive to be the degenerate secular and materialist bias of American society. To Islamic radicals, the U.S. is the villainous successor of the European colonial empires that have sought to dominate the Middle East since the time of the crusades. In their holy war against the West, terrorism is an acceptable instrument for carrying out the will of God. Because they are motivated by apocalyptic zeal, and not sober political calculations, their choice of possible targets is much wider and more indiscriminate than that of other terrorists. Since they are less predictable, they can be more dangerous than Palestinian or other Middle Eastern terrorists.

Islamic radicals also often have a different audience in mind than Palestinian nationalists. Instead of using terrorism to influence Western powers to change their policies, they often use terrorism to punish Western powers and inspire other Muslims to rise up against the West. This focus on the Muslim audience rather than an American audience helps explain how the bombers of the World Trade Center could rationalize their bloody actions. The bombing was meant to demonstrate the power of Islamic radicals and the vulnerability of the U.S., not to lead the U.S. to rethink its Middle East policy.

The Threat of State-Sponsored Terrorism

The Middle East is a hotbed of state-sponsored terrorism. Five of the seven states that have been branded by the U.S. government as sponsors of international terrorism— Iran, Iraq, Libya, Sudan, and Syria—are located in the region. (Cuba and North Korea are the other two on the State Department's list of states that sponsor terrorism.) Moreover, 22 of the 41 major international terrorist groups described in the State Department's annual report on global terrorism are based in the Middle East. The region not only is infested with more terrorist groups than any other region, but these groups subscribe to a wider variety of ideologies and causes, ranging from Marxism to secular Arab, Armenian, Kurdish, and Palestinian nationalism to radical Islamic fundamentalism. Each year the Middle East is the world's foremost exporter of terrorism, with most of the spillover afflicting Western Europe.

Because of the heavy concentration of terrorist states and terrorist groups, most new trends in terrorism develop in the Middle East, then spread quickly to other regions. Radical Palestinian groups such as the Marxist Popular Front for the Liberation of Palestine (PFLP) pioneered the tactic of airline hijackings after the 1967 Arab- Israeli war. When improved airport security measures made hijacking more difficult, Palestinian groups such as the 15 May organization were in the forefront of the trend of airline bombings.

Most terrorist groups prior to 1970 were autonomous organizations of indigenous dissidents that pursued their own agendas without outside support. During the 1970s the Soviet Union and its satellites greatly expanded their support for terrorist groups. Moscow often used Middle Eastern client states such as Iraq, Libya, Syria, and the former People's Democratic Republic of South Yemen as intermediaries to mask Soviet arms, training, intelligence, and logistical support for a wide variety of terrorist groups.

The radical Arab states, which regularly used terrorism as a tool of repression against internal opposition, sought their own terrorist surrogates to wield as weapons against Israel, Western powers, and other Middle Eastern states. Libya, Syria, and Iraq courted Palestinian splinter groups or created their own Palestinian puppet organizations to buttress their claims to Arab leadership. These puppets also were used as proxy terrorists who, if caught, would not bring down retaliation on the head of the state sponsor.

The 1979 Iranian revolution brought Iran into the forefront of international terrorism. Iran organized, trained, equipped, and financed Shiite revolutionary movements such as Hezbollah in Lebanon and Ad Dawa (The Call) in Iraq and the Gulf States. Under Iranian supervision, Hezbollah unleashed a lethal terrorist campaign in 1983 to drive the Western peacekeeping forces out of Lebanon, bombing the U.S. Embassy in Beirut in April and the Marine barracks in October.

After Ali Akbar Hashemi Rafsanjani was elected President in 1989, Iranian support for international terrorism was toned down and the Western hostages held by Hezbollah in Lebanon gradually were released by the end of 1991. But assassinations of Iranian exile leaders continued at an alarming pace. Government-sponsored terrorism also was supplemented by terrorism financed by Iranian so-called charitable foundations, many of which are controlled by radical clerics opposed to many of Rafsanjani's policies. One of these, the Fifteenth of Khordad Foundation, has put a $2 million bounty on the head of Salman Rushdie, condemned to death as a blasphemer by Ayatollah Khomeini in 1989.

President Rafsanjani's power steadily has been eroded by radical rivals who have gained dominance over the Iranian parliament. He is a lame duck, prohibited by the Iranian constitution from running for re- election for a third term in 1996. As the struggle to succeed him intensifies, there is a good chance that Iran's support for terrorism will escalate. The West and the U.S. make convenient targets for hard- liners in their fight to seize power. In fact, Iran already has become more aggressive in supporting terrorism. In addition to suspected Iranian involvement in the July bombings in Buenos Aires and London, three Iranians await trial in Thailand for an attempt to bomb the

Israeli Embassy in Bangkok in March. In April, the British government charged that it had clear evidence of growing contacts between Irish Republican Army terrorists and Iranian embassies in Europe. In May, more than 300 Iranian Revolutionary Guards arrived in Bosnia to organize Muslim militias and terrorist groups, according to U.S. intelligence sources.

The U.S. has an historic opportunity to crack down on Middle East terrorism. The end of the Cold War and collapse of the Soviet Empire have deprived Middle Eastern terrorist states of superpower backing. The embryonic peace agreement between Israel and the PLO has reduced one source of terrorism, although Palestinian rejectionists both within and outside the PLO continue their terrorist war against Israel. Iraq's defeat in the Gulf War and subsequent isolation has constrained state support from that quarter, particularly as long as Baghdad moderates its policies in an effort to wriggle out of U.N. sponsored economic sanctions. Iran and Libya are isolated and beset by substantial economic problems caused in part by low oil prices. Sudan's radical Islamic regime is drained by a long-running civil war and a grim economic situation. Syria faces a precarious future as President Hafez al-Assad, not in the best of health, plots his personal political endgame.

All of these Middle Eastern regimes, which have exported so much terrorism-related misery, are simultaneously vulnerable on a number of different fronts. In the past they have been able to shrug off Western demands to halt their support of terrorism. But now that they have lost Soviet backing and have become increasingly dependent on the West for economic support, that is no longer true. The West now has more influence and leverage over these states. Moreover, many of these regimes are threatened by internal political opposition, or the prospect of such opposition in the near future. The U.S. and other Western powers, therefore, gain potential leverage by supporting or threatening to support opposition groups hostile to terrorist regimes.

While the threat or actual use of force is the ultimate deterrent to terrorism, experienced terrorist states and groups often are successful in concealing their responsibility for terrorist outrages to avoid military reprisals. To deter terrorism, Washington must convince its allies and other concerned states to increase the diplomatic, economic, military, and political costs of state-supported terrorism. A unified Western campaign to curtail Middle Eastern terrorism now has a greater chance for success than ever before. Only the U.S. can forge and lead such a coalition.

To build an international consensus to combat terrorism and to follow through and act on that consensus, the Clinton Administration must drop its short-sighted plan for downgrading the State Department's Office of Counterterrorism. This reorganization plan would fold that office into a new Bureau for Narcotics, Terrorism and Crime and demote the Coordinator for Counterterrorism from the current equivalent of an Assistant Secretary of State to the level of a Deputy Assistant Secretary. L. Paul Bremer, a former Ambassador-at-Large for Counterterrorism, noting that the office would be "gutted," charged that: "The Clinton Administration has neglected the terrorist threat, with our public officials paying only lip service to the problem." Congress has temporarily blocked the Administration's plans. Under the leadership of Representative Benjamin Gilman (R-NY), the House voted on April 18, 1994, to retain an independent Office of Counterterrorism. But the Administration has not given up on its reorganization plan, which originated in the Bush Administration as a cost-cutting measure.

Congress will again have to wrestle with the reorganization plan after April 30, 1995, when the Gilman amendment expires. At that time, Congress should consider insisting that the Administration permanently shelve its plans to downgrade State's counterterrorism office. This office instead must be given the bureaucratic clout to champion tough anti-terrorism policies against other bureaus in the State Department, or in other departments, that have little or no interest in combating terrorism. Therefore, the Coordinator for Counterterrorism, who is the U.S. government's senior full-time counterterrorism official, must have direct access to the Secretary of State, and not be relegated, as the Administration plans, to the bottom of a cumbersome reporting chain. To secure the diplomatic clout that is needed to impress U.S. allies and terrorist nations, the Coordinator should be restored to the status of ambassador-at-large, as was the case during the Reagan Administration.

Washington should aggressively raise the profile of the counterterrorism issue by injecting it into every multilateral diplomatic forum and every high-level bilateral meeting with officials from allied governments or terrorist regimes. The U.S. should ensure that the issue of terrorism appears automatically on the agenda at every G-7 summit. The Coordinator for Counterterrorism should become a permanent fixture at the summits as the prime mover in a multilateral working group on counterterrorism.

As a Form of Low-intensity Warfare

Terrorism is the most ubiquitous kind of low-intensity conflict. Yet, it is too often treated primarily as a law enforcement issue. While bringing the rule of law to bear on terrorists is desirable, it is not always possible, particularly when terrorists are being protected by a state sponsor. In cases of state-supported terrorism, which the CIA estimates comprise up to 80 percent of all international terrorism, it is not realistic to rely solely on law enforcement agencies to fight terrorists.

State-supported terrorism is in effect an act of war and should be approached as a form of surrogate warfare. The U.S. should not unnecessarily hobble itself in this war against terrorism by treating state-sponsored foreign terrorists the same as it treats domestic terrorist groups. Counterterrorist forces should not require courtroom standards of evidence before they take action. Adopting a narrow legalistic approach to fighting terrorism would lead to American paralysis and terrorism would proliferate unchecked.

The U.S. should make use of the full arsenal of its weapons against terrorism by relaxing self-imposed restrictions on special operations. For example, Executive Order No. 11905, signed in 1976, was designed to prohibit assassinations of foreign leaders, but it also has been interpreted as prohibiting commando assaults on terrorist groups. This executive order should be refined to permit such special operations, particularly against terrorist groups that have killed Americans in the past, such as Hezbollah or the Abu Nidal organization. Counterterrorist teams also should be deployed to apprehend terrorists in anarchic areas such as Lebanon or Afghanistan, and not just in international waters or airspace.

The U.S. should also make greater use of non-violent covert actions, such as the dissemination of disinformation to create dissension inside terrorist groups and psychological warfare to aggravate the terrorists' sense of vulnerability and to encourage distrust of their state sponsors. Agents of influence, wherever they can be inserted, would help to disrupt terrorist operations and turn terrorists against each other. Sabotage operations also should be launched against the safe houses; logistics support networks, and financial assets of terrorist groups.

Middle Eastern states have relied heavily on state-sponsored terrorism because it is a cost-effective tool to their foreign policies. The U.S. should work with its allies and other concerned states to raise the diplomatic, economic, political, and military costs of supporting terrorism so high that it outweighs the strategic benefits.

Diplomatic Sanctions

Countries victimized by terrorism in the past have broken relations or reduced the size of the diplomatic mission of the state sponsor. This helps limit the threat of terrorism, because much of it is directed, supported, and financed by intelligence personnel operating under diplomatic cover.

But diplomatic sanctions usually have been unilateral, ad hoc responses that have had little effect on terrorist states. Washington should propose an agreement among the G-7 and NATO allies that would require all of them to expel large numbers of diplomats, if not break diplomatic relations completely, with states that support terrorist attacks. Moreover, diplomatic personnel of these states should be expelled for each confirmed terrorist attack by a surrogate terrorist group.

This measure would raise the public uproar over terrorism and increase the costs of each attack. This may give pause to some terrorist states, particularly those such as Iran and Sudan, that want the West to bail them out of dire economic predicaments. At a minimum, reducing the diplomatic presence of terrorist states will make it harder for them to support terrorism out of their embassies. For example, the expulsion of diplomats greatly undermined Iraq's ability to export terrorism during the 1991 Gulf War.

Regardless of whether it can gain G-7 support for such an agreement, the U.S. should pressure its allies to pare down the diplomatic presence of Iranian and Sudanese diplomats in their countries. Diplomats from Iran and Sudan have been implicated in the July bombing in Buenos Aires and in the 1993 bomb plots in New York City. The

Iranian diplomatic presence particularly should be cut back in Germany and Venezuela, which are centers for Iran's intelligence and terrorist networks.

Economic Sanctions

Washington should persuade its allies to participate in developing a multilateral version of the State Department's list of states that support terrorism. Once placed on the list, a terrorist state should be denied economic assistance, arms sales, and preferential trade privileges from all participating states. Further, the allies would be committed to voting against financial aid for that state in international financial institutions such as the World Bank. If Western Europe and Japan presented a united front in threatening to impose sanctions, it could have a sobering effect on the five Middle Eastern terrorist states. All, with the possible exception of Libya, will require Western or Japanese economic assistance, loans or renegotiation of existing loans in the near future. Iran already is staggering under the financial burden of its $30 billion foreign debt. Iraq owes foreign creditors more than $14 billion, Syria owes $16.5 billion, and Sudan's foreign debt is in excess of $16 billion. Now that the Soviet Union has dissolved, they have no place else to go. The U.S. should convince its allies to take advantage of their financial leverage and elevate counterterrorism to the forefront of economic aid and loan renegotiation decisions.

Trade sanctions against terrorist states will be more difficult to extract from the Western Europeans and Japanese since they see Iran, Iraq, and Libya as potentially lucrative export markets and important sources of oil supplies. France and other countries already are impatient to lift the U.N.-sponsored economic sanctions on Iraq. To block this, Washington should make Iraq a high-priority test case for Western anti-terrorism cooperation. The U.S. should stress Iraq's abortive plot to assassinate former President George Bush during his visit to Kuwait in April

1993 and Baghdad's continuing terrorist attacks on the Kurds and on U.N. personnel in northern Iraq.

To test Baghdad's intentions, Washington should request the extradition of Abdul Yasin, an Iraqi who participated in the plot to bomb the World Trade Center, who returned to Iraq. (Yasin was seen outside his father's house in Baghdad by an ABC News reporter earlier this year.) If Baghdad balks at observing the terms of the extradition treaty that it signed with the U.S., then it clearly will be in violation of U.N. Security Council Resolution Number 687 (April 1991), which called on Iraq to abandon its support of terrorism. This violation could become a justification for maintaining the U.N. sanctions on Iraq.

The Europeans have been more cooperative in imposing economic sanctions on Libya for its refusal to extradite two suspects in the 1988 Pan Am flight 103 bombing over Lockerbie, Scotland. But these U.N.-imposed sanctions have fallen short of an embargo on Libyan oil. The U.S. should expand the sanctions to include Libya's oil exports. Washington should work through the U.N. Security Council to impose an oil export regime similar to the one imposed on Iraq: oil revenues would be funneled into a U.N.-administered escrow account that could be used to pay reparations to the families of victims of Libyan terrorism. This could be a model to punish other terrorist states that block international efforts to apprehend terrorists.

Another terrorist state that is extremely vulnerable to concerted international economic sanctions because of its crumbling economy is Sudan. It already has sought to appease the West by turning over the notorious Venezuelan-born terrorist Illich Ramirez Sanchez, alias "Carlos the Jackal," to France on August 15. (Carlos was a terrorist playboy who had outlived his usefulness to Syria, which had harbored him until 1991. Carlos's leftist politics did not endear him to Sudan's radical Islamic regime.) Iran will be a more difficult case because of the reluctance of America's allies, particularly Germany and Japan, to sacrifice their short-term commercial interests in exporting to Iran. Now that Iran is having difficulty repaying its debts, foreign creditors may be more willing to consider trade sanctions against Tehran. In any case, the U.S. could strengthen its case for economic sanctions against Iran if President Clinton blocks the proposed $750 million sale of up to 20 Boeing 737 jetliners to Iran and prohibits U.S. oil companies, the largest purchasers of Iranian oil, from buying Iran's oil exports. (American oil companies currently are prohibited from importing Iranian oil into the U.S. but are allowed to buy it for resale elsewhere.)

The U.S. should drive up the prospective political costs of state-sponsored terrorism. This can be done by supporting opposition groups in countries that engage in international terrorism. All Middle Eastern terrorist states have generated domestic opposition. Washington should provide diplomatic, economic, and even military support to the most viable opposition groups in terrorist states. The Kurds in Iraq, the resistance movements in southern Sudan, pro-Western exile groups and the increasingly restless Azeris, Baluch, and Kurds in Iran, and Libyan dissidents all merit increased American and Western support. The Assad regime in Syria has brutally eliminated most domestic opposition, but President Assad's persistent health problems and the recent death of his son and heir apparent, Basil, has increased uncertainty about the political durability of Syria's minority Alawite regime. Although there may be no viable opposition inside Syria in the short run, the U.S. should increase its diplomatic support for an independent Lebanon free from Syrian domination.

Mobilize Reluctant Allies

Western Europe has borne the brunt of the spillover of

Middle Eastern terrorism, yet historically has been reluctant to take determined action against it. Too often, European states have sought to appease terrorist states and cut separate deals with them, rather than take a unified stand against terrorism. Last October, Germany hosted a visit by Iran's Minister of Intelligence and Security, Ali Fallahiyan, the overseer of much of Iran's terrorist operations. France appeased Iran last December by expelling two suspected Iranian terrorists whose extradition had been sought by Switzerland for the 1990 assassination of an Iranian opposition leader in Geneva.

The U.S. must drive home to its allies that appeasement of terrorism is a self-defeating policy that only encourages more terrorism. France may be ripe for persuasion, now that an upsurge in terrorist attacks against French citizens in Algeria led Paris to crack down on exiled Algerian radicals in France in early August. France now criticizes the U.S. and Germany for allowing exiled Algerian radicals to continue to operate freely within their borders. Washington should cooperate with France and closely monitor the activities of Algerian radicals in the U.S., while pressing Paris to support greater international cooperation in isolating terrorist states, particularly Iran.

Germany and Japan, the two biggest exporters to Iran, are the weak links in Western efforts to isolate Iran. Both states argue that they aid Iranian "moderates" by maintaining good trade and diplomatic relations with Iran. This rationale has grown increasingly threadbare in view of Iran's continued support of terrorism. Besides, Iran's "moderates" are losing ground to more radical elements in Tehran who are likely to escalate terrorism unless confronted with firm international pressures. The U.S. should strongly warn Germany and Japan, first privately and increasingly in public, that appeasement only encourages Iran and other terrorist states to believe that terrorism is cost-free. Worse, by conducting preferential trade relations with Iran and granting it foreign aid and loans, Germany and Japan are subsidizing Iran's terrorism.

Washington also should press its allies to establish a high-level central office for coordinating counterterrorism policies. These offices could act as liaisons with allied counterterrorism agencies. Modeled on the U.S. Office of Counterterrorism, these offices would help raise the profile of counterterrorism as an international issue and make international cooperation more effective and timely. Washington also should lobby all its allies to adopt stiffer penalties for terrorism, including longer jail terms and the seizure of the assets of terrorist groups or states. The Europeans, in particular, should be pressed to stop releasing terrorists before their sentences have been completed.

Washington also should press Saudi Arabia to halt the flow of financial aid to radical Islamic movements. Substantial sums of money from private Saudi religious foundations and individuals have bankrolled Sheik Abdul Rahman and other radical fundamentalists. Riyadh placed restrictions on the flow of these funds outside the country in 1993 but needs to more carefully control the activities of the Islamic foundations to prevent them from meddling in the internal affairs of other Muslim countries.

Maintain the Option to Retaliate Unilaterally

The use or threat of use of military force is essential for punishing and deterring state-sponsored terrorism. The military response should be designed to raise the cost of terrorism above the price a terrorist state is willing to pay. The U.S. should not get bogged down in a tit-for-tat exchange by limiting its attacks merely to terrorist training camps. Instead, it should strike targets that the terrorist state highly values, such as its internal security forces and secret police. For example, if Iran or one of its surrogates, such as Hezbollah, lashes out at an American target, the U.S. should not content itself with destroying a few easily replaceable terrorist camps in Lebanon or Iran. Rather, the U.S. should attack Iran's Revolutionary Guards which train terrorists and provide internal security, as well as Iran's Ministry of Intelligence and Security.

A sharp and decisive military reprisal not only can have a deterrent effect on the terrorist state attacked, it also can have a strong demonstration effect on other states that support terrorism. For example, the April 1986 air strikes against Libya had a significant impact on Syria as well as Libya. According to the State Department, Libya reduced its involvement in international terrorism from 19 incidents in 1986 to six in 1987, while Syrian involvement fell from 34 in 1985 to six in 1986 and to one in 1987.

Special operations are an important option for fighting terrorists close to innocent civilians, in hostage rescue operations, and in efforts to apprehend terrorist leaders. The Pentagon must make an effort to maintain the strength and readiness of the Special Operations Command which includes the elite "Delta Force," Army Special Operations Forces, Navy Seals, Marine Reconnaissance teams, and a special assault unit from the 101st Air Assault Division. These forces should be periodically dispatched on anti-terrorism training exercises in friendly Middle Eastern states to give them familiarity with the region and experience with desert warfare.

Stand Firmly Behind States Threatened

Middle Eastern terrorists pose much more of a threat to secular and moderate regimes in the Muslim world than to the West. Islamic revolutionary movements have used terrorism to undermine and demoralize ruling governments, polarize societies, and intimidate secular opposition. Terrorists have become the shock troops of Islamic revolutionary movements seeking the overthrow of the governments of Egypt and Algeria. The U.S. has a major stake in both countries. A radical Islamic revolution in either of them would send shock waves throughout the Arab world.

Washington should steadfastly support the governments of Egypt and Algeria in their efforts to reach an accommodation with political opposition groups while firmly suppressing terrorists. American diplomats should not meet publicly with radical Islamic leaders because this could undermine the existing government. Nor should Washington permit radical Islamic leaders, such as Tunisian revolutionary Rashid el-Ghanoushi, to visit America unless they reject terrorism. Nor should it pressure any government to enter talks with any group that supports terrorism. Whenever possible the U.S. should share its intelligence on terrorist groups and their supporters with the governments battling revolutionary terrorists.

In addition to supporting moderate Arab regimes threatened by terrorism, the U.S. should cooperate closely with Turkey and Israel in combating terrorism. Both countries are valuable sources of intelligence on international terrorism and should be furnished with American intelligence on terrorist activities in a timely manner. The U.S. also should maintain relentless pressure on Syria to halt its support for the Kurdish Workers Party and the Armenian Secret Army for the Liberation of Armenia, two terrorist groups that have killed scores of Turks. Moreover, Washington should strongly back Israel's demand that any Syrian-Israeli peace agreement must include guarantees that Syria will cease its support for Palestinian terrorists and help end Hezbollah's rein of terror in Lebanon.

Upgrade Counterterrorism Intelligence

Fighting terrorism effectively requires detailed and timely intelligence about the operations of terrorist groups, their support networks and their state sponsors. The FBI has made effective use of intelligence information to pre-empt at least 78 terrorist plots since 1982. But the new breed of radical Islamic terrorists, organized in informal amorphous groups, presents a new challenge for intelligence-gathering. To maintain and expand its intelligence network, the FBI should make a systematic effort to recruit Arab-Americans and American Muslims.

The CIA needs to upgrade the volume and quality of its human intelligence on terrorist groups and states. It must develop a more extensive network of agents dedicated to counterterrorism intelligence and infiltrate terrorist groups on a long-term basis. The CIA should make every effort to recruit American and foreign personnel with extensive knowledge of and experience in the cultures and societies of their terrorist adversaries. The CIA's Counterterrorist Center, created in 1986 by President Reagan after the hijacking of TWA flight 847, should be expanded and devote more resources to surveillance of the new breed of radical Islamic terrorists.

The National Security Agency and various defense intelligence agencies should be directed to give counterterrorism a higher priority in their intelligence-gathering efforts. The Defense Department also should consider dedicating more of its reconnaissance satellites to gathering information on possible military targets related to terrorism, such as terrorist bases and training camps in terrorist states and the Syrian- controlled areas of Lebanon. In addition, the U.S. should improve its efforts to reward informants who provide useful information about terrorist activities.

The State Department's International Counterterrorism reward program provides monetary awards of up to $2 million for information on terrorist activities against Americans. It has led to the defection of more than ten terrorist informants and the prevention of nearly a dozen acts of terrorism against Americans. This program should be publicized more widely in the Middle East. A recent report that a valuable informant was treated shabbily by the U.S. government is disconcerting because it could lead the trickle of informants to dry up. Informants who risk their lives to provide important intelligence should be promptly rewarded for their efforts.

Laws to Improve Internal Security

Sheik Abdul Rahman and two of the World Trade Center bombers entered the country illegally. They eventually were caught but were allowed to remain in the country pending subsequent legal proceedings. This situation is intolerable. Congress should reform the immigration laws to accelerate deportation proceedings and simplify and consolidate the lengthy procedural hearings and appeal system that permit illegal and undocumented aliens to evade immigration controls. Applicants for political asylum should be screened to weed out and immediately deport those without a credible basis for asylum.

Tougher penalties should be imposed on the production or use of fraudulent passports and visas. Nine of the original 35 indictable counts in the 1993 New York bombing plots involved visa or passport offenses. The recently passed crime bill contains a measure that will double the maximum prison terms for such crimes from 5 to 10 years (and increase to 20 years if the documents were used to facilitate terrorism) and boost fines from $2,000 to $250,000. A companion measure sponsored by Representative Gilman, which currently is under consideration by the House Judiciary Committee, would allow the government to seize the assets of criminals convicted of creating or using false documents for terrorism or drug smuggling. If passed, this measure would make it harder for terrorists to obtain false documents.

Finally, the U.S. government should automatically deny visas to members of groups that advocate, support, or participate in terrorism. Unfortunately, the 1990 Immigration and Naturalization Act killed the provisions of the 1952 McCarran-Walter Immigration and Nationality Act that allowed the U.S. government to restrict the entry into the U.S. of members of a group deemed a threat to U.S. security. The State Department now wrings its hands over denying visas solely because of membership in a terrorist group. This loophole, which puts the nation at risk, needs to be closed. Congress should pass legislation that enables the U.S. government to deny visas to foreigners because of membership in terrorist groups rather than requiring proof of personal involvement in terrorist acts, as is now the case.

Restore Order in Anarchic Areas

Many of the World Trade Center bombers were supporters of the radical Afghan group Hezbi Islami (Party of Islam) led by Gulbuddin Hekmatyar, a virulently anti-Western Islamic militant. Some reportedly were trained in Hezbi Islami camps and fought in the Afghan war. The U.S. should drop its short-sighted hands-off policy in Afghanistan that has led it to remain neutral in the fighting between Hekmatyar's Islamic zealots and the provisional government of President Burhanuddin Rabbani. With a limited commitment of financial aid, the U.S. can greatly strengthen the ability of the moderate Afghan forces to defeat Hekmatyar's drive to transform Afghanistan into a revolutionary Islamic state. By bolstering Rabbani's regime, the U.S. could help end the anarchy that gives terrorists a foothold in Afghanistan.

The U.S. also should revive its efforts to build a stable and independent Lebanon. Syria has sought to keep the Lebanese weak and divided to assure its own dominance there. It has vetoed the efforts of the Lebanese government to extend its control into southern Lebanon and disarm Hezbollah. The U.S. should insist that Syria abide by the terms of the 1989 Taif agreement, which require Syria to withdraw its 40,000 troops to eastern Lebanon and permit the Beirut government to extend its control over its own territory. Only then will Lebanon cease to be a staging area for international terrorism.

Middle Eastern terrorism has become more unpredictable and audacious. Radical Islamic terrorists inspired by Iranian, Algerian, and Egyptian revolutionary movements have overshadowed Palestinian nationalist terrorists as a threat to the West. These new terrorists often are supported by networks of radical Islamic activists who live in Muslim communities in the West. Even more worrisome is the training, arms, financial support, and guidance which radical Islamic terrorists receive from such states as Iran and Sudan.

International terrorism is not likely to be eradicated, but it can be weakened considerably if increased diplomatic, economic, political, and military pressure is brought to bear on the state sponsors of terrorism. The U.S. must lead an international campaign to raise the costs of terrorism. This will require a coordinated, firm, and relentless international effort. This kind of cooperation paid off in disarming Iraqi terrorism during the Gulf War, and it can work again. The U.S. must convince its allies that they now are involved, whether they want to be or not, in an international war against terrorism.

To do so, the Clinton Administration must do more to stop international terrorism. It must shelve its misguided plan to downgrade the State Department's Office of Counterterrorism, toughen its approach to terrorist states, and remain vigilantly on guard against terrorist movements. Only then will its allies sacrifice their short-term commercial interests to advance the long-term security interests of the West and other targets of Middle Eastern terrorists.

4

The New Terrorism and their Origins

The suicidal collision of hijacked commercial airliners into the World Trade Center and the Pentagon on 11 September 2001 was the most destructive terrorist attack in world history. Before the deaths of approximately 3,000 people in those attacks, the most devastating single terrorist attack had claimed the lives of about 380 people. The 2001 disaster took place at a time when experts had been defining a new form of terrorism focused on millennial visions of apocalypse and mass casualties. The catastrophic attacks confirmed their fears.

The State Department's Patterns of Global Terrorism, published in early 2002, revealed that terrorist attacks have scaled back in number in recent years, even though more casualties have occurred. The late 1980s were a high point for the number of terrorist attacks, with the incidence of attacks exceeding 600 annually in the years 1985-88. With the exception of 1991, the number of terrorist attacks after 1988 decreased to fewer than 450 every year, reaching their recent low point in the years 1996-98, when the number of attacks was about 300.The number of attacks has increased slightly since 1998, when there were 274 attacks, but the level has not reached the number realized in any of the years of the 1980s.

This is not a linear progression from a large number to a small number of attacks, but the trend revealed is one of a decreasing incidence. Yet even if the frequency has decreased, the danger has not. Osama bin Laden and the al Qaeda network of international terrorists are the prime examples of the new terrorism, but Islamic radicalism is not the only form of apocalyptic, catastrophic terrorism. Aum Shinrikyo, the Japanese religious cult, executed the first major terrorist attack using chemical weapons on a Tokyo subway in 1995. The bombing of the Murrah Federal Building in Oklahoma revealed similar extremism by American right-wing militants. Other plots by Christian Identity terrorists have shown similar mass-casualty proclivities.

Nadine Gurr and Benjamin Cole labeled nuclear-biological-chemical (NBC) terrorism as the "third wave of vulnerability" experienced by the United States beginning in 1995. David Rapoport made a similar assessment that religiously motivated modern terrorism is the "fourth wave" in the evolution of terrorism, having been preceded by terrorism focused on the breakup of empires, de colonialization, and anti-Westernism. The National Commission on Terrorism found that fanaticism rather than political interests is more often the motivation now, and that terrorists are more unrestrained than ever before in their methods. Other scholarly sources have reached similar conclusions. Terrorism is increasingly based on religious fanaticism. Warnings about the dangers of nontraditional terrorism were raised frequently in pre-2001 literature. For instance, Ashton Carter, John Deutch, and Philip Zelikow declared in the pages of Foreign Affairs in 1998 that a new threat of catastrophic terrorism had emerged.

Earlier concerns about alienating people from supporting the cause are no longer important to many terrorist organizations. Rather than focusing on conventional goals of political or religious movements, today's terrorists seek destruction and chaos as ends in themselves. Yossef Bodansky's Bin Laden quotes from S. K. Malik's The Quranic Concept of War: Terror struck into the hearts of the enemies is not only a means, it is in the end in itself. Once a condition of terror into the opponent's heart is obtained, hardly anything is left to be achieved. It is the point where the means and the ends meet and merge. Terror is not a means of imposing decision upon the enemy; it is the decision we wish to impose upon him. Today's terrorists are ultimately more apocalyptic in their perspective and methods. For many violent and radical organizations, terror has evolved from being a means to an end, to becoming the end in itself.

The National Commission on Terrorism quoted R. James Woolsey: "Today's terrorists don't want a seat at the table they want to destroy the table and everyone sitting at it." Some analysts argue that the evolution of terrorism represents continuity rather than change that mass-casualty bombings have long been characteristic of terrorist methods, and that radical extremism has always dominated terrorist motivations. Walter Laqueur's most recent book warns against trying to categorize or define terrorism at all because there are "many terrorisms," and he emphasizes the particularities of various terrorist movements and approaches. (Laqueur, however, recognizes some evolving strains of terrorism, especially the Islamist variant.) Bruce Hoffman discussed the definition of terrorism at length in his 1998 book, Inside Terrorism, and his final definition includes "political change" as the desired end-state of terrorist activity. This would be more consistent with traditional means-end constructions of terrorism. Richard Falkenrath pointed out in a pre-9/11 article that mass-casualty terrorism is still an aberrant occurrence.

A recent survey of terrorism suggests historical and intellectual links between the fascism of fanatical Islamist terrorism today and the totalitarian movements of the 20th century, further emphasizing continuity rather than change. Most recent scholarship, however, has taken the perspective that contemporary terrorism represents a significant departure from the past. Various factors have led to the development of this new type of terrorism. Paul Wilkinson pondered the increase in indiscriminateness among terrorists, and he posited several possible reasons accounting for this upsurge. First, the saturation of the media with images of terrorist atrocity has raised the bar on the level of destruction that will attract headline attention. Second, terrorists have realized that civilian soft targets involve lower risk to themselves. Finally, there has been a shift from the politically-minded terrorist to the vengeful and hard-line fanatic.

While Wilkinson's factors accurately describe developments in terrorist strategy and tactics, there are more fundamental forces at work. The world has undergone a variety of changes on several levels. While it is impossible to link all social changes to terrorism today, it is possible to track several distinct factors that have converged to evolve a form of terrorism that is unprecedented in the level of threat it poses around the world. This will explore these factors from cultural, political, and technological perspectives. Cultural Factors Islamic radicalism is the most notorious form of the new culture of terrorism, but it is far from the only variety of cultural trends motivating terrorist activity. Numerous cults, whose emergence in many cases has been synchronized with the turn of the new millennium, have also posed an increasing threat.

Finally, the American religious right has been active with escalating and destructive objectives, although law enforcement presence has restrained these groups. It is important to distinguish religious terrorists from those terrorists with religious components, but whose primary goals are political. Religiously motivated terrorist groups grew six fold from 1980 to 1992 and continued to increase in the 1990s. Hoffman asserted that "the religious imperative for terrorism is the most important characteristic of terrorist activity today." This may not be as much an entirely new phenomenon as a cyclic return to earlier motivations for terror. Until the emergence of political motives such as nationalism, anarchism, and Marxism, "religion provided the only acceptable justifications for terror." However, terrorism in modern times has not, until recent years, been so dominated by religious overtones. At the time when modern international terrorism first appeared, of the 11 identifiable terrorist groups, none could be classified as religious.

Today's terrorists increasingly look at their acts of death and destruction as sacramental or transcendental on a spiritual or eschatological level. The pragmatic reservations of secular terrorists do not hold back religious terrorists. Secular terrorists may view indiscriminate violence as immoral. For religious terrorists, however, indiscriminate violence may not be only morally justified, but constitute a righteous and necessary advancement of their religious cause. In addition, the goals of secular terrorists are much more attuned to public opinion, so senseless violence would be counterproductive to their cause, and hence not palatable to them. As Hoffman observed, the constituency itself differs between religious and secular terrorists. Secular terrorists seek to defend or promote some disenfranchised population and to appeal to sympathizers or prospective sympathizers. Religious terrorists are often their own constituency, having no external audience for their acts of destruction.

Aum Shinrikyo has been included in typologies of terrorism that include radical Islamists as part of a group of religiously motivated organizations that attack symbols of the modern state. In many ways, the dynamics of cultist followings make groups such as Aum Shinrikyo (also known as Aleph) more dangerous than religious terrorists rooted in conventional and broadly based religious traditions or denominations. There is no constituency of more moderate adherents to share common beliefs with the radical group while at the same time posing a restraining influence. For the fundamentalist Islamic or Christian radical, authoritative figures from either of those religions can condemn violence and de-legitimize the terrorist, at least in the eyes of the average faithful.

Another feature of religious cults that makes them incredibly dangerous is the personality-driven nature of these groups. Cultist devotion to one leader leaves followers less able to make their own moral decisions or to consult other sources of reasoning. If that leader is emotionally or mentally unstable, the ramifications can be catastrophic. The more dangerous religious terrorist groups from traditional faiths may often share this feature of the cult: a charismatic leader who exerts a powerful influence over the members of the group.

According to many analysts, Aum Shinrikyo demonstrated its comparatively more threatening potential in its sarin attack in the Tokyo subway. As D. W. Brackett wrote, "A horrible bell had tolled in the Tokyo subway.... Terrorists do not follow rules of engagement in their operations but they do absorb the lessons to be learned from successful acts of violence." If for no other reason than providing an example to others, Aum Shinrikyo has gained notoriety as one of the more dangerous terrorist elements. Despite setbacks such as the incarceration of key leadership figures, the group continues to pose future threats. The ability of Aum Shinrikyo to recruit individuals with a high level of education and technical knowledge also has been a significant aspect of the threat posed by the cult.

In the past, cults were not viewed as national security threats; they were more dangerous to unwary individuals who might succumb to the cult's influence. Even the emergence of cultist mass suicides did not alter this perception. However, the recent appearance of cults willing and able to adopt destructive political goals has revised the more benign view of the cult phenomenon. Since cults are often fundamentally based on the violence of coercion, they can be accustomed to the mindset necessary to adopt terrorist methods. Although cults more often practice a mental violence with psychological control and extreme invasions of privacy, they do occasionally engage in physical abuse. The most dangerous cults are also fascinated by visions of the end of the world—which, like radicals from more mainstream religions, cultists often believe that they are instrumental in bringing about. The nature of the cult's mythical figure can also be indicative of the level of threat. A vengeful deity is more threatening than a suffering savior. This sign is somewhat unpredictable, however, because cults can switch their principal myths as circumstances change.

In summary, cults are a particularly dangerous form of religious terrorism because they can appear quickly without warning, have no rational goals, and can become agitated due to the apprehension and hostility with which they are viewed by the society at large. Whether initiated by cultists or by extremists from more established religions, the violence of religious terrorists can be particularly threatening in comparison with that of the political terrorists of earlier years. As Hoffman notes, "For the religious terrorist, violence is a divine duty... executed in direct response to some theological demand... and justified by scripture."

Religion can be a legitimizing force that not only sanctions but compels large-scale violence on possibly open-ended categories of opponents. Terrorist violence can be seen as a divinely inspired end in itself. One explanation that has been proffered to account for violent Islamic extremism views revenge as the principal goal of the terrorists. This reasoning makes political change or conventional political objectives irrelevant, and it is consistent with observations that violence is itself the objective. Fundamentalist Islam "cannot conceive of either coexistence or political compromise. To the exponents of Holy Terror, Islam must either dominate or be dominated."

A recent study that traced the Islamic theological doctrine to the Middle Ages noted recent philosophical developments that explain the preponderance of religious mass-casualty terrorism coming from adherents of Islam. Remarkably, a recent analysis of bin Laden's fatwa, published in Studies of Conflict and Terrorism, found that the content of the fatwa was "neither revolutionary nor unique, as it encapsulates broad sentiments in the Muslim world, especially that of Islam's being on the defensive against foreign secular forces and modernization." However, some of the content of the fatwa does fall directly within the paradigm of contemporary religious terrorism.

Consider the following excerpts: Praise be to God, who revealed the book, controls the clouds, defeats factionalism, and says in his book: "But when the forbidden months are past, then fight and slay the pagans wherever ye find them...." On that basis, and in compliance with God's order, we issue the following fatwa to all Muslims: The ruling to kill the Americans and their allies—civilians and military—is an individual duty for every Muslim who can do it in any country in which it is possible to do it. In an article published shortly after 9/11, Steven Simon and David Benjamin noted that many al Qaeda attacks, including the major planning phase of the 9/11 attacks, took place during favourable times for the Palestinians in the Middle East peace process, and that no foreign policy changes by the US government could possibly have appeased the bin Laden is radical.

While Islamic terrorists are the most notorious of today's violent radicals, others such as right-wing Christian extremists also exhibit many characteristics of the new terrorism. Mark Juergensmeyer, in his book Terror in the Mind of God: The Global Rise of Religious Violence, identified three elements that Islamists, radical Christians, and other religious terrorists share: They perceive their objective as a defense of basic identity and dignity; losing the struggle would be unthinkable; and the struggle is in deadlock and cannot be won in real time or in real terms.

In the past, right-wing Christian terrorists conducted racially motivated or religiously motivated acts of violence discriminately against chosen victims, and confrontation with the state was limited to instances when the state interfered with the political or religious agenda of the terrorist groups. Today, some such groups are directly hostile to the government, which adherents believe is engaged in a widespread conspiracy threatening the existence of the "white Christian way of life." A recent FBI strategic assessment of the potential for domestic terrorism in the United States focused on such groups as Christian Identity and other ultraconservative movements associated with Christian fundamentalism.

The most extreme of these fanatics attribute a subhuman status to people of color, which in their eyes mitigates any moral compunction to avoid harming such individuals. In addition, they view themselves in a perpetual battle with the forces of evil (as manifested through non-white races and a powerful, sinister government) that must culminate in the apocalyptic crisis predicted by the Book of Revelations. The Christian terrorists view it as their duty to hasten the realization of this divine plan, which permits and even exhorts them to greater levels of violence. That violence is directed against existing social structures and governments, which are viewed to be hopelessly entangled with such "dark forces" as Jewry, enormous financial conglomerates, and international institutions trying to form an ominous "new world order."

While Christian violence in the United States has been discriminately focused for decades against racial minorities and "immoral" targets, it recently has expanded into attempted bombings and poisoning municipal water supplies. These indiscriminate attacks demonstrate a willingness to tolerate greater levels of collateral damage in efforts to generate mass levels of casualties. The bombing of the Murrah Federal Building in Oklahoma City was the pinnacle of this trend, and although Timothy McVeigh accepted responsibility for that attack, some speculate that there was additional involvement by other conservative militia or Christian terrorists.

Effective domestic law enforcement in the United States has largely prevented these groups from achieving widespread violence on the level of Oklahoma City, making that incident a tragic exception among a larger number of foiled plots. While there is certainly no cooperation between foreign Islamist and US-domestic Christian radicals, there is a disquieting similarity in their views. August Kreis of the paramilitary group Posse Comitatus responded to the collapse of the World Trade Center towers with this disconcerting rant: "Hallelu-Yahweh! May the WAR be started! DEATH to His enemies may the World Trade Center BURN TO THE GROUND!" Jessica Stern's recent book, Terror in the Name of God: Why Religious Militants Kill, which compiles interviews with international terrorists conducted over five years, does not begin with an example from the Guantanamo Bay detention facility or the streets of the Middle East.

Her introductory example is a former Christian terrorist in a Texas trailer park. While Islamic terrorism is the most salient threat to the United States, it is not the only danger posed by the new trend of a culture of religious violence and extremism. A cluster of several cultural features among new international terrorist groups indicates the high level of threat. These aspects include a conception of righteous killing-as-healing, the necessity of total social destruction as part of a process of ultimate purification, a preoccupation with weapons of mass destruction, and a cult of personality where one leader dominates his followers who seek to become perfect clones. These aspects taken together represent a significant departure from the culture of earlier terrorist groups, and the organizations that these characteristics describe, represent a serious threat to the civilized world.

Political and Organizational Factors

A number of developments on the international scene have created conditions ripe for mass-casualty terrorism. Gross inequalities in economic resources and standards of living between different parts of the world are a popular reason given for the ardency and viciousness of contemporary terrorists, although governmental collapse in "failed states" as a breeding ground for terrorists presents a more convincing variation on this logic. However, there is no "comprehensive explanation in print for how poverty causes terror," nor is there a "demonstrated correlation between the two." The intrusion of Western values and institutions into the Islamic world through the process of free-market globalization is an alternative explanation for the growth of terrorism, which is the weaker party's method of choice to strike back.

The process of globalization, which involves the technological, political, economic, and cultural diminution of boundaries between countries across the world, has insinuated a self-interested, inexorable, corrupting market culture into traditional communities. Many see these forces as threatening their way of life. At the same time that globalization has provided a motivation for terrorism, it has also facilitated methods for it. One of the major consequences of globalization has been a deterioration of the power of the state.

The exponential expansion of non-governmental organizations (NGOs), regional alliances, and international organizations has solidified this trend. Although certainly not a conventional humanitarian-based NGO like the Red Cross or Doctors without Borders, al Qaeda has distinguished itself as among the most "successful" of non-governmental organizations in pursuing its privately-funded global agenda. The trend among terrorists to eschew direct connections with state sponsors has had several advantages for the enterprising extremist. Terrorist groups are more likely to maintain support from "amorphous constituencies," so extreme methods are more acceptable because such methods can be used without fear of alienating political support. Harvey Kushner described this development as a growth of "amateur" groups as direct state sponsorship has declined. Lawrence Freedman pointed out that the Taliban-ruled Afghanistan was not so much a state sponsor of terrorism as it was a "terrorist-sponsored state."

Terrorists do, however, continue to enjoy the benefits of indirect state sponsorship. Although the opportunity for state sponsorship has arguably diminished as a result of the Bush Administration's war on terror that has been prosecuted in the aftermath of the 9/11 attacks, state sponsorship remains widespread. In fact, developments in counterterrorist measures may propagate some dangerous trends of modern terrorism. When terrorists cannot rely on direct state sponsorship, they may become less accountable and harder to track. States must conceal their involvement by exercising less control and thus maintain less-comprehensive intelligence of radical terrorist organizations. Many states have been on the US government list of state sponsors for more than a decade, including Cuba, Iran, Iraq, North Korea, Libya, and Syria. More recently, Sudan and Afghanistan became government sponsors of terrorism.

Many state sponsors cooperate with one another to promote terrorist violence, making terrorist activity further disconnected from the foreign policy of any single state. Iran has funded training camps in Sudan, and the Palestinian Islamic Jihad has received support from both Iran and Syria. Further exacerbating the problem is the method of funding, which often has no measures for accountability. Iran's support for terrorist organizations can include no particular target selection, and it occasionally results, with the funds disappearing, in no terrorist attacks. This unpredictability is tolerated by state sponsors because of the occasional destructive payoff and the obfuscation of evidence connecting the state to the terrorist. Iran has consciously created a decentralized command structure because of these advantages.

A further advantage of maintaining arm's length from extremist operatives is for self-protection. The government intelligence organization of Sudan evidently monitored Osama bin Laden while he lived in that country, apparently to prevent his activists from eventually doing harm to even that extremist government. While the American operations in Afghanistan and Iraq have diluted the threat from those states, other sponsors have possibly been left off official lists for political reasons. (It has been frequently argued that inclusion of a state on the list of state sponsors of terrorism reflects its relationship with the United States). Pakistani intelligence reportedly has been involved in sponsoring violent terrorists, both in Afghanistan and in the contentious Kashmir.

Additionally, the Kingdom of Saudi Arabia has been at the center of controversy over sponsorship and proliferation of radicalism and violence. Laurent Murawiec, an analyst at the RAND Corporation, attracted public attention by pointing out the dangers of Saudi support for radical Islamists and specifically Osama bin Laden in a briefing to the Defense Policy Board in 2002. While no official publication of the RAND Corporation documents this analysis, Murawiec highlighted evidence of Saudi support for the Islamist agenda through Islamic educational venues and financial backing. So while globalization has helped remove many of the restraints that state sponsorship once imposed, terrorists can still enjoy the funding and protection that sponsorship provides.

Another factor of globalization that benefits terrorism is targeting: "In today's globalizing world, terrorists can reach their targets more easily, their targets are exposed in more places, and news and ideas that inflame people to resort to terrorism spread more widely and rapidly than in the past." Among the factors that contribute to this are the easing of border controls and the development of globe-circling infrastructures, which support recruitment, fund-raising, movement of materiel, and other logistical functions. In addition to international political changes, developments in organizational practice have enhanced the lethality of terrorists. As corporations have evolved organizationally, so have terrorist organizations.

Terrorist groups have evolved from hierarchical, vertical organizational structures, to more horizontal, less command-driven groups. John Arquilla, David Ronfeldt, and Michele Zanini note that terrorist leadership is derived from a "set of principles [that] can set boundaries and provide guidelines for decisions and actions so that members do not have to resort to a hierarchy—'they know what they have to do.'"

The authors describe organizational designs that may "sometimes appear a cephalous (headless), and at other times poly cephalous (Hydra-headed)." Paul Smith observed that the multi-cellular structure of al Qaeda gave the organization agility and cover and has been one of its key strengths. This flexibility has allowed al Qaeda to establish bases using indigenous personnel all over the world. It has infiltrated Islamic nongovernmental organizations in order to conceal operations.

Jessica Stern has evolved in ways that provide unprecedented opportunities for terrorists. The collapse of the Soviet Union and the possibility of proliferation of nuclear weapons to non-state users is the primary factor that has significantly increased the danger of nuclear terrorism. However, nonnuclear weapons of mass destruction and information technology also have created opportunities for terrorists that are in many ways more threatening than radiological terrorism because these alternatives are more probable. Some theorists have argued that weapons of mass destruction do not represent a weapon of choice for most terrorists, even in these changing times. Stern writes that "most terrorists will continue to avoid weapons of mass destruction (WMD) for a variety of reasons," preferring the "gun and the bomb."

Brian Jenkins agreed that most terrorist organizations are technologically conservative, but he also noted that the self-imposed moral restraints which once governed terrorist actions are fading away. As the trends in the preceding sections reach fullness, increasing the proclivity toward mass-casualty terrorism, terrorists may turn more to these weapons that will better fit their objectives and moralities. Walter Laqueur's New Terrorism emphasizes the availability of very powerful weapons of mass destruction as the major current danger facing the industrialized world. Aside from the nuclear variety of WMD, biological and chemical weapons pose serious dangers.

Biological weapons are limited because human contact is required to spread the effects, but as the Asian brush with Severe Acute Respiratory Syndrome (SARS) demonstrated, the associated panic and uncertainty can take a large economic and political toll—not to mention the cost in human suffering for those exposed to the pathogen, perhaps without knowing how or even whether they have been infected. Biological weapons can come in a variety of forms, including viruses, bacteria, and rickettsia (bacteria that can live inside host cells like viruses). Chemical toxins differ from biological weapons in that they are non living pathogens and require direct infection and contact with the victim. This negates the continual spread of the weapon, but it entails more direct and possibly more damaging effects. Chemical agents appear in several types: choking agents that damage lung tissue, blood agents that cause vital organs to shut down, blister agents (also known as vesicants) that damage the skin, and—most lethal—nerve agents.

Various methods allow the agent to infect its victim, including inhalation, skin absorption, and ingestion into the digestive tract. Exacerbating the danger is the fact that many deadly chemicals, or their components, are commercially available. The State Department's annual report on terrorism asserted that the events of 11 September 2001 confirmed the intent and capability of terrorist organizations to plan and execute mass-casualty attacks. The report also stated that these unprecedented attacks may lead to an escalation of the scope of terrorism in terms of chemical, biological, radiological, or nuclear methods.

The report further cited evidence discovered in military raids of Afghan terrorist facilities, the use of poison by Hamas to coat shrapnel in improvised explosives, and an unnamed group arrested in Italy with maps of the US embassy and possessing a compound capable of producing hydrogen cyanide. Activities of cults such as Aum Shinrikyo and American terrorist plans to poison municipal water facilities provide further evidence of the WMD threat. Another key development is recent advances in communications and information technology.

This technology provides both assistance to the terrorists and an opportunity for targeting as industrialized societies place greater reliance on information infrastructures. Terrorists will likely avoid dismantling the internet because they need the technology for their own communication and propaganda activities. Accordingly, terrorists may be more interested in "systemic disruption" rather than the total destruction of information networks.

While the consequences of a major disruption of American or global information infrastructures could be catastrophic financially or socially, terrorists have not shown the inclination or capability to undertake massive strikes in this area. There have been limited attacks along these lines, but the major use of information technology has been as an aid for terrorists rather than as a target of their activity. The reported use of the internet and e-mail by al Qaeda to coordinate the strikes on the World Trade Center and the Pentagon provides a dramatic example of this sort of coordination. As Paul Pillar noted, "Information technology's biggest impact on terrorists has involved the everyday tasks of organizing and communicating, rather than their methods of attack."

Technology also has increased the ability of terrorists to conduct mass-casualty attacks. As noted earlier, the worst single terrorist attack before 9/11 claimed the lives of about 380 people. The yield of contemporary radiological, chemical, and biological weapons could dwarf that number, given the goals of today's terrorists as exemplified by the World Trade Center and Pentagon attacks, the Oklahoma City bombing, the sarin gas attack on the Tokyo subway, and other, less-successful attacks of the past decade. Technological developments and their availability as spread by the globalized market economy have unavoidably expanded the dangers of terrorism in the new century.

The practice of terrorism has undergone dramatic changes in recent years. The categorical fanaticism that is apparent in terrorist organizations across a spectrum of belief systems is a major part of this change. In the past, terrorists were more likely to be dominated by pragmatic considerations of political and social change, public opinion, and other such factors. Today, a phenomenon that was a minute rarity in the past—terrorists bent on death and destruction for its own sake—is more commonplace than ever. In addition, the statelessness of today's terrorists removes crucial restraints that once held the most extreme terrorists in check or prevented them from reaching the highest levels in their organizations.

Terrorists can still enjoy the funding and shelter that only a national economy can mobilize, but they are on their own to a greater degree in greater numbers than in the past. Organizationally, terrorists are using the non-hierarchical structures and systems that have emerged in recent years. Finally, the potential availability of nuclear, chemical, and biological WMD technology provides the prospect that these trends could result in unprecedented human disasters.

Terrorism has quantitatively and qualitatively changed from previous years. Whether it is Gurr and Coleman's "third wave of vulnerability" or Rapoport's "fourth wave of terrorism," contemporary terrorism is a significant departure from the phenomenon even as recently as during the Cold War.

The US National Security Strategy has recognized terrorism, in the memorable phrase "the crossroads of radicalism and technology," as the predominant security threat in the post-Cold War world. The cataclysmic impact of 9/11 on Spring 2004 both the American strategic consciousness and the international security environment can scarcely be over stated. Those attacks resulted from a combination of cultural, political, and technological factors and were a revelation to the world of the emergence of the new terrorism.

Mutant *Jihads*

The strategic decision to carry out 9/11 was made in the early 1990s, almost ten years before the barbaric attacks on New York and Washington took place. The decade-long preparations—and the testing of America's defenses and political tolerance to terrorism that took place before September 11th—were a stage in the much longer modern history of the *jihadist* movement that produced al-Qaeda and its fellow travelers. Decades from now, historians will discover that the United States, the West and the international community were being targeted by a global ideological movement which emerged in the 1920s, survived World War II and the Cold War, and carefully chose the timing of its onslaught against democracy.

Undoubtedly, the issue that policy planners and government leaders need to address with greatest urgency, and which the American public is most concerned about, is the future shape of the terrorist threat facing the United States and its allies. Yet developments since 2001, both at home and overseas, have shown that terror threats in general—and the *jihadi* menace in particular—remain at the same time resilient and poorly understood.

The *jihadi* war against the Soviet Union during the Cold War—and the struggle against the United States and some of its allies thereafter—are all part of a single continuum. Over time, *jihadi* Salafists and Khomeinist radicals alike have become proficient in selecting their objectives and infiltrating targets. Indeed, an analysis of the security failures that made 9/11 possible clearly demonstrates that the hijackers exploited systemic malfunctions at the national security level. Learning these lessons is essential for better counterterrorism planning in the future. But the *jihadists* are also learning, and the advantage will go to the side which can adapt most quickly. If the jihadists learn to understand and anticipate their opponents, their tactics and strategies will mutate. The first strain of mutating Islamist ideology is that of al-Qaeda and its affiliates. In his now-historic April 2006 speech, Osama Bin Laden confirmed his commitment to global, total and uncompromising *jihad*. "It is a duty for the Umma with all its categories, men, women and youths, to give away themselves, their money, experiences and all types of material support, enough [to establish *jihad* in the fields of *jihad*] particularly in Iraq, Palestine, Afghanistan, Sudan, Kashmir and Chechnya," Bin Laden has maintained. "Jihad today is an imperative for every Muslim. The Umma will commit sin if it did not provide adequate material support for *jihad*."

Bin Laden's latest *risala* (message) is as important as his initial declarations of war and of mobilization, laying out his most comprehensive vision so far. As this "world declaration" makes clear, the global Salafi agenda accepts no truth other than radical Islamist dogma. All non-Islamist governments must be brought down, and pure, pious ones erected in their stead. Global *jihadism*, in its Salafi-Wahhabi form, is ideologically at war with the rest of the world. The conflict is universal in nature. It encompasses the entire West, not just the United States and Europe. Russia, India, and at some point even China, in addition to moderate Muslim governments, must be brought down. Like no other document to date, Bin Laden's speech outlines the final fantasy of the *jihadi* mind: world domination.

The second branch of *jihadism* is smaller, and concentrated in the hands of a single regime: the Islamic Republic of Iran. Since its inception, Khomeini's Islamic Revolution has seen itself as universal in nature. And today, flush with oil dividends, it is rapidly expanding its influence in Lebanon, the Persian Gulf, Iraq, and Afghanistan. Similar to its Salafi counterpart, the Khomeinist worldview seeks to erect Islamist regimes, launch radical organizations and expand its ideology. But unlike in Wahhabism, the chain of command is narrow and tightly controlled; Iran's

Supreme Leader, the Ayatollah Ali Khamenei, is the unquestioned ideological head, while Iran's radical president, Mahmoud Ahmedinejad, decides the time, place and scope of the battles.

Future battlefields

By understanding the objectives of these forces, it is possible to extrapolate some theaters of likely confrontation in the years ahead.

Iraq

Today, U.S.-led forces in Iraq are battling al-Qaeda and other Salafi forces in the so-called "Sunni Triangle." In the south, meanwhile, Coalition forces have engaged Iranian-supported militias, such as Muqtada al Sadr's Mahdi Army. U.S. and Iraqi forces will continue to battle on both of these fronts, in Iraq's center and south. The Salafi strategy will center on classical terrorist attacks, while Iranian-supported forces are likely to attempt to infiltrate and take control of Iraqi forces. U.S.-Iraqi counterterrorism cooperation will continue to expand, but a decisive victory for Baghdad cannot take place before Iranian and Syrian interference has receded—and that will not happen until both of those regimes are weakened from the inside. Hence, American support for democratic and opposition forces in Syria (and by extension Lebanon) and Iran is the surest way to ensure success in Iraq.

Afghanistan

The consolidation of the Karzai government in Kabul is essential to American strategy, both as a bridge to a younger generation of Afghans and as a counterweight to the appeal of the Taliban. Al-Qaeda is committed to preventing such a development. It has a vested interest in causing the country's post-Taliban government to fail, and in preventing a new generation of citizens from being exposed to non-Salafi teachings. U.S. and NATO forces therefore face a long-term struggle against *jihadists* in that country, both on the military and the socio-cultural level. Sustaining engagement there will depend on two factors: American public support, and the outcome of the struggle between fundamentalists and the government currently taking place in Pakistan.

Pakistan

Many of the components of the worldwide war with *jihadism* are concentrated in Pakistan. So far, Pakistan's radical Islamists have been able to block their government from taking back control of the country's western tribal areas and uprooting the fundamentalist organizations in its east. But potentially even more dangerous is the possibility that *jihadists* could take control of Pakistan's nuclear arsenal. In this context, the most serious threat to the United States would be the collapse of the Musharraf government and the Pakistani military at the hands of radical Islamists. Should this happen, the U.S. would be under direct nuclear threat from a nuclear-armed al-Qaeda regime—one that would have tremendous control over many other Muslim countries.

Asia

A major shift in south Asia will not only impact Afghanistan and Pakistan, but is likely to spill over into Bangladesh, Malaysia, Indonesia, and the southern Philippines, with ripple effects on U.S. allies Australia, Thailand, and India. The U.S. will be deeply and adversely affected by the expansion of *jihadism* in Asia.

Iran

While the Salafi threat is likely to extend east into Asia, Khomeinism is likely to expand westward, from Iran to southern Lebanon via Iraq's Shi'ite areas and Syria's Alawite-dominated regime. Since its inception, the radical regime in Tehran has had a vision of itself as a great power, and consequently perceives itself to be on a collision course with the "Great Satan": the United States. The imperial vision of a Shi'a Crescent from Afghanistan to the Mediterranean held by Iran's leaders mirrors the Sunni Caliphate envisioned by al-Qaeda and its followers—albeit one with a modern twist: nuclear weapons. Bolstered by its partnership with Syria and the strength of its proxy force in Lebanon, Tehran today envisions a global confrontation with the United States. As such, the Iranian regime represents a cardinal threat to democracies in the region and, by extension, to the United States.

Syria

Ever since Hafez al-Assad chose to permit Iran to expand its influence in Lebanon, a Syrian-Iranian axis has existed in the region. During the Cold War, Damascus was able to outmaneuver the U.S. on a number of fronts, chief among them Lebanon. By 1990, the latter had been abandoned by Washington to Syria. The Ba'athist domination of Lebanon, in turn, led to the ascendance of Hezbollah. But America's post-9/11 *volte-face* brought the dangers of Syrian-occupied Lebanon into sharp focus. By 2005, Syria had been forced out of Lebanon, but Bashar al-Assad remains defiant. Today, in the aftermath of Hezbollah's war with Israel, Syria, like Iran, finds itself hurtling toward confrontation with the United States.

Lebanon

Since the 1970s, Lebanon has been a key battlefield between the forces of terror and the West. The country houses a dense conglomeration of anti-democratic forces, ranging from Hezbollah to pro-Syrian groups to extreme Salafists. Since the 1983 attacks on the U.S. Marine barracks, the United States has altered its strategy toward Lebanon several times, but today, Washington finds itself forced to contain a rising Hezbollah and support a struggling "Cedar Revolution."

Sudan and the Horn of Africa

All the indications suggest that al-Qaeda is planning to open a new battlefield in Africa. In the speeches of Bin Laden and other Islamist leaders, Sudan represents a central arena of confrontation with the infidels, and a major launching pad for world *jihad*. The *jihadists* aim to thwart the international community in Darfur and reignite a holy war in southern Sudan. In addition, fundamentalists are expanding their influence in Somalia, and conspiring against U.S. ally Ethiopia. Here again, the U.S. and other democracies find themselves on a collision course with radical Islamists, even though international engagement in Africa today is essentially limited to humanitarian assistance.

Europe

With the Madrid and London attacks, the many plots foiled in Great Britain, France, Germany and Italy, the violence in the Netherlands and Scandinavia, the French "intifada" and the "Cartoon *Jihad*," Europe has well and truly become the next battlefield. Transatlantic cooperation could give way to tensions between America and its European partners, as European *jihadis* become a danger to the United States. Indeed, *jihadi* penetration of Europe, particularly Western Europe, is expected to facilitate the infiltration of North America.

Russia

Since the 2002 Moscow theater hostage-taking and the subsequent Beslan school massacre, *jihadism* has engulfed Russia. Wahhabism has already taken hold in Russia's southern provinces, and *jihadists* are thinking beyond Chechnya, toward the dismemberment of the Russian Federation. Russian strategy, for its part, has been peculiar; while Moscow has confronted fundamentalists at home head-on, it nonetheless pursues a policy of support for Iran and Syria—and, by extension, Hezbollah. In doing so, Russia's foreign policy has become antithetical to its own national security. The U.S. and Russia have a solid basis for collaboration against international terrorism, but unless Moscow abandons its tolerance of Tehran's radicalism, the two countries will miss a strategic opportunity to defeat world terror in this decade.

Latin America

While the Soviet legacy has mostly dissipated in Latin America, with Fidel Castro's regime in Cuba the last ailing vestige of the Cold War, it has taken just one decade for new threats to emerge. The populist regime of Hugo Chávez in Venezuela not only poses a challenge to liberal democracies in the region, it also serves as a conduit for foreign *jihadi* threats. With an alliance with Iran in the making and with an al-Qaeda and Hezbollah presence in the country, Venezuela is facilitating the activities of a network of forces inimical to U.S. interests. Deeper in the continent, meanwhile, both al-Qaeda and Hezbollah have successfully put down roots in the Andes and the Tri-Border Region between Brazil, Paraguay and Argentina. With the long and porous Mexican-American border a major vulnerability, another future threat to the U.S. is brewing to its south.

Canada

Finally, American security is also at risk from the north. Not only is Canada considered a passageway by which international terrorists can enter the United States, it has also become a site for the proliferation of *jihadi* groups. The arrests made in Toronto in the summer of 2006, and the coordination between U.S.-born radicals and their Canadian "brothers," are signs of a new era—one in which Islamists view the United States and Canada as one strategic arena for operations. Washington therefore will increasingly need to coordinate its counterterrorism strategies with its northern neighbor, despite the differences in political culture, institutions and attitudes.

The American front

For the United States, winning the War on Terror depends on two battlefields. The first is overseas, where Washington must confront *jihadi* forces and help allies to win their own struggles with terrorism. This will require the United States to support democratic change abroad, both as a counterweight to *jihadist* lobbies and as a means of assisting Arab and Muslim democrats to win the conflict within their own societies.

The second, however, is closer to home. Homeland security planners must be thinking seriously about a duo of unsettling questions. First, are *jihadists* already in possession of unconventional weapons on American soil, and how can the U.S. government deterring them? This crucial issue tops all other challenges, for a terrorist nuclear strike on the U.S. has the potential to transform international relations as we know them. Second, how deeply have *jihadist* elements infiltrated the U.S. government and federal agencies, including the Federal Bureau of Investigation, the Department of Homeland Security, the Department of Defense, and various military commands, either through sympathizers or via actual operatives?

As the recent scandal over the National Security Agency's domestic surveillance program has shown, the answers are fraught with complications. Five years into the War on Terror, the U.S. has not fully made the transition from the pre-9/11 legal counterterrorism framework to one based on intelligence, prevention and robust police action. And, without a national consensus about the seriousness of the *jihadi* threat, America will lose its own war of ideas.

The future enemies of the United States will be a mutation of current and past terrorist foes. In confronting these forces, knowledge of their ideologies, objectives and determination will make all the difference.

5

International Efforts Against New Terrorism

As in the case of the intensification of its internal efforts, the EU has also intensified its international efforts against terrorism after the September 11 terrorist attacks. Thus, in this chapter, the EU's international efforts with its global partners on counterterrorism cooperation will be evaluated by emphasizing on remaining divergences and disagreements on the ways to confront terrorism. In this context, the divergences between the EU and the US approaches on tackling terrorism and convergences on counterterrorism cooperation between the EU and the US will be analysed. Under the Euro-Mediterranean Cooperation on terrorism, firstly, the Barcelona Process will be observed in order to explain the important parts of the EU's approach on terrorism.

Then, the counterterrorism cooperation of Euro-Mediterranean Partners will be examined. Before the elaboration of the EU-Russia disagreements on Chechen conflict, the counterterrorism cooperation between the EU and Russia will also be pointed out in brief. Transatlantic Cooperation Since the September 11 terrorist attacks, there has been a growing divergence between the EU and the US on the ways to confront terrorism, which mainly stems from both sides' different strategies. However, beyond these divergences, the EU and the US have a considerable convergence in terms of cooperation in the areas of police and judicial cooperation, transport and border security.

Transatlantic Divergences

Growing Division between Europe and the US: Despite the end of Cold War, the Bill Clinton administration believed in the value of European support and made significant efforts to persuade European allies to adopt the Atlantic Alliance to better deal with the new types of threats in regions beyond Europe. In addition, despite growing American power to confront new threats, the Ex President Bill Clinton was convinced that the US should do everything possible to provide agreement among Europeans before resorting to unilateral action, not only on issues like Balkans, but also on global issues like the Middle East. That liberal commitment to consensus with Europeans changed to a significant degree with the arrival of G.W. Bush to the Whitehouse, and then again, even more so, after the September 11 terrorist attacks.

G.W. Bush gave his first foreign policy speech in November 1999 stating that "in the defence of our nation, a president must be a clear-eyed realist" and during 2000 presidential election campaign he criticized the liberal foreign policy perspective of the Clinton administration. The Bush administration, influenced by realist world view, took the Office in January 2001 and dedicated itself to establish "unipolar world". By acting unilaterally in the first months of his administration, the US withdrew from the "ABM Treaty", refused to join "International Criminal Court (ICC)", refused to approve the "Biological Weapons Convention" (WPC) and the "Comprehensive Test Ban Treaty" (CTBT), regardless of the opposition of the European countries, China, and Russia.

Indeed, these oppositions to unilateral policies of the Bush administration came into most significant degree, at least from Europeans' point of view, when the US rejected the "Kyoto Protocol" on global warming. On the other hand, indeed, the Bush administration did not systematically avoid working with Europeans within multilateral forums. On some specific issues, notably in its efforts to stop nuclear proliferation of North Korea, reinforcement of "Road Map" for the Middle East, NATO's further enlargement with seven new members, the Bush administration preferred a liberal multilateral approach that sought the support of Europeans. In fact, the Bush administration's willingness to use multilateral forums on these specific issues were no more than to show the willingness of Bush administration to accomplish some specific realist foreign policy goals of the US.

Therefore, the divisions between the US and Europeans on international matters began significantly with the arrival of the Bush administration to the Whitehouse. However, it was the September 11 terrorist attacks that expanded and accelerated the gaps between European and American approaches on international matters, particularly the ways of tackling the threat of terrorism. Initially, the September 11 attacks seemed to have brought Europe and the US closer together opening a new period of transatlantic cooperation based on a common threat, terrorism. The European Allies of NATO immediately invoked Article 5 of the North Atlantic Treaty and supported UN Security Council resolution which gave US international legitimacy to respond to the attacks.

After the initial shock of the attack wore off, the transatlantic relations started to deteriorate again. Significant differences emerged over how to deal with the threat of terrorism. Now, both had to choose broad strategies according to their respective strengths and conceptual understanding of how the post-Cold War World works. On the one hand, Europeans, have a long experience with the terrorism phenomenon, and believe that the root causes of terrorism lies in the economic and social alienation of communities and military force cannot eradicate the sources of terrorism.

In addition, before September 11, the EU's strategic priorities were not global military issues, but economic and political integration, Eastern enlargement, and the completion of the monetary union. September 11 attacks did not change that. On the other hand, September 11 terrorist attacks were so massive for the US that they regarded these attacks as an act of war against the US and inclined to use unilateral military force combined with greater American power and resources.

This unilateral perspective of the US administration took place in its Afghanistan operation by rejecting the multilateral support of NATO's European allies. The US did not prefer NATO forces in Operation Enduring Freedom in Afghanistan in order not to share the command structure of military forces with NATO allies. Instead, the US received bilateral military support from its European allies for Operation Enduring Freedom and symbolic NATO support, in particular, NATO AWACS (early warning aircraft) patrolled the US air space and NATO frigates patrolled the Eastern Mediterranean in order to free up the US assets for deployment.

Indeed, the US's unilateral military operation in Afghanistan by leaving out NATO troops was the evidence of the US foreign policy's alignment to realism's self-help principle in which the realists claim, for survival, states do not depend on international institutions but actively involve in self-help arrangements which are manifested in the use of force. In addition, as Nora Bensahel points out, many Europeans were dissatisfied with the symbolic role that NATO played in Operation Enduring Freedom as a response to September 11 terrorist attacks and attributed it to US unilateralism and arrogance. Operation Enduring Freedom in Afghanistan confirmed the Bush administration in its view that the Cold War norms of alliance no longer applied, even though the NATO invoked the collective defense commitment, Article 5, for the first time in its history.

However, the real turning point for transatlantic relations was the US President G.W. Bush's January 29, 2002, State of Union Address in which he stated an "axis of evil" that included Iraq, Iran, and North Korea, and warned that these regimes, by seeking weapons of mass destruction, pose "a grave threat and growing danger" because they "could provide these arms to terrorists [and] attack our allies or attempt to blackmail the United States". However, the US would not "permit the world's most dangerous regimes to threaten the US with the world's most destructive weapons".

Beyond these remarks President G.W. Bush put an important message for Europeans to consider: *"My hope is that all nations will heed our call, and eliminate the terrorist parasites who threatened their countries and our own...But some governments will be timid in the face of terror. And make no mistake about it: if they do not act, America will...America will do what is necessary to ensure our nation's security. We will be deliberate, yet time is not on your side. I will not wait on events, while dangers gather. I will not stand by, as perils draws closer and closer. The United States of America will not permit the world's most dangerous regimes to threaten us with the world's most dangerous weapons".*

As Philip H. Gordon and Jeremy Shapiro argue, the above mentioned speech implied a strategic doctrine of unilateral preemptive war that would emerge later in the year and the implication of speech was clear for Europeans: If the US deemed force necessary to deal with the threat to the US security, no nation or alliance should or could stand in the way. On the other hand, as Simon Serfaty argues, the speech, relying on self-help and statism, deepened

Europeans' fears that, as had been shown in Afghanistan, America's European allies were being moved to secondary role even for the treatment of issues which were of direct concern to them.

The European reaction to the speech was tough and swift. German Foreign Minister Joscha Fisher said "The international coalition against terrorism is not the foundation to carry out just anything against anybody, and particularly not on one's own". He also complained that alliance partners should not be treated like "satellites". In addition, French Foreign Minister Hubert Vedrine called the speech "simplistic" and "absurd".

Moreover, Chris Pattern, the EU Commissioner for External Affairs, warned that "whoever might you are, even you are the greatest superpower in the world, you cannot do it all on your own". Finally, the French Prime Minister Lionel Jospin urged the US not to define its policy only for single goal by stating the problems of the international community "cannot be reduced simply to the struggle against terrorism, however vital that struggle may be. Nor can such problems be solved by overwhelming military power". In fact, these remarks were implicit message to the US's realist statist and self-helf approach of acting unilaterally in contrast that Europeans underline the necessity of liberal multilateral cooperation for fighting against terrorism.

The President G.W. Bush's endorsement of the unilateral military "preemption" doctrine in a speech at West Point, New York, in June 2002, confirmed the European view that the Bush administration had a simplistic approach to foreign policy that reduced everything to the military aspects of war on terrorism. While speaking at West Point, President Bush described a "threat with no precedent" that required "new thinking". He added, [d] eterrence means nothing against shadowy terrorist networks with any nation or citizens to defend Containment is not possible when unbalanced dictators with weapons of mass destruction can deliver those weapons on missiles or secretly provide them to terrorist allies. We cannot defend America and our allies hoping for the best... if we wait for threats to fully materialize, we will have waited to long".

Thus, the President Bush promised to "take the battle to the enemy, disrupt his plans, and confront the worst threats before they emerge", and he concluded his message, "in the world we have entered, the only path to safety is the path of action.

And this nation will act...Americans to be forward-looking and resolute, to be ready for preemptive action when necessary to defend our liberty and our lives". Indeed, the President Bush's West Point speech implied that the US had a right and duty to apply preemptive action not only against an imminent threat, but also, if Washington decided, against a potential threat. In September 2002, President Bush's January 29, 2002 State of the Union Address and June 2002 West Point Speech given an official status in the National Security Strategy (NSS) of the US.

By putting the military power of the US as a defining factor of international relations, NSS indicates the willingness to use US military forces without multilateral support by stating "[w]e will not hesitate to act alone, if necessary, to exercise or right of self defense by acting preemptively against such terrorists". The two important speeches of President Bush and the statements of the NSS confirmed the US alignment with key realist assumptions such as statism, survival, and self-help while implementing its foreign policy to deal with the threat of terrorism. In contrast, indeed, it was the realist US foreign policy that caused great concern to many European governments and the majority of the European public who supported liberal multilateral cooperation against unilateral approach of the US to get rid of terrorism.

The implications of speeches made by President Bush and the statements of the NSS came into force after the US invasion of Iraq in March 2003. In 2002, Europe-US clash over Iraq led to the serious deterioration of transatlantic relations. The dispute shook the European-American relations to its core and posed a challenge to the main institutions under pining the world order during the post World War II period. The United Nations Security Council, the main international body for international peace and security, failed in March 2003 to reach a consensus on the resolution of Iraq dispute. NATO, the most important and enduring military alliance in the history of the world, not only failed to unite on Iraq, but also failed to respond to a request from one of its members, Turkey, to arrange its defence measures.

The EU, in the midst of the constitutional convention for the continent's political unification, was profoundly divided by France, Germany, Belgium, Luxembourg, and Greece on the opponent side and the UK, Spain, Italy, Poland, Hungary, Denmark, Portugal, the Czech Republic, who also signed "Letter of Eight" on January 30, 2003, to express solidarity to the US, on the proponent side of military operation in Iraq. The intra-European divergences on Iraq also spilled over into relations between Western and Eastern Europe with the publication of "Vilnius 10 Text" by Albania, Bulgaria, Croatia, Estonia, Latvia, Lithuania, Macedonia, Slovakia and Romania to show the same solidarity with the US as the publishers of Letter of Eight did.

Philip H. Gordon enumerated the arguments for and against the war on Iraq in his paper: *Iraq: The Transatlantic Debate* in order to explain the reasons of divergences between Europeans and the US, and Europeans themselves. Philip H. Gordon puts six war arguments used by the war's advocates. The first argument of war's advocates was that nuclear weapons could lead Saddam Hussein to risk aggression against his neighbours and seek to dominate the Middle East. As the war's adherents claimed, the worst nightmare scenerio was that the Iraqi regime might obtain nuclear weapons. In that situation, Saddam Hussein could attack neighbouring countries in order to seek the domination in the region.

A second argument was that if nothing is done to stop Saddam Hussein's development of WMD, these weapons could be passed to Islamic terrorists. The third argument that war's advocates claimed that it was no longer possible to manage rigorous and detailed inspections to ensure that Saddam Hussein's regime did not possess nuclear weapons and WMD because Iraq is too big to be inspected properly. In addition, WMD could easily be hidden or transported to other countries such as Iran and Syria.

The fourth argument was that the cost of existing *status quo* had become too high. Saddam Hussein's vicious rule, sanctions on Iraq, humanitarian suffering, threats to Iraq's neighbours, the need for troops in Saudi Arabia, the no-fly zones, Saddam Hussein's support for Palestinian terrorists and periodic disruption of oil markets posed a great danger to the interests of the West and the region. Upholding international law and the authority of the UN Security Council was the fifth argument.

War's advocates argued that the regime of Saddam Hussein had flouted the authority of the UN by defying 16 Security Council resolutions for the past 11 years. Therefore, expecting the enforcement of other resolutions or the implementation of other WMD non-proliferation regimes was impossible in Iraq. The last argument of war's advocates was that the only threat of military action would have forced Iraqi regime to disarm.

Opponents of war had often pressured Iraq by political tools, however without a credible military dimension these attempts were proving futile. On the other hand, the opponents of war in Iraq (France, Germany, Belgium, Luxembourg, Greece) firstly claimed that military operation in Iraq could not be too easy as the proponents of war claimed. Iraqi regime change would not be a repeat of Gulf War, when the forces were fought in the desert and the main objective was kicking Iraqi army out of Kuwait.

This time, Saddam Hussein would have fought for his survival perhaps by using his so-called WMD, so the causalities of war could be much more on invading forces and civilians. In addition, to involve in an urban combat could defeat coalition force's technological superiority. The day after problem was the second argument of opponents of war. The opponents' impression was that the US had no vision for post-Saddam Hussein Iraq, most importantly, including how to convince Iraqi ethnic and religious groups to cooperate. The third argument of opponents was that the Iraqi invasion would have undermined the war on terrorism. The invasion of Iraq, if things go bad, would have led to the US bombings of Arab civilians, broadcast throughout the Arab world; an Israeli incursion in West Bank under cover of Iraq invasion leading to high Palestinian terrorist attacks; potentially violent invasion could have fueled resentment of West in Arab world to intensify attacks on Western societies.

This would have undermined the efforts to prevent terrorism in the world. Finally, opponents of war claimed that the unilateral US invasion would be illegal, unless explicitly authorized by the UNSC. Even a unilateral US action would be dangerous for international security because China, Israel, Russia and anyone else could emulate the US's unilateral way against its neighbours to increase their spheres of influence.

Therefore, the unilateral US action could destroy the order of international system in the long run. Robert Kagan theoretically analysed the reasons for these divergences between the US and many European governments and the majority of the European public. Robert Kagan claims that European opposition to the US was the result of different philosophical and psychological ways of perceiving the world. In that way, Europeans live in a Kantian world where the rules are paramount and the use of military force is the last resort. Robert Kagan also argues that Europeans' temptation in that way is due to the power gap between European states and the US.

Thus, the best choice for militarily weak Europe to sustain its global influence is to insist on conducting international politics by the world of norms. On the other hand, according to Robert Kagan, Hobessian US rule of law does not matter in the face of danger. Due to the US's overwhelming military power, the US is capable of acting unilaterally even if the whole world is against them which is not the case for Europeans. Thus, the unilateral US action could not be accepted by Europeans. However, it is simplistic to explain the European attitude by reducing it only to the military power differences between Europe and the US as Robert Kagan argues. In fact, European societies demanded their governments act according to the long existing liberal European values and standards such as human rights, democracy, the rule of law, and multilateralism which are institutionalised in the EU during its nearly 50 years of history.

The European Union and the US Security Strategies

The divergences between European states concerning the war in Iraq, which was analysed in the previous section, increased the need for a common strategic approach of all the EU countries. Therefore, Javier Solona, High Representative of the CFSP of the EU, prepared the "European Security Strategy" which he entitled "A Secure Europe in a Better World" that was accepted by the European Council on December 12, 2003.

In fact, the publication of the ESS not only created common strategic approach for the EU, but also revealed the strategic divergences between the EU and the US on the confrontation of increasing threat of terrorism and other emerging threats. Thus, in this part, the main themes of the ESS and the NSS will be compared in order to analyse these strategic divergences between the EU and the US, which stems from the implementation of strategic objectives of both papers. In fact, as Jean-Marc Rickli argues, the two papers are relatively similar in their threat assessment conclusions.

Both papers acknowledged the danger of terrorism, failed states, or in the words of the NSS rogue states, weapons of mass destruction which pose serious danger to their citizens, their territory and to the international community. The NSS indicates that rogue states are the primary threat because they not only provide a sanctuary for terrorists but also breed them. The ESS concurs with this analysis, while pointing out the crucial role of the regional conflicts as enabler of terrorism, extremism, state failure and organized crime.

Yet, the ESS and the NSS conclude that the major threat is the use of weapons of mass destruction. While the ESS points out that "the most frightening scenario is one in which the terrorist groups acquire weapons of mass destruction", the NSS puts that "the gravest danger our Nation faces lies at the crossroads of radicalism and technology. Our enemies have openly declared that they are seeking weapons of mass destruction, and evidence indicates that they are doing so with determination".

The greatest difference between the ESS and the NSS stems from the implementation of both papers. In this way, the ESS adopts a two-pronged strategy: extending the zone of security in the EU's neighbourhood and "effective multilateralism". To extend the zone of security in the EU's neighbourhood, the ESS considers the Balkans and

Mediterranean as the key regions for the success of European strategy by stating that "[o]ur task is to promote a ring of well governed countries to the East of the European Union and on the borders of the Mediterranean with whom we can enjoy close and cooperative relations".

In order to ensure well governed countries in the Balkans and Mediterranean region, the ESS indicates the importance of the extension of the benefits of economic and political cooperation to these regions. In this context, the EU adopts a liberal approach by pursuing its foreign policy interests through an international agenda which includes developmental, economic, environmental, and cultural matters, in addition to security matters, to solve terrorism and other emerging threats by its root causes. The ESS emphasizes that today's problems are so complex that no country can tackle it by its own, so the solution of these complex problems depends on "effective multilateralism" by upholding and developing international law under the framework of the UN Charter.

In addition, the ESS identifies the UNSC as the primary international body responsible for the maintenance of peace and security. Thus, the EU underlines the importance of multilateral cooperation to fight against terrorism and other emerging threats. The EU's multilateral perspective reflects its liberal approach on international matters, because they are liberals who claim that the international community can improve the world and promote justice by cooperation-particularly through international institutions, as multilateralism is a preferred approach for global problems in the anarchical environment of international system. However, NATO took less prominent place in the ESS. In fact, NATO is considered as a toolbox for the EU missions and as a bridge in transatlantic relations.

On the other hand, the US strategy, unlike the European strategy, based on the instrumentalisation of cooperation in favour of the US interests in line with the perceptions of realists who argue that for survival states must selfishly pursue their national interests, the most vital being national security. To this end, when the nature of threat has become unclear and volatile, the NSS puts that coalitions can no longer be fixed, but depend on missions. Therefore, even though the US "will work with others to defuse regional conflicts", it would not inhibit its freedom of action by fixed pattern of cooperation.

Likewise, international organizations' roles are subordinated to the mission as well. Thus, according to the NSS, NATO must "act wherever American interests are threatened, creating coalitions under NATO's own mandate, as well as contributing to mission based coalitions". In the same vein, the NSS indicates the US encouragement to develop the ESDP that is compatible with NATO and thus compatible with the US interests. Moreover, the NSS considers the UN exclusively for soft security matters.

The strategic divergences in two papers are echoed in the means favoured to implement them. The NSS significantly emphasizes the importance of the US military power. The NSS considers military force as an appropriate tool to destroy terrorist organizations, prevent rogue states before they use weapons of mass destruction, protect the US national interests, and strengthen "America's homeland security to protect against and deter attack". In other words, the NSS puts the military force of the US as a vehicle to carry out the US hegemony in line with realist perceptions which claims that the most important resources in the pursuit of the national interests are material capabilities, especially offensive military ones. The NSS also considers non-military means.

However, as Jean-Marc Rickli points out, non-military means subordinated to the military means and apply in soft security issues. On the other hand, the perspective of the ESS aims to provide a balance between military and civilian instruments in order to pursue more coherent and capable policies. The ESS puts that developing military capabilities is needed in order to address new threats.

From one point of view, this should be considered as the rise of realist "hard power" perception for the EU, however in the ESS military factor is handled as one mean together with the civil ones for the implementation of the EU policies. Besides, the ESS draws the role of military power to a minor degree and as a post conflict tool by stating that in the failed states "military instruments may be needed to restore order", and in regional conflicts "military assets and effective policing may be needed in the post conflict phase".

Thus, while the ESS perspective offers a constructive way for "restoring order" by military means, it provides destructing way of causes of terrorism by civilian soft power means. In this context, the ESS states that "proliferation may be contained through export controls, attacked through political, economic and other pressures while the underlying causes are also tackled" and "dealing with terrorism requires a mixture of intelligence, police, judicial, military and other means". To sum up, as the liberals claim, today's complex security issues requires comprehensive understanding of both "hard power" and "soft power" policies, the EU acknowledge this approach in its security strategy.

The most striking divergence between the ESS and the NSS emerge when they deal with terrorism and other threats. The ESS refers "preventive engagement" by stating that "[w]e needs to be able to act before countries around us deteriorate, when signs of proliferation are detected, and before humanitarian emergencies arise. Preventive engagement can avoid more serious problems in the future". Even though the ESS's preventive engagement also encompasses military hard power, the ESS envisages military hard power as a useful tool to restore order in failed states for humanitarian means only in the post conflict phase under the framework of the UN.

In fact, the ESS dominates civilian soft power instruments for its preventive engagement approach. In this context, the ESS's preventive engagement incorporates various instruments of civilian soft power for crisis and post crisis situations under the framework of the UN with the aim of fighting terrorism and other emerging threats from their root causes. Thus, the emphasize of the ESS both on soft and hard security instruments for its preventive engagement approach, even though soft security tools given more emphasize, justifies the claim of liberalism that military hard power has become less effective to solve problems in the complex and interdependent environment of international relations, so that the international security environment requires the combination of "hard power" and "soft power" policies.

On the other hand, the NSS adopts "preemption" concept. The NSS states that deterrence no longer works against people willing to sacrifice their lives and concludes that the US will strike before their enemies to do so. In addition, preemption concept of the NSS is closely related with unilateralism: "while the US will constantly strive to enlist the support of international community, we will not hesitate to act alone, if necessary to exercise our right of self-defense by acting pre-emptively against such terrorists". These statements of the NSS are a clear justification of the US's alignment to realism's key assumptions such as self-help and survival while pursuing its foreign policy to confront the terrorism.

Transatlantic Convergence

Despite their growing divergences on the ways for tackling the terrorism and other threats, as Valsamis

Mitsilegas argues, the September 11 terrorist attacks acted as a catalyst for the intensification of law enforcement cooperation between the EU and the US. Since September 11, the EU has made improving the law enforcement cooperation with the US a top priority as part of its international efforts to combat terrorism. The Bush administration and Members of Congress have welcomed these initiatives of the EU to prevent other terrorist attacks against the US and root out terrorist cells in Europe.

The dialogue between the EU and the US officials on police, judicial, and border control policy matters have increased substantially since September 11 terrorist attacks. The EU officials meet with their respective the US counterparts at least once a year, and the EU-US working group of senior officials meet once every six months in order to discuss their police and judicial cooperation against terrorism. In 2004, Europol posted two liaison officers in Washington to work with the US officials, and the US posted an FBI liaison officer in The Hague, Netherlands, to work with Europol officials on counterterrorism.

The EU and the US officials also bridged the many gaps between their respective terrorist lists. In addition, the EU and the US established a high-level policy dialogue on border and transport security including passenger data-sharing, cargo security, biometrics, visa policy, and sky Marshalls. Beyond the increasing dialogue, the EU and the US also signed agreements concerning police and judicial cooperation, and transport and border security against terrorism. Europol- US Agreements In 2001 and 2002, two information sharing agreements were signed between Europol and the US.

The first agreement was concluded on December 11, 2001. The purpose of the agreement is "to enhance the cooperation of the EU Member States, acting through Europol, and the US in preventing, detecting, suppressing, and investigating serious forms of international crime in the areas mentioned in Article 3, in particular through the exchange of strategic and technical information defined in Article 2". Article 2 of the agreement provides Europol and the US law enforcement authorities to share both "strategic" information, including threat tips, crime patterns, and risk assessments, and "technical" information including stengthening administrative structures, forensic police methods, investigative procedures, methods of training the officials, criminal intelligence analytical methods, identification of law enforcement expertise.

Areas of criminality to which the agreement applies are arranged in Article 3 of the agreement. According to Article 3, the cooperation established in this agreement shall relate to following criminal activities: (i) unlawful drug trafficking; (ii) trafficking in nuclear and radioactive substances; (iii) illegal immigrant smuggling; (iv) trade in human beings; (v) motor vehicle crime; (vi) crimes committed or likely to be committed in the course of terrorist activities against life, limb, personal freedom or property; (vii) forgery of money and means of payment.

In addition, illegal money laundering activities in connection with these forms of crime or specific manifestations thereof and related criminal offences are put into the areas of criminality. This agreement does not include personal data sharing. In fact, agreement on the exchange of personal data, the issue of most interest to the Americans, was deferred to second agreement concluded in 2002. The disagreement on personal data exchange stemmed from the fact that the EU laws specify that the EU can only transmit personal data to another state with the same legal framework to protect the privacy of such data. In this context, the US structure differed from the EU one because the US does not have a central authority that is responsible for the supervision and control of the use of personal data and also there is no structured data protection legislation.

In order to solve this problem, the US proposed that the principles of such protection, rather than specific institutions set up to protect data, be examined. If the Parties should agree that the purposes of both sides were similar, and that different institutions and laws accomplished the same goal in practice, that understanding might form the basis for agreement. After an exchange of information on their respective principles and institutions to protect personal data, the EU and the US signed the "Supplemental Agreement between Europol Police Office and the United States of America on the Exchange of Personal Data and Related Information" in December 2002 allowing the transfer of such data for law enforcement purposes.

The "supplemental" agreement intensified the level of cooperation between Europol and the US law enforcement agencies. This intensified cooperation allow for an unprecedented dimension of personal data exchange in terms of quantity and sensivity of the data. In this context, the exchange of a wide range of personal data- transmission of information is provided in the "supplemental" agreement for purposes including "the prevention, detection, suppression, investigation and prosecution of any specific criminal offences, and for any specific analytical purposes".

Therefore, the exchange of information is not limited to data related to the "fight against terrorism", but encompasses "any offence". Article 5 (4) puts that the grounds for refusing or postponing assistance must be limited "to the greatest extent possible". In the Exchange of Letters accompanying the Agreement, it is noted that Article 5 (4) of supplemental agreement "is to be understood not to permit the imposition of generic restrictions with respect to the sharing of personal data, additional to the express requirements of the Agreement as a precondition to be imposed by either Europol or one of its Member States".

This serves to prevent refusals of the EU Member States to transmit data to the US "on the grounds that the data protection system in the US *per se* contains inadequate safeguards". The exchange of sensitive personal data is also provided in the "supplemental" agreement.

Accordingly, Article 6 of the Agreement puts that the transmission of personal data revealing race, political opinions, or religious or other beliefs, or concerning health and sexual life is possible "only upon the transmitting Party's determination that such data is particularly relevant to a purpose set forth in Article 5, paragraph 1".

Article 7 (1) (a) and (b) defines US authorities competent to receive Europol data- these include the US Federal authorities, but also "the US or local authorities provided that they agree to observe the provisions of the Agreement, in particular Article 5 (1)". On the other hand, Article 7 (2) permits access to the US data to the "competent law enforcement authorities of the Member States of the European Union or for use within Europol". The Exchange of Letters defines "competent authorities" as those authorities who are "responsible for functions relating to the prevention, detection, suppression, investigation and prosecution of criminal offences". Article 7(3) of the Agreement permits the onward transmission of information to international organizations or third parties only "with the prior written consent of the Party that supplied the information, unless already in the public domain".

Europol's Joint Supervisory Body (JSB) reacted to this provision by claiming that Europol must not consent the onward transmission of Europol data by the US in any case. The Exchange of Letters states that the US "takes note of the fact that under its legal framework Europol is not allowed to provide authorization for onward transmission beyond that reflected in this Agreement". According to Nicolaos Lavranos, this limitation is worthless because the scope of the agreement is so broad that onward transmission can always be possible within the scope of the agreement.

Judicial Cooperation Agreements

The EU and the US signed two agreements on extradition and mutual legal assistance to simplify the extradition process, and increase better prosecutorial cooperation. Two points should be noted before the examination of agreements: first, the Agreements do not intend to substitute existing bilateral agreements between the Member States of the EU and US, but to supplement them. While all 15 Member States had a bilateral extradition agreements with the US, 11 of 15 had mutual legal assistance agreements with the US while the agreements have been signed. Second, the Agreements considerably extend the ambit of cooperation between the EU and the US, because scope of the Agreements is very broad.

The Extradition Agreement

The Extradition Agreement defines extraditable offences which are "punishable under the laws of both the requesting and requested State by deprivation of liberty for a maximum period of more than one year or by a more severe penalty". It adds to this an attempt or conspiracy to commit, or participation in the commission of, an extraditable offence and requests for enforcement of the sentence of a person convicted of an extraditable offence when the period of deprivation of liberty remaining to be served is at least four months. Article 4 (4) of the agreement states that extradition may be refused for extraterritorial offences unless they are also extraterritorial offences in the requested State in similar circumstances.

Beyond the some main provisions of the extradition agreement mentioned above, the death penalty provision of agreement merits further attention. Even though the bilateral agreements between the EU Member States and the US contain assurances that suspects extradited to the US would not face death penalty, the US officials were reluctant to agree to such a blanket guarantee with the EU as whole in the negotiations of the agreement. In contrast, the main objective of the EU in the negotiations were to obtain a guarantee that the death penalty would not be imposed or carried out on extradited individuals from a Member State to the US.

The discussions on death penalty was solved in favour of the EU's demands in Article 13 of the extradition agreement which states that in cases where extradition is sought for offences punishable by death, the requested State "may grant extradition on the condition that the death penalty shall not be imposed on the person sought, or if for procedural reasons such condition cannot be complied with by the requesting State, on condition that the death penalty if imposed shall not be carried out". Therefore, the US accepted the EU demands that suspects extradited to the US would not face death penalty.

On the other hand, Amnesty International (AI) criticized the Article 13 of the extradition agreement. Amnesty International considers that Article 13 leaves an unacceptable margin of discretion with regard to conditioning and refusing extradition in the face of the death penalty. It is not consistent with Protocols 6 and 13 of European Convention on Human Rights and with the EU Charter of Fundamental Rights which prohibit extradition where there is a risk of death penalty.

Mutual Legal Assistance Agreement

Mutual Legal Assistance Agreement between the EU and the US contains innovative elements. The provisions of Mutual Legal Assistance Agreement enable the use of modern communication techniques and facilitate mutual legal assistance by simplifying the exchange of the requests. Article 4 of the Agreement concerns identification of bank information. Article 4 (1) (a) stipulates that requested State shall promptly communicate a requesting State its inquiries on bank account or accounts of "identified natural or legal person suspected of or charged with criminal offence".

Article 4 (1) (b) also states that the actions described in Article 4 (1) (a) may also be taken for the purpose of identifying "information regarding natural or legal persons convicted of or otherwise involved in a criminal offence", "information in the possession of non- bank financial institutions" or "financial transactions unrelated to accounts". Article 5 (1) of the Agreement enables the establishment of "Joint Investigative Teams" which can operate in the respective territories of each Member State of the EU and the US to facilitate criminal investigations and prosecutions involving one or more Member States of the EU and of the US. The procedures under which these teams will operate will be "as agreed between the competent authorities responsible for the investigation or prosecution of criminal offences as determined by the respective States concerned".

Beyond the identification of bank accounts and establishment of joint investigative teams, the provisions of the Agreement also contain various forms of mechanisms for assistance. These mechanisms include video conferencing for taking testimony (Art.6), expedited transmission of requests, including by fax and e-mail (Art.7), and mutual legal assistance to administrative authorities investigating a case with a view to criminal prosecution (Art.8). The Agreement also comprises a provision on limitations on the use of information to protect personal and other data (Art.9) and on requests for confidentiality (Art.10).

Border and Transport Security

The EU and the US have also concluded several agreements in the area of border control and transport security. In April 2004, the EU and the US signed a customs cooperation agreement. The Agreement tries to extend the US Container Security Initiative (CSI) throughout the EU. CSI stations the US customs officers in the foreign countries' ports to help pre-screen the US-bound cargo containers. The primary aim of pre-screen is to ensure that containers do not contain dangerous materials such as WMD. On May 28, 2004, the EU and the US signed an agreement on transfer of PNR (Passenger Name Record) data.

The agreement permits airlines operating flights to or from US to provide US Customs and Border Protection (CBP) with PNR data (including phone numbers, addresses, credit card numbers) in their reservation and control systems within 15 minutes of a flight's departure. The European Parliament has lodged a case against PNR agreement in the EU Court of Justice by claiming that the agreement breaches EU citizens' data privacy rights. The EU and the US also tries to improve international information exchanges on lost and stolen passports and increase travel document security by using the interoperable biometric identifiers such as digital finger scans and photographs. The aim of cooperation on biometric identifiers is to minimize the EU-US conflicts on new US rules for its Visa Waiver Program (VWP).

Even though the US law had required machine-readable biometric passports from the citizens of VWP countries by October 26, 2004, the US Congress extended the deadline for biometric requirements for VWP passports to October 26, 2005, in order to allow more time for the solution of technical problems. However, European participants to VWP do not seem to meet 2005 deadline. Therefore, the EU lobbies with the US to extend the deadline to 2006.

The EU and the US discussed the use of armed air marshals for some transatlantic flights. Some EU Member

States-such as France and the UK- opposed to use of armed air marshals by claiming that guns on board planes would increase the security risks. Thus, in April 2004, the US officials pledged to consider alternative measures that could be put in place for European opposition to armed marshals, and the EU and the US agreed that cancelling flight should be a measure of last resort.

EU-Mediterranean Cooperation

Terrorism and the Barcelona Process: According to the EU perspective, stability and development in the Mediterranean region is essential for security at home and abroad. At the same time, the EU believes that the root causes of terrorism lie in the economic, political, and social inequities that exist in the southern shores of the Mediterranean and these inequities can only be addressed with the promotion of well governed countries in the region. In order to do so, the EU tries to extend the benefits of economic and political cooperation to the Mediterranean region to eradicate the deepest causes of terrorism and other key threats by pursuing its foreign policy interests through an international agenda including economic, political, developmental, social matters, in addition to security matters.

By adopting this liberal approach, the EU moves away from the US's realist perception that reduces fight against terrorism excessively on military matters. In that context, the Barcelona Process that incorporates various cooperation areas and the subsequent adoption of Valencia Action Plan under its framework after the September 11 terrorist attacks to promote regional security and development serve as a critical piece of the EU perspective on fight against terrorism. The Euro-Mediterranean Conference of Ministers of Foreign Affairs, held in Barcelona on November 27-28, 1995, started the Euro-Mediterranean Partnership (Barcelona Process), a wide framework of political, economic and social relations between the Member States of the EU and 12 Partners of the Southern Mediterranean (namely, Morocco, Algeria, Tunisia, Cyprus, Malta, Egypt, Israel, Jordan, Syria, Lebanon, Turkey and the Palestinian Authority).

In fact, the Barcelona Process represents the beginning of the new security concept- which replace the Cold War's power politics with, in addition to security factor, more emphasize on political, economic, social and environmental factors of international system - for the EU and Mediterranean countries relations. After the collapse of the Soviet Union, the EU saw numerous south-south struggles and a range of new transnational threats (particularly terrorism, illegal trafficking in arms, drugs and persons, immigration and various regional conflicts) rather than nuclear threat or potential for North-South conflict of the Cold War era. These new transnational threats meant that the massive differential in wealth that characterized the two sides of the Mediterranean was no longer compatible with long-run stability and prosperity within the EU.

The EU believed that the European security had become more tied to economic, political and social development of the southern countries than to military preparedness or non- proliferation. The Barcelona Declaration defined three objectives of the Euro- Mediterranean Partnership.

These are:

- The definition of a common era of peace and stability through the reinforcement of political and security dialogue (political and security chapter).
- The construction of a zone of shared prosperity through an economic and financial partnership and the gradual establishment of a free trade zone by 2010 (economic and financial chapter).
- The rapprochement between peoples through a social, cultural and human partnership aimed at encouraging

between cultures and exchanges between civil societies (social, cultural and human chapter).

The ultimate goal is to develop free and flourishing civil societies. The Euro-Mediterranean Partnership comprises two complementary bilateral and regional dimensions:

1. Bilateral dimension: EU carries out a number of activities bilaterally with each country. The most important are the Euro-Mediterranean association agreements which the EU negotiates with Mediterranean partners individually. They reflect the general principles governing the new Euro-Mediterranean relationship, even though they each contain characteristics specific to the relations between the EU and each Mediterranean partner.

2. Regional dimension: Regional dialogue represents one of the most innovative aspects of the Euro-Mediterranean Partnership, covering the cooperation in political, economic and cultural fields. Regional cooperation has a very important strategic impact as it deals with problems that are common to many Mediterranean partners while it emphasizes the national complementarities.

Regional dimension supports and complements the bilateral actions and dialogue taking place under the Euro-Mediterranean Association Agreements. The MEDA programme is the main financial instrument for the Euro-Mediterranean Partnership. The MEDA programme devoted 3.44 billion Euro for 1995-1999, 879 million Euro in 2000, and 5.35 billion Euro for 2000-2006 in order to enhance Euro-Mediterranean cooperation.

Counterterrorism Cooperation

Counterterrorism cooperation between the EU and the Mediterranean Partners can only be seen at the declaratory level, but should not be underestimated. In fact, both sides showed their willingness to overcome problems, particularly definitional problem, and to enhance their cooperation. On April 22-23, 2002, at Valencia Euro-Mediterranean meeting, both sides declared that they are determined to give unconditional support to the convening of an International Conference on Terrorism under the UN auspices, to fully support the UN resolutions 1368 and 1373, and to pursue and bring to justice those who perpetrate, plan and sponsor terrorist acts.

Following the terrorist attacks in Morocco, on May 16, 2003, the Mid-term Euro-Mediterranean meeting held in Crete, Spain, on May 26-27, 2003. The meeting concluded that the fight against terrorism should be regular subject in the political dialogue between Partners and that Senior Officials should continue their dialogue through ad-hoc meetings. The meeting also concluded that "differences regarding the definition of terrorism should not prevent partners from identifying areas where they can cooperate". The Euro-Mediterranean meeting at Naples, on December 2-3, 2003, went further in declaring Partners' commitment to fight against terrorism "in all its forms and manifestations wherever and whomsoever committed" without getting any opposition from Syria.

It is also concluded that the dialogue on terrorism would be continued at the level of senior officials, including ad hoc meetings, and cooperation would be pursued "under existing and future regional and bilateral programmes for training and technical assistance to improve the capability to fight against terrorism". Dublin Euro-Mediterranean Mid-Term meeting held in Dublin, on May 5-6, 2004, following the Madrid train station bombings. The conference concluded that the recent terrorist attacks showed that the cooperation for fight against terrorism must be a priority objective and Partners need to move to the stage of concrete operational joint activities both at regional and bilateral levels. At bilateral level, foreign ministers mandated the Justice and Security subcommittees "to take forward such joint activities at expert level with the aim of improving and assisting the development of counter-terrorism standards and capabilities".

In addition, it is put that the fight against terrorism should also be pursued under the framework of the EU Plan of Action to Combat Terrorism which was adopted in the wake of the September 11 terrorist attacks. November 29-30, 2004, Euro-Mediterranean meeting at The Hague stated that the EU and some countries of the region, particularly Morocco, Algeria and Tunisia, have stepped up the dialogue and cooperation on counterterrorism which could be extended to other partners. It is also noted that Ad-hoc meetings on fight against terrorism were held in April 2004, focusing primarily on the ways to prevent the financing of terrorism, and November 2004, concentrating on enhanced cooperation with some Mediterranean Partners.

Euro-Mediterranean conference, held in Luxembourg on May 30-31, 2005, emphasized that state-to-state cooperation has proved important, but it should be reinforced by mutually agreed measures to confront the global terrorism threat. Both sides underlined the importance "to adopt all relevant UN Conventions, and to fully implement the commitments pertaining to the ones they have ratified, as well as these commitments which derive from the UNSC Resolutions concerning the fight against terrorism". In this context, Foreign Ministers also encouraged the signature, ratification and implementation of recently agreed Convention for the Suppression of Acts of Nuclear Terrorism under the UN framework. In addition, meeting concluded that disagreements on the definitions of terrorism hinder regional dialogue on fight against terrorism.

Therefore, Foreign Ministers supported the join efforts to reach the largest possible consensus on the draft of the

UN Comprehensive Convention against Terrorism that promises to close gaps on the UN's twelve existing conventions on terrorism and, in this context, which also tries to provide universally accepted definition of terrorism. Conclusively, the conclusions of Euro-Mediterranean Conferences should be considered as important step. These conclusions should pave the way for future Euro-Mediterranean Cooperation for counterterrorism in a practical way.

The EU-Russia Cooperation

The EU and Russian relations have significantly improved since the collapse of the Soviet Union and creation of the Russian Federation. The ratification of "Partnership and Cooperation Agreement (PCA)" between the EU and Russia in 1997 has formed the legal basis for bilateral relations. The PCA indicates a new level of EU-Russian relations upgraded to partnership based on common respect for democratic principles and human rights.

The Agreement designated the main areas of cooperation between the EU and Russia: political and economic cooperation. In June 1999, the EU adopted "Common Strategy on Russia", which is valid for a period of four years, built upon existing bilateral relations extending coherence to include the consolidation of democracy, the rule of law and public institutions, the integration of Russia into a common European economic and social sphere, reinforcement of stability and security in Europe and beyond, and a commitment to common challenges on the European continent such as organized crime, illegal immigration and environment. In addition, through TACIS (Technical Assistance to the Commonwealth of Independent States) programme, created in 1991, the EU has provided financial assistance for the reinforcement of democracy and the rule of law and promotion of a market economy.

Counterterrorism Cooperation between the EU and Russia

Joint Statements and Areas of Cooperation

The September 11 terrorist attacks brought counterterrorism cooperation to the table of EU-Russian political dialogue. At the summit level, the EU and Russia issued two related joint statements. In fact, these statements are also important to form the framework of practical counterterrorism cooperation in the future, as in the case of Euro-Mediterranean Conferences' conclusions. The first statement was issued following the EU-Russia Summit in Brussels on October 3, 2001, in which the two Parties pledged to increase cooperation to form an international coalition against terrorism.

In addition, as part of this statement, the EU and Russia agreed to exchange information on: (i) the activities of individuals or groups belonging to terrorist networks or maintaining links with such networks; (ii) tickets of dubious authenticity; (iii) supplies of arms, explosives and dual-use goods; (iv) financial transactions which should be used in support of terrorist intrigue; (v) new forms of terrorist activity, including chemical, biological or nuclear threats On November 11, 2002, the EU and Russia issued a second statement on fight against terrorism after their Brussels summit.

The statement emphasized the need to bring to justice the perpetrators, organizers and sponsors of terrorist acts and stressed the role of the UN as the main legal and political authority in counterterrorism struggle. In addition, through the issue of statement, both parties declared that they agreed on areas of the EU-Russia cooperation in fight against terrorism to intensify cooperation related to counterterrorism. In this context, the EU and Russia reiterated the areas of cooperation on exchange of information stressed by Statement on International

Terrorism on October 3, 2001, and agreed to increase their cooperation on the following issues (i) enhanced cooperation in all relevant international and regional fora; (ii) early signature and ratification of relevant counterterrorism conventions and protocols, and smooth and rapid implementation of relevant UN Security Council Resolutions; (iii) early finalization of the UN Comprehensive Convention against Terrorism and the international convention for the suppression of acts of nuclear terrorism; (iv) enhancing common efforts to stop the financing of terrorism, including freezing of funds and other financial assets of terrorists; (v) Strengthening cooperation with and support to third countries to implement UNSCR 1373 (2001), including reinforcement of technical cooperation to third countries for their capacity buildings in the field of counterterrorism.

More practically, the statement also stressed that an agreement between Europol and Russia on the exchange of technical and strategic information was to be finalized as soon as possible.

Europol-Russia Agreement

The negotiation process of Europol and Russia agreement on the exchange of technical and strategic information was finalised in the late 2003 and Parties signed the "Agreement on Cooperation between the European Police Office and the Russian Federation". The Agreement lays the basis for enhanced police and judicial cooperation on terrorism and other serious crimes between EU and Russia. Before analysing some main provisions of the Agreement, it is important to mention that Agreement does not include the exchange of personal data between Europol and Russia.

Article 2 of the Agreement states that "the exchange of personal data shall be carried out on the basis of a separate agreement between the Parties". According to Article 4 of the Agreement, Europol and Russia "shall cooperate in the area of prevention, detection, suppression and investigation of crimes" in areas such as terrorism and its financing, money laudering, illicit trafficking in explosives, nuclear and radioactive materials, narcotic drugs, poisonous substances, and illegal immigration.

Article 5 of the Agreement determines the ways of Europol-Russia cooperation. In this context, Article 5 (1) states that Parties shall cooperate on the exchange of strategic and technical information of mutual interest including information on: (i) forms, methods and means of committing crimes; (ii) new types of narcotic and psychotropic substances discovered in illicit trafficking, the technologies and the materials used to produce such substances, as well as new methods for the examination and identification of such substances; (iii) channels for transferring illegally acquired funds; (iv) crime situation and development reports, threat assessments; (v) new forms and methods of combating crime; (vi) legal and administrative measures to develop main trends of law enforcement activities; (vii) modern forensic police methods and investigating procedures; (viii) advanced forms and methods of personnel training; (ix) centres of excellence; (x) methods of information processing and analysis; (xi) criteria for the evaluation of law enforcement activities.

Exchange of law enforcement experience including the organization of conferences, internships, consultations and seminars; exchange of legislation, technical literature, manuals and other related law enforcement materials; training are also put as ways of cooperation between Europol and Russia. In addition, "cooperation within the framework of this Agreement is carried out on the basis of requests for assistance, or on the initiative of one of the Parties, if this Party presumes that such assistance is of interest to the other Party". Moreover, Agreement contains provisions to deny assistance.

In this context, assistance may be denied completely or partially if "the Russian Federation considers that the execution of the request may damage its sovereignty, security, public order or other essential State interests, or contradicts its legislation or international obligations" or "Europol considers that the execution of the request conflicts with its purposes and tasks". Finally, Article 13 of the Agreement puts that the provisions of this agreement "shall not affect rights and obligations arising out of any other bilateral or multilateral agreements to which the Europol or Russian Federation are a party, including Mutual Legal Assistance Treaties". The provisions of Agreement "shall also not affect any working law enforcement relationship" between the EU Member States and Russia.

Disagreements between the EU and Russia over Chechen Conflict

Before analysing the EU-Russian disagreements on Chechen conflict, it is worth mentioning that for Russia the issue of terrorism is primarily linked to Chechnya and it is very important for Russian foreign policy that Russian efforts in Chechnya be recognized by the international community as combating terrorism. Even though the EU-Russia relations has significantly improved after the end of Cold War, even upgraded to strategic partnership, the issue of Chechnya has always remained as a significant problem between Partners. The most sticking point is the EU's insistence on political solution of the Chechen conflict, based on the territorial integrity of Russia, the creation of representative institutions and respect for human rights, while Russia sees its military actions as the only way to stop Chechen conflict and terrorist actions it generates.

At the beginning of the second Chechen war in October 1999, the EU and Russia engaged in a heated discussion in Helsinki. The EU urged Russia to avoid use of military force and to negotiate with political leaders of Chechens.

However, Russian President V. Putin wanted the EU not to interfere its internal affairs on how to conduct Chechen conflict. In April 2004, Russia complained on a critical draft UN human rights resolution on Chechnya, proposed by the EU. The draft resolution strongly condemned the serious violations of international human rights law and international humanitarian law in Chechnya.

The draft resolution also urged the Russian government to ensure free unimpeded access for the UN, aid agencies, the media and non-governmental organizations to the region. Russia described the draft resolution as an "unfriendly" act and Deputy Foreign Minister Vlademir Chizkov claimed that the EU proposal "does not reflect the partnership relations between Russia and EU". In addition, the tension between the EU and Russia has also increased in September 2004, when the EU foreign ministers demanded that Russia provide the EU information on how the Beslan School siege tragedy could have happened. Russian reaction to this demand was immediate and angrily, calling the EU's inquiry an insolent, odious, offensive and clear interference to Russian internal affairs. Even though the EU and Russia later called this incident a misunderstanding, the disagreements on Chechen conflict between Partners again came to the surface.

Moreover, on March 9, 2005, the EU reacted to the killing of Chechen leader Aslan Maskhadov by Russian forces by calling on Russia to respect human rights and work for a political settlement to the conflict. On the other hand, in the aftermath of the Beslan school siege, Yuri Baluyevski, the chief of the general staff of Russia's armed forces, declared that Russia would carry out preemptive strikes on terrorist bases in any region of the world. Interestingly, the speech did not take much attention from the EU which argues that a policy of preemptive strikes is too risky for international security. Only the EU's official spokeswoman Emma Udvin reacted to this speech, saying that she could not be sure whether the speech represented government policy of Russia. Emma Udvin also added that 25 nations of the EU is against "extra-judicial killings" in the form of preemptive strikes. In fact, the EU reflects its liberal world view in Chechen conflict by constantly making pressure to Russia to solve the conflict through political settlement under the framework of international law. However, Russia is in the side of realist power politics by reducing the option of settlement only to military means.

6

Defeating New Terrorist

F-16 Program in the Fight Against Terrorism

On February 18th 2008, the Pakistani people went to the polls and elected moderate leaders who are working to set a stable, prosperous, democratic path for Pakistan into the future. The journey along this path is going to be a difficult one as Pakistan faces increasing economic challenges and the serious threat of growing instability in the border regions. The United States wants to see this new government succeed, not only because it represents the desires of the Pakistani people but because we believe that a moderate government with a democratic mandate is the most effective partner in the fight against terrorists and violent extremism.

During Prime Minister Gillani's visit to Washington in late July, we saw the United States and Pakistan committed to maintaining and strengthening broad-based partnership; and the United States committed to steps that can help Pakistan deal with economic problems and increase its effectiveness in countering the extremist threat. The Administration's request to re-direct Foreign Military Financing [FMF] in 2008 and beyond to support F-16 Mid-Life Updates [MLU] speaks directly to these two commitments. Updates to Pakistan's F-16s will make these aircraft far more effective against terrorist targets, while helping with these payments will provide the newly-elected Pakistani government valuable fiscal flexibility as they deal with rising food and fuel prices. The new Government of Pakistan stands behind these requests and has committed to assume subsequent payments with national funds beginning in December 2009.

The sale of F-16s to Pakistan became a transformative element of the U.S.-Pakistan bilateral relationship over 20 years ago, and this historical context is important to understand and remember as we determine how to handle the questions of F-16 financing today. Not only has a component of Pakistan's national defense, the F-16 become an iconic symbol of our bilateral relationship and our commitment to each other.

In the early 1980s, the U.S. Government initially agreed to sell Pakistan 111 F-16 aircraft. This decision was influenced by our close partnership with Pakistan during the Soviet invasion of Afghanistan. By October 1990, however, Pressler sanctions were imposed when President [George Herbert Walker] Bush was unable to certify that Pakistan was not developing a nuclear weapon. The Pressler sanctions led to a decade-long suspension of security assistance to Pakistan and a deficit of trust between our two countries that we are still working to overcome.

The suspension of our security assistance programs required under Pressler meant the suspension and eventual cancellation of an additional sale of F-16 aircraft that would have augmented the 40 F-16s Pakistan purchased in 1982. That cancellation has been viewed as a symbol of the collapse of our relationship during the 1990s, a period which remains highly emotional for many Pakistanis. The suspension of our security assistance also precluded Pakistani military officers from attending U.S. military schools, which has produced nearly a generation of

Pakistani military officers who have not traveled to the United States to learn side-by-side with American officers.

The New Face of Chechen Terrorism

On July 5, 2003, two female suicide bombers blew themselves up during a rock concert at the Tushino airport in Moscow. This attack was followed on July 9 by an attempted bombing of a restaurant in downtown Moscow, on Tverskaya-Yamskaya street. In addition, a number of explosive devices of the same type as was used on the previous occasions was found stored in Tolstopaltsevo outside Moscow on July 24. While the use of terrorist tactics in the Chechen war is not new, these events are a novel pattern.

Foreign Islamic extremists of Arab origin began to engage in suicide bombings in Chechnya already in mid-2000. These were carefully coordinated attacks on military targets by mainly male suicide bombers who used the Middle Eastern method of exploding trucks loaded with explosives near the target. Units of Chechen fighters then often followed up the attacks by conventional means. Similar attacks have continued to occur since, including devastating ones aimed at a government building in Znamenskoe, in Chechnya, on May 12, 2003 and a military hospital in Mozdok, North Ossetia on August 1, 2003.

Chechen women took part in fighting already during the First Chechen War, in 1994-1996. However, they only recently turned to suicide attacks against civilians, another method learnt from the Middle East. Examples include a suicide bombing in the Chechen town of Iliskhan-Yurt on May 14, 2003, and the suicide bombing of a bus in Mozdok on June 5, 2003. Underlying factors no doubt include a feeling of hopelessness among Chechen women, many of whom have lost family members in the war. Besides, many are likely destitute. It is hardly coincidental that female suicide bombers have become known as the "black widows."

The key factor that made several Chechen women turn to terror was probably the failed hostage-taking in the Dubrovka theatre in southern Moscow on 23 October 2002. A unit of Chechens, including many women, took hundreds of civilians' hostage. In the First Chechen War, hostage-taking operations such as Shamil Basaev's 1995 raid on Budennovsk were pivotal episodes with regard to the outcome of the war. Basaev launched what appeared to be a suicidal operation against a Russian target, yet emerged victorious with only few casualties. In addition, his raid resulted in widespread international media attention on the Chechen cause as well as outspoken Russian public criticism of the war as many Russians blamed their own government for its incompetence and heavy-handed tactics.

In 2002, the Chechens who took part in Dubrovka hostage-taking probably hoped to duplicate the success of Basaev's raid seven years earlier. For this reason, the operation was probably intended to take hostages rather than kill Russians. The goal might have been to regain some measure of sympathy from the West, the support from which had diminished since the American War on Terror began in 2001. However, the Dubrovka operation produced little sympathy for the Chechen cause abroad and none whatsoever in Russia. Besides, the response of the Russian security organs, to gas both hostage-takers and hostages (more than a hundred of whom were killed by the gas) and then slaughter all the hostage-takers probably persuaded many Chechens that the only remaining solution was to engage in suicide bombings of the type that the Arab extremists in Chechnya have long favoured.

Despite the fact that the increased numbers of female suicide bombers would seem to be a natural reaction to the events in Dubrovka rather than any kind of premediated war strategy among the Chechens, the phenomenon indicates a fundamental shift in the nature of the war in Chechnya. The earlier cases of Chechen terrorism and hostage-taking were either aimed at military targets or, if not, were never planned to result in large numbers of killed civilians. Basaev's 1995 hostage-taking in Budennovsk was in practice aimed at a military target: a garrison town hospital in which Russian military personnel was recuperating. Besides, interviews with Chechens who participated in the raid indicate that the hospital was only a secondary target, chosen when the primary target could not be reached. Even the suicide bombings committed by foreign extremists in Chechnya were aimed at military targets, typically barracks or headquarters of the Russian Interior Ministry Forces in Chechnya.

The Chechen suicide bombers are unlikely to change the outcome of the war in Chechnya militarily. Chechnya remains unstable, and any Russian reaction to the suicide bombings in the form of increased repression - in Chechnya or directed at Chechens living in Russian cities such as Moscow - will no doubt only encourage yet more Chechens to engage in terrorism. Yet, the Russian securities organs have stepped up surveillance of Chechens present in the Russian cities - and could hardly do otherwise when suddenly faced with a real threat of terrorism.

However, the new threat of terrorism brings implications for the political and social development of Russia. Since 1999, Russian President Vladimir Putin has gradually increased the powers of the state, motivating this with the need to protect Russian society from Chechen terrorism. Yet the Russian claims of Chechen involvement in the 1999 apartment building explosions in Moscow and elsewhere have never been substantially proven, and except in the Northern Caucasus, the threat from terrorism was always minimal. The security organs never, or only seldom, had to face a genuine need to use their new powers to fight real, not imagined terrorists. Beginning with the Dubrovka hostage-taking, this situation has changed. President Putin and the Russian security organs will henceforth have to deliver the security that the increased state powers were meant to provide.

Russia from now on will have to live with sudden acts of terrorism aimed at civilians in Moscow as well as other major cities. Whether this will alter the public image of President Putin remains to be seen. He has hitherto enjoyed the image of a tough commander-in-chief of a small victorious war in the Caucasus. However, if Putin cannot deliver the security that he has promised, even he - and certainly the security organs - may eventually lose the support of the public.

On the Chechen side, it remains unclear to what extent the Chechen leadership under President Aslan Maskhadov is able to prevent, or even influence, the shift in tactics. Maskhadov immediately condemned the Dubrovka hostage-taking. He has also condemned other attacks aimed at civilians. Yet, the Chechen leaders no doubt realize that the foreign support lost since 2001 will hardly be regained as long as some Chechens engage in suicide bombings. On the other hand, a situation that pushes men and women so far over the edge that they choose to become suicide bombers is not one that can be solved by logic and negotiations alone. The war in Chechnya is unlikely to be over soon.

Living in a Time of Terrorism

Terrorism haunts our times. People throughout the world live with frightening memories of terrorist attacks and with the uncertainties of possible future attacks. Terrorist networks continue to operate in many countries, some with ability to strike far from their home base. While terrorism has a long history, its threat to peace has intensified in our time. On September 11, 2001, when the world was again shaken by terrorism's murderous destruction and its ability to terrorize millions, the United States experienced its own vulnerability to international terrorism. The attacks of that day can only be condemned.

Our hearts and prayers continue to go out to all those lives were shattered by the events of that day. Since then the United States has been engaged in a struggle against terrorism in which some actions have provoked controversy and division in this country and around the world. Terrorism and counterterrorism are complex, crucial, and long-term concerns for all people who seek a more peaceful world.

"We of the Evangelical Lutheran Church in America share with the Church of Jesus Christ in all times and place the calling to be peacemakers." This opening sentence in the ELCA social statement "For Peace in God's World" reminds us that in these times also God calls us "to proclaim the Gospel of God's final peace and to work for earthly peace." This message draws on that social statement to give a theological perspective on earthly peace, recall the role of governments, call for public vigilance of counterterrorism and for international cooperation, affirm the Gospel's gift of living beyond fear, and highlight the importance of interfaith encounters.

Earthly Peace

"Since we are justified by faith, we have peace with God through our Lord Jesus Christ" (Romans 5:1). In light of the Gospel's promise of peace, Christians recognize both the goodness and limits of earthly peace.

Earthly peace is not the same as the promised peace of God's present and future eternal reign. As a human achievement built in the middle of strife, earthly peace is often fleeting and always partial. It is difficult to build and maintain. It is easily and frequently disrupted by violence and war. All the more, then, is earthly peace a most precious gift. It embodies God's intention for creation, serves human and planetary good, and gives space to proclaim the Gospel, keeping hope in God alive.

This distinction between God's eternal reign of peace and earthly peace offers perspective for approaching terrorism. Terrorism threatens earthly peace, not the peace given in the Gospel. The struggle against terrorism belongs to earthly peace and shares its characteristics. This struggle is not a matter of God's ultimate salvation, which God has already secured for us and for all creation in the cross of Christ. It will not end sin and evil or bring about God's reign of peace. Our task is rather to restrain destructive acts and promote just peace among finite, sinful human beings within the constraints of our historical context.

Because earthly peace is a precious yet fragile good, there is reason for all to be vigilant, self-critical, and active in preventing and suppressing terrorism, holding terrorists accountable, and addressing what gives rise to terrorism. Complacency and wishful thinking endanger peace; pride and self-righteousness endanger peace as well.

In pursuing earthly peace, we must make judgments about good and evil, recognizing that we make them as sinful human beings who are accountable to God for our judgments. Terrorist acts are rightly called "evil," and the cause to protect innocent people from them is good and worthy. Yet counterterrorism should not be seen as the righteous waging a holy war against God's enemies, even when terrorists may understand themselves to be fighting a holy war.

Religious leaders and others who criticize counterterrorism measures need to resist the temptation to be self-righteous in their judgments. "Because all are sinners before God, efforts to build earthly peace must recognize sin's persistent, pervasive, and subtle power. We easily deceive ourselves about our own righteousness. Even our best intentions can produce harmful results."

Acting in a good cause does not mean being free from sin. We act "knowing what we do or do not do falls short of what love requires. No matter what conscientious people decide, they remain under God's judgment and in need of God's mercy given in the cross of Christ." Living in forgiveness encourages a spirit of humility, which recognizes legitimate disagreements about counterterrorism as well as the burdens and risks that decision-makers face before an uncertain future.

The Role of Governments

Terrorism may be understood as violence or the threat of violence directed toward civilians to create a climate of fear and uncertainty. State actors use terror to maintain their grip on power. Non-state actors use terror to disrupt a political, social, or economic order. Terrorism is political violence. It is planned and organized violence that aims to undermine a society's civic peace. Terrorists kill and injure civilians in order to generate fear and panic in society. Because terrorists aim to influence an audience, "terrorism is theatre" and terrorism is "propaganda by deed."

According to both international law and the just war tradition, some political violence may be justified (like wars of self-defense), while other political violence is not (like wars of aggression). The principles for deciding about wars include right intention, justifiable cause, legitimate authority, last resort, declaration of war aims, proportionality, and reasonable chance of success. The principles for conducting war include noncombatant immunity and proportionality.

By these principles, terrorism is one kind of unjustifiable political violence. Just as human rights laws and just war principles condemn violent acts by a state to terrorize its people, so the same standards condemn terrorist acts by non-state actors. Many such terrorist acts fail to meet any of the just war standards. Even when the terrorists' cause is viewed as just, terrorism cannot be justified because it intentionally targets noncombatants. Few people claim to be terrorists; yet if they intentionally kill or threaten to harm civilians to generate fear in order to disrupt a social order, they are terrorists.

Lawful governments are authorized by God to protect society and secure the blessings of just order. Without minimal civic peace, people cannot carry on their daily activities that allow life to go on or attain the benefits of a just society. "We also advocate an earthly peace that provides security from violence and aggression, seeks just order in place of tyranny or anarchy, checks unrestrained power, and defends and enhances the life of people who are poor and powerless."

Governments often abuse and violate their authority under the guise of seeking security. They may deny the rightful aspirations of an oppressed group, violate human rights, or inflict their own unjustifiable violence on people in the name of fighting terrorism. They may use terror to guard the interests of an elite ruling group instead of protecting the security of all citizens. In their counterterrorism activity, governments have the obligation to adhere to basic human rights, the rule of law, and just war standards.

The security that governments—including that of the United States—can provide from the threats of terrorism has limits. Human beings, finite creatures that we are, are always vulnerable; eliminating vulnerability would also do away with freedom. Governments cannot provide perfect or total security; when they claim or seek to do so, they become agents of arrogant pride and the injustice and insecurity that flow from pride. If they are to secure freedom for vulnerable people, governments must recognize their limits in providing security.

International Cooperation

Different perceptions of the nature and seriousness of the threat of terrorism are often a major reason for disagreements within and among nations on what should be done in response to it. Faith provides perspective in approaching terrorism, but it does not give Christians or the Church special knowledge or competence in evaluating this threat. Like other concerned citizens, Christians must rely on others—terrorism analysts, government, media, international voices—for information in forming judgments about the threat of terrorism.

The credibility of such individuals and institutions depends on their provision of trustworthy information and unbiased interpretations to the public. Assessing the reliability and significance of the information and interpretations, however, belongs to the responsibility of citizens. Careful and critical public discussion is essential to sort out truth from deceit and genuine security concerns from self-serving manipulation.

Policy makers face risky and difficult decisions in calculating what kind of security is either too little or too much, determining priorities and allocating expenditures, and balancing security with other responsibilities of government. Public scrutiny is needed to ensure that the costs and burdens of security measures are shared fairly and that the needs of people who are poor and marginalized are met. Continuing public vigilance is essential to evaluate whether or not the security measures are needed, effective, and, above all, respectful of the rights and freedoms guaranteed by the Constitution and in accord with the best of our country's traditions.

Security measures and practices that make people their

target only because they belong to a particular ethnic or religious community endanger the well-being of the particular community and betray the nation's commitment to equal treatment under the law. Government policies and practices that deny or weaken due process for people accused or suspected of terrorist activities jeopardize these protections for all.

In tracking potential terrorists, laws and practices that invade or infringe upon civil liberties without proper judicial oversight threaten the security that comes from being a free people. Policies, practices, and attitudes that are hostile to immigrants living in the United States and that unduly curtail the legal arrival of immigrants, refugees, and asylum seekers fail to live up to our country's tradition of welcoming newcomers in a fair and generous way.

Security from terrorism requires nations to cooperate with one another and with international organizations. Nations must work together to find and track terrorists, to cut off their funds, to prevent terrorists from crossing international borders, to provide protection for high-risk targets, and to improve readiness to respond in the event of new terrorist attacks. International conventions can provide a common framework for national laws and their effective enforcement. It is therefore significant that all 191 nations in the United Nations in 2001 united in condemning terrorist acts and in pledging to work together to prevent and suppress them.

Even with this important cooperation, deep differences exist in the international community about how to respond to terrorism. These differences are evident in opposing views on the political roles of the United Nations and the United States, as may be illustrated in these questions: Are the interests and worldviews of the members of the Security Council so divergent that they render the United Nations ineffective in addressing the threat of terrorism? Or is the dominant power of the United States, with its "war on terrorism," a greater danger to peace than terrorism itself?

Many in other nations perceive that the United States too often acts arrogantly and without sufficient consultation, agreement, and participation of other nations. Citizens in the United States need to hear and evaluate this perception of their nation's actions.

According to the social statement "For Peace in God's World," the United States with its "vital leadership role in world affairs...cannot and should not withdraw or isolate itself from the rest of the world. Neither should it seek to control or police the world." Like all nations, the United States in pursuing its interests has "an obligation to respect the interests of other states and international actors and to comply with international law. Nations should seek their own common good in the context of the global common good."

Whenever military action is considered, citizens have responsibility to hold their government accountable to just war principles. "At their best, these principles provide a moral framework, ambiguous and imprecise though it be, for public deliberation about war, and guidance for persons deciding what to do when faced with the dilemmas of war." Especially contentious in the struggle against terrorism is the meaning of three of these principles: legitimate authority (who authorizes war?), last resort (questions of pre-emption), and reasonable chance of success (does this military action increase or decrease the threat of terrorism?).

Public vigilance also is needed in times of war to judge whether the war is being rightly fought according to the principles of discrimination (noncombatant immunity) and proportionality (determining whether the evil effects are more or less than the evil prevented). In clarifying and applying these principles, "Christians need to be prepared to say 'no' to wars in which their nation participates."

Living Beyond Fear

Fear generated by the threat of terrorism may be a reasonable response to danger, alerting us to take steps to address it. Yet fear can become part of the fabric of society and make people its captives. Fear then paralyzes, divides people, fosters distrust, and clouds judgments. The Gospel promises freedom from living in debilitating fear. Through Word and Sacrament the Holy Spirit surrounds children, youth, and adults with God's unfailing love. "There is no fear in love, but perfect love casts out fear" (1 John 4:18). In faith we may carry on our lives with the confidence that nothing—including terrorism—"will be able to separate us from the love of God in Christ Jesus our Lord" (Romans 8:39). Living from the security of faith in God, Christians in a fearful society may exhibit courage to evaluate soberly the threat of terrorism without ignoring it or becoming all-consumed by it.

The Gospel also frees "us from fear to see others as brothers and sisters for whom Christ died and lives." Believing that God's love in Christ Jesus extends to all, we are freed to attend to the interests and welfare of those who might be considered "enemies." We are better enabled to know and feel the vulnerability of others around the world and to work for a just peace in light of our mutual vulnerability.

As people freed by the Gospel, we need to deepen our understanding of what drives an international terrorist network to carry out attacks such as those of September 11. Is the motivation envy, hate, and resentment toward a prosperous, powerful, and stable society? Is it the belief that the "West" continues to wage a centuries-long crusade against the Islamic world? Is it fear of the freedom of Western societies? Is it the belief that under the guise of freedom a moraliy corrupt culture is undermining a cherished way of life? Is it because an extremist strain of

Islam has captured the imagination of millions of Muslims who see themselves unjustly alienated by the "West"? Is it reaction to United States policy in the Middle East? Is it due to the mysterious presence of evil in the human heart?

To explore such questions is not to justify or explain away terrorist acts, much less to blame the victims for them, but to seek to understand by viewing the world from perspectives of other religions, peoples, and nations. A world with less hate and misunderstanding is a more secure one. Trying to understand may help us to check our own hatred and spirit of revenge, to see our own country's part in the world's tangled web of evil, and to approach our responsibilities as repentant and forgiven sinners.

Terrorism haunts our times, but so do hunger and poverty, corrupt and brutal political systems, harsh discrimination and social inequalities, civil wars, environmental degradation, and epidemic diseases. These are sources of insecurity and hopelessness for millions, and they belong to a world that "is increasingly interconnected." To neglect or be indifferent to these realities while countering terrorism is both morally wrong and shortsighted.

Earthly peace in God's creation "is built on the recognition of the unity and goodness of created existence, the oneness of humanity, and the dignity of every person." A simple yet profound condition for peace is the acknowledgement of the common humanity of all people as God's beloved creatures. This belief too compels us to strengthen our compassionate understanding of peoples throughout the world and to broaden our moral horizon to embrace their suffering and well-being as our concern.

This concern takes form in the search for just peace in a global society. This search envisions "a culture of peace," "an economy with justice," and "a politics of cooperation." The comprehensive naming of cultural, economic, and political "tasks" to keep, make, and build peace today in "For Peace in God's World" points to the breadth of this search. Enduring human security for all depends on building just peace.

Interfaith Encounters

History shows that religions, including Christianity, may be a source of both violent conflict and peacemaking. In a time often thought to be secular, religion has taken on new public significance: Two decades ago terrorists tended to frame their activity in political and ideological terms; in recent times an increasing number view their activity in religious categories. Most notably, the network responsible for September 11 as well as other terrorist acts identifies itself as Muslim and claims to be acting to fulfill a supposed divine obligation.

Worldwide, millions of Christians will join with millions of Muslims in condemning the belief that God sanctions terrorist acts. Similarly, Christians will insist that for them the struggle with terrorism is not a religious war and do all that they can to make sure it does not become a war between Christians and Muslims. They will understand that it is their moral duty to reject blanket condemnations of Islam, all notions that blame all Muslims for specific terrorist acts, and all attitudes and actions that unjustly discriminate against Muslims on account of their religion. Christians will work with others to protect the religious freedom of Muslims.

"Peace is difference in unity. It requires both respect for the uniqueness of others—finite persons in particular communities—and acknowledgment of a common humanity." "This vision calls us to engage differences, not to ignore or fear them. The hope for earthly peace challenges people to strengthen their own particular communities in ways that promote respect and appreciation for people in other communities, for all share a common humanity."

In many situations today, religious differences are a source of enmity. Religion is used to incite people to violence. The Church faces new challenges in being a reconciling presence among the religions of the world. We need to learn from Jews, Muslims, Hindus, Buddhists, and others, discovering the ways they strive for peace, correcting distorted images, and working for mutual understanding. We rejoice where people of different religions work together to overcome hostility.

Our times bid us to intensify our efforts to work with humility and persistence for mutual understanding among all religions, especially among Christians, Muslims, and Jews. This challenge has many dimensions and is only at a beginning stage. It includes personal relationships in neighborhoods, schools, and work places; meetings among congregations, mosques, and synagogues; cooperation with common projects; and scholarly discussions of sacred texts, historical relationships, and living beliefs and practices. It calls for recognizing the great diversity within each religion and for understanding friendly and hostile encounters in multiple contexts.

Christians, Muslims, and Jews belong to particular communities that appeal to their own sacred texts and traditions as their authority in matters of life and belief. Fruitful and respectful dialogue will explore how each community draws on what is authoritative in its life to address how societies should order their life together. Some topics, for example, might be: On what bases does each community reject hatred for those who do not belong to their community? What beliefs and practices in each community foster tolerance and respect for others with different beliefs, and what beliefs and practices further pride as well as disdain for the other communities? How does each community make distinctions between justifiable and unjustifiable political violence? What beliefs in each community lead to a principled commitment to a legal order that guarantees religious freedom for all? Christians, Muslims, and Jews should find agreement in denouncing the belief that terrorist acts are a divine obligation. They should also find agreement in recognizing that religious faith can and should be a powerful force for peace.

Prayerful Quest

The Holy Spirit calls us in the Church "to proclaim the Gospel of God's final peace and to work for earthly peace." In the Gospel we find consolation in our sorrow, freedom from fear, and hope to carry on the "elusive quest to build earthly peace," even when terrorism and other evils haunt our times.

May we in this quest turn to God in prayer, asking forgiveness for our sins, wisdom for discernment, and renewal for our spirits; and interceding for those who suffer from terrorism and war, for those who govern the nations, for those who would harm the innocent, for those who help the wounded, and for those who provide security for the endangered. O God, it is your will to hold both heaven and earth in a single peace. Let the design of your great love shine on the waste of our wraths and sorrows, and give peace to your Church, peace among the nations, peace in our homes, and peace in our hearts; through your Son, Jesus Christ our Lord.

Canada's Response to Terrorism

Near-term prevention

The essential goal of preventing further terrorist attacks on the United States, Canada or any other potential target states in the near term will not be accomplished through military attacks on Afghanistan or any other state identified as a sponsor of terrorism. That goal must be pursued through increased care and vigilance at home and in all states vulnerable to terrorist attacks. We welcome and encourage continued attention to the broad range of security measures that is required, emphasizing due regard for a constructive balance between prudent care and the preservation of the rights and freedoms that define our society.

Justice requires that those who participated in or share responsibility for the September 11 attacks be brought to trial as quickly as possible. Moral and political legitimacy, as well as justice, require also that the international community be meticulous and uncompromising in its attention to due process. We are encouraged by apparent high levels of international cooperation among law enforcement and investigative agencies, and also urge international involvement and cooperation in the trial process.

United Nations Secretary-General Kofi Annan has reminded the international community that "United Nations conventions already provide a legal framework for many of the steps that must be taken to eradicate terrorism – including the extradition and prosecution of offenders and the suppression of money laundering. These conventions," he said, ""must be implemented in full." We endorse the international call on Afghanistan to deliver for trial those accused who now find refuge in that country, and we encourage the United States and the international community to provide the Government of Afghanistan with the evidence gathered and to encourage direct discussions toward the early delivery for trial of the accused. For such appeals to have any prospect for success, they must have the active support of the broad international community, especially states within the region.

In the face of the continued and persistent refusal of the Government of Afghanistan to live up to its obligations under international law, the United States and its partners should now go to the Security Council to seek assistance and authority for all international direct interventions needed to apprehend the accused. We fear that relying on military attacks, some of which are already resulting in the displacement and deaths of civilians, will erode essential regional support and cooperation for the pursuit of the accused, and that a predictable result will be the infliction of widespread damage on an already mutilated Afghanistan, without the successful apprehension of the accused.

Long-term Prevention

American, British, and Canadian political leadership, among many others, have emphasized that efforts toward the reduction and eradication of terrorism must be long-term and multi-dimensional. It is highly regrettable, therefore, that states have allowed attention to shift prominently to military measures. The essential non-military character of the struggle against terrorism must be restored. The concept of human security which Canada has emphasized in recent years is key to addressing the roots of terrorism. This concept means that the safety and well-being of people must be rooted in political, social and economic conditions and institutions that are sustainable and that have the confidence of the people they are intended to serve. Now, in the face of the menacing threat of terrorism, is not the time to ignore that fundamental reality.

Further, as Foreign Affairs Minister John Manley has recognized, Canada will have to provide increased resources for human development in troubled societies if we are to be effective in helping to build conditions inimical to terrorism. The peacebuilding tools that Canada and others have been developing in the post-Cold War era have much to offer, both for the general campaign against terrorism and for discouraging support for terrorism in particular states such as Afghanistan. The September 11 events demonstrate with extraordinary horror that the world is irreversibly interdependent. Safety for any people or nation is inseparable from the collective safety of the international community itself. Security is mutual. It is the product of cooperation and requires multilateral work. Fortunately, as Secretary-General Annan has noted, the United Nations "provides the forum necessary for building a universal coalition and can ensure global legitimacy for the long-term response to terrorism."

We call on the United States, and by association Canada, the United Kingdom and others, to make a full, unambiguous commitment to multilateralism by seeking explicit Security Council authorization for multinational intervention in Afghanistan. Without that authority, and without defining the specific, limited objectives that such an authorization should set out, military action will increasingly tend toward the kind of open-ended assault on a vulnerable people that the September 11 terrorists were trying to provoke to advance their own perverse interests.

Commitments and Values

All the elements of the struggle against terrorism — near term measures to prevent additional attacks, the pursuit, capture and trial of those accused of participating in or sharing responsibility for the September 11 attacks, and long term measures towards the reduction and eradication of terrorism — must be guided by methods and processes that honour the laws, values and freedoms that terrorism threatens. Canada must work to demilitarise the international struggle against terrorism, and we must resist pressures to curtail immigration, to reduce access to safe havens for refugees, and to change national priorities to increase military spending at the expense of social programs and development assistance. A fundamental commitment to seek the safety and well-being of all people, from America to Afghanistan and beyond, must be at the core of the campaign against terrorism – a commitment that must now be pursued with new energy and diligence.

7

The Effects of War and Terrorism on Children

At the outset, it must be noted that virtually no research examines directly the psychological effects of terrorism on children. As a result, implications for prevention and intervention must come from related research that does not focus specifically on terrorism. Three broad areas of research are reviewed. First, we review the behavioural and psychological effects of various forms of trauma, focusing particularly on the effects of 'distant traumas,' as this form of traumatic exposure appears most similar in form to the threat of terrorism. Throughout the review, we compare what is known about the responses of children to what is known about the responses of adults. Research generally indicates that most children recover quickly from exposure to traumatic events unless they are directly involved in harm to themselves or their family. However, a small minority can develop chronic problems following exposure even to distant trauma. While severity of traumatic exposure is a strong predictor of outcome, aspects of the child and the child's ecology also play a role.

This diversity of event- and child-related factors provides a range of potential targets for interventions designed to promote resilience. In the second section of this review, we summarize key principles to consider when evaluating the potential benefits of such interventions. Protective interventions, whether occurring naturally in the lives of children or implemented by professionals, can target many different processes at different system levels, ranging from cells (eg, medication) to social policy (eg, mandated school emergency planning). Regardless, many of the adverse effects of trauma and the moderating effects of protective factors or interventions are thought to operate by influencing functional aspects of the central nervous system. Moreover, there are individual and developmental differences in how the system responds to trauma. Therefore, in the third section, we review developmental plasticity in neural systems that are responsive to threats.

Stress, Trauma, and Psychopathology

At some point before they reach adulthood, most children are exposed to one or more traumatic event involving 'actual or threatened death or serious injury, or other threat to one's physical integrity'. Some of these events are personal, caused either by accident or by deliberate violence against the child. Others, like natural disasters and mass accidents, can involve whole families or communities. Traumatic events can be placed on a continuum based on the degree to which a child is exposed directly to extremely frightening and prolonged stressors that carry long-term impact on personal well being or access to social supports. The most extreme traumas involve high degrees of threat, targeted directly at the child over long periods of time, that produce a loss of social supports.

For example, one form of extreme trauma might involve witnessing a period of prolonged violence directed towards a parent that ultimately culminates in death of a parent. Alternatively, milder traumas involve exposures that either are brief in duration, only mildly threatening, or produce an increase in the availability of social support. For example, one form of relatively mild trauma might involve brief exposures to inter parental arguments that culminate in divorce and an actual decrease in exposure to violence. A wealth of epidemiological studies examine the association between childhood psychopathology and these various forms of stress exposure, including direct exposure to a violent act, as well as relatively milder and more common stressful life events, such as breakup of a romantic relationship or relatively mild illnesses.

In general, the types of psychopathology exhibited by children following what DSM-IV calls 'extreme stressors,' as well as less severe life events, show broad similarities to the types of psychopathologies exhibited by adults. In particular, there are quite strong predictions from traumatic stress to emotional disorders, defined in DSM-IV as mood and anxiety disorders.

Some evidence suggests that traumatic events in children may also lead to behaviour problems, such as those included in DSM-IV oppositional defiant disorder, conduct disorder, and attention deficit hyperactivity disorder (ADHD). However, these associations emerge with less consistency. Moreover, since few studies rely on prospective community-based longitudinal designs, findings in many available studies may be influenced by biases related to referral patterns or retrospective recall.

Therefore, it remains unclear the degree to which some psychiatric problems that emerged after a traumatic event might actually represent exacerbations of preexisting problems. For example, pre-traumatic behaviour problems may actually shape the degree to which a child is exposed to various forms of traumatic stress. Some researchers treat traumatic exposure as a continuum, from relatively mild to severe, and place more emphasis on the magnitude of overall stress, or the impact of moderating factors, than on the precise nature of the event. This view of trauma suggests that traumatic events produce a broad, generalized increase in risk for various forms of psychopathology. From this perspective, the specific psychiatric outcome may have more to do with characteristics of the child than of the event.

Other research suggests that different forms of stress may be associated with different forms of psychopathology. Research in this area has categorized events based on the typical reaction produced by such an event in most children. For example, events that involve exposure to dangerous circumstances, such as exposure to violent acts, typically produce characteristic signs of fear in a child, whereas events that involve exposure to loss of vital relationships, such as decreased contact with a loved one, typically produce characteristic signs of dysphoria.

Such distinctions between fear- and grief-related reactions can be made relatively reliably, even among preschool children. In this area of research, events involving fear have been shown to exhibit close links to anxiety disorders, whereas events involving loss have been shown to exhibit close links to mood disorders. It would follow from this perspective that the unique features of terrorism may contribute to risk for specific psychopathology in children. Beyond the specific aspects of one or another traumatic event, different forms of trauma may be linked to psychopathology through the relationship between specific traumas and correlated patterns of other risk factors.

These associated risk factors, acting in concert with specific aspects of the trauma, may mediate trajectories in symptom profiles. For example, parental psychopathology and disruption in the parent–child relationship might predict particularly high risks for psychopathology following exposure to domestic violence. Concerning contributions from parental psychopathology, considerable research examines the association between mood and anxiety disorders in parents and their children, as reviewed elsewhere. This literature is not reviewed in the current summary, since few family-based studies have examined directly interactions between parental psychopathology and the psychological effects of traumatic exposure. Similarly, characteristics of the child, including their developmental stage or aspects of their psychobiology, may moderate the response to traumatic exposures. These influences are discussed below.

Exposure to Terrorism

While exposure to traumatic events is very common during childhood, terrorism adds unique dimensions to traumatic exposure. For example, children may become targets of people who hate them for political rather than for personal reasons.

Such events have the potential to increase children's perceptions of the uncertainty and risk in the world and cause psychological harm, even if experienced only at second or third hand. Terrorism is a form of undeclared war that often targets the civilian population as well as, or instead of, the military. As such, terrorism often avoids formal engagement in battles in favour of unannounced attacks, often perpetrated (or carried out) by small groups operating from within a society rather than as an external, invading force.

Terrorists can use rumors of potential disasters and traumatic events as effectively as real acts of terror. Children may face particular danger on their own account (eg, as the children of the President), as members of a specifically targeted group (eg, families of military personnel), as a vulnerable class of society (eg, because the death of children is so horrifying), or simply as randomly selected individuals. It is perhaps this combination of targeted hate and random violence that is particularly frightening.

Terrorism combines two threats: of deliberate harm to a child's community and of random harm to children and their families. These characteristics pose special challenges to the emotional balance of a community, and they require unique responses from communities and care providers.

In other respects, however, terrorism shares key dimensions of other traumas. Features of traumatic events and experiences can be quantified with respect to their potential impact on the psychological well-being of individual children. These features include:

- The degree of exposure to the event (victim, member of victimized group; victim of event's consequences (eg, famine following war), friend killed; witness to horrific events; exposure through media);
- The amount of family support available during the experience and in the aftermath (parents killed, parents psychologically unavailable, parents supportive);
- The amount of life disruption (orphan refugee, refugee with family, home and/or school damaged, little effect on home/school life); and
- The amount of social disorganization (social order collapses into chaos, emergency systems overwhelmed, or work effectively). Given the dearth of data examining the psychological effects of trauma in children and adolescents, data on other traumas provide important insights on terrorism, particularly given these similarities between terrorism and other traumas.

While traumatic exposure among children is common, exposure to some specific types of traumatic events is uncommon in the United States. Most American children have been extraordinarily protected from the extreme end of these dimensions, though there are important exceptions to this rule. Aside from children growing up in military families, it is rare for native-born children growing up in America to be direct victims of war or terrorism, to have parents killed in such events, or to become refugees as a result of them. Even so, most American children have been indirectly exposed to war and terror through media coverage or effects on family and friends, or effects on daily life (eg, security procedures). Moreover, the US is home to growing numbers of child and adolescent refugees who have been exposed to war and terrorism at first hand. Finally, large subpopulations of American children have been exposed to violent acts through circumstances endemic to some geographic areas in America, such as portions of large urban areas.

In this section, we briefly summarize literature examining the possible effects of terrorism on children, emphasizing what is known about the impact of indirect exposure to war and terrorism because this is the form of terror most likely to impact American children. Indirect exposure may occur through various avenues:

- Children learn about the acts of terrorism against their country through coverage on TV, the internet or other media, and through people they know talking about it;
- Children respond to how their parents react to such events; and,
- Events lead to changes in home or school life, such as increased police presence or surveillance, economic hardship, increased distrust of 'foreigners,' or even the erosion of civil society. In discussing such potential effects, Terr *et al* (1999) proposed the term 'distant trauma' to refer to 'the reaction (memory, thinking, symptoms) to a disastrous event, experienced at the time of the event, but from a remote and realistically safe distance.'

In an attempt to elucidate the risk children face when exposed to terrorism as opposed to other forms of trauma, we summarize literature on five different types of exposure, involving different levels of random violence, aggressive acts, and targeted hate:

- Personal exposure to war and terrorism,
- Natural disasters,
- Man-made accidents,
- Mass shootings, and

- Indirect exposure to war and terrorism.

We do not review the extensive literature on childhood sexual abuse, as this literature has been reviewed extensively and appears less relevant to research on terrorism. Nevertheless, the summary of research in these five areas is informed by the considerable existing research on domestic, physical and sexual abuse, as summarized extensively in recent publications.

Finally, research methods vary considerably across the five classes of traumatic exposure, and few studies have been conducted on any single class of event. Moreover, the current review adopts a broad perspective, focusing on behavioural outcomes as well as implications for research on interventions and neurobiology. As a result, the current summary does not provide a quantitative meta-analysis of outcome data, but rather broadly reviews exemplary studies.

For interested readers, Pine and Cohen (2002) recently provided such a semi-quantitative review, based on data in prospective community-based studies of trauma exposure during childhood. In general, rates of post-traumatic stress disorder (PTSD) in the reviewed studies rarely exceed 25% of exposed children, unless large groups of children are exposed to very high degrees of extreme trauma. Similarly, the magnitude of the risk in these studies for any form of psychopathology, including PTSD as well as other emotional or behavioural disorders, typically involves a two-to-four-fold increased risk for some clinically impairing condition in the exposed as compared to unexposed groups.

Personal Exposure to War and Terrorism

The psychological effects on children of war or terrorism have been studied through research on various events occurring since World War II. Examples include the Holocaust, the Belfast riots in Northern Ireland, the Iraqi occupation of Kuwait, the ongoing saga of ethnic rivalry in

Sri Lanka, the effects of the current situation in the Middle East, and ethnic cleansing in Cambodia or Rwanda.

As found in research on adults, virtually all of these studies find a dose-response effect: the more directly a child lies in harm's way, the more severe the risk of PTSD. Similar dose gradients have been observed in research on child maltreatment. Clearly, 50–80% of children will show at least some signs of PTSD when they directly experience intense threats, as posed, for example, by tear-gas attacks, witnessing the murder or beating of their parents, or by near-death experiences.

Many studies of trauma in children have found that direct injury to self, parents, and other close people is associated with more trauma symptoms.

Moreover, traumatic experiences during war rarely occur in isolation, and high cumulative exposure levels are related to higher symptom levels, with rates of acute PTSD symptoms surpassing 75% in some situations. The study of children from refugee camps is equivocal from the viewpoint of 'distant trauma'.

Several researchers have concluded that events threatening survival of self or parents are much more likely to lead to PTSD than experiences related to forced removal from home, as typically experienced in refugee camps. However, refugee camps can still be extremely dangerous environments where children are exposed to horrifying trauma.

Also, the exposure of these children is real, rather than 'from a remote and realistically safe distance.' On the other hand, these children may be less exposed to direct trauma than children living in regions actively involved in a war. The majority of studies in this area have found relatively high rates of PTSD in refugee camps, generally exceeding 10%, and surprisingly low rates of other emotional and behavioural symptoms.

Exposure to Distant Trauma

In this section, we review the literature on the effects of *distant* or *indirect* traumatic exposure to natural disasters, mass accidents, school shootings, war, and terrorist attacks. When considering the potential effects of future terrorist attacks, distant trauma is the most likely type of exposure for most American children.

Natural Disasters

While natural disasters can involve violence and extreme threat, they lack the element of targeted hate. Nevertheless, research on natural disasters informs the potential reactions of children to terrorism since natural disasters involve indirect traumatic exposure that can affect large groups of children who are not directly harmed physically by the event. Considerable heterogeneity exists in the outcome following such traumatic events. On the whole, children seem to be remarkably resilient in the face of natural disasters unless the disaster results in death or injury to family members, or dislocation of home life. However, in a minority of cases, children can develop chronic psychopathology following this form of trauma.

What factors contribute to the resilience that most children show, and what predicts the adverse outcomes that occur in the minority of cases? As noted above, effects on family members can moderate outcomes of direct exposures, but few studies examine moderators of associations between childhood psychopathology and the indirect effects of natural disasters. Asarnow *et al* provide one of the few such studies using a pre–post, quasi-experimental design; in this study, investigators assessed participants in a family-genetic depression study both before and after the 1997 Northridge, California earthquake.

The level of exposure was generally quite mild, but there was extensive exposure to the media reports of death and destruction. On the whole, children fared quite well. Pre-earthquake anxiety disorders, but no other diagnoses or family characteristics, predicted an increased level of post-earthquake PTSD scores, over and above the impact of resource loss.

These events may be the result of human error or culpable incompetence, but not of deliberate intent to harm. As in research on the effects of war, these events show a dose–response effect for children directly exposed to the trauma. In terms of indirect exposure, effects on children not directly implicated appear fairly modest and short-lived, with odds ratios rarely exceeding, in terms of risk for psychopathology. For example, Terr *et al* examined the impact of the *Challenger* disaster on three groups of children: those who had made the trip to Florida for the launch, many of whom were third-grade classmates of astronaut and teacher Christie McAuliffe's son, students from Christie McAuliffe's home town in Concord, New Hampshire, who watched the launch live on television, and a group on the West coast who heard about the explosion later.

Children who had the closest relationship to McAuliffe and saw the explosion live (regardless of whether it was in person or on TV) tended to suffer the most, suggesting a psychological 'dose–response' effect. There were less severe PTSD symptoms among the West coast group. Symptoms diminished sharply by a year later in all groups. Interestingly, contrary to research reviewed later on other traumatic exposures, children with previous traumatic exposures tended to react less to *Challenger* than did other children.

A particular subtype of man-made accident is damage to nuclear reactors, with its risk of future illness. Given this unique aspect of the event, one might anticipate a stronger association with psychopathology, relative to other accidents. However, as of this writing, children also appear resilient in the aftermath of such accidents. Studies of the effects of the Three Mile Island near-meltdown in 1981, and of the Chernobyl disaster in 1986 have shown few long-term effects on indirectly exposed children so far. Bromet and colleagues also found that the main effects on the children were mediated by maternal anxiety or depression.

School Shootings

Like exposure to terrorist acts, school shooting incidents contain elements of both randomness and deliberate intent to harm, as well as being rare events with large potential impact. These incidents also occurred in a setting where adults have been entrusted by parents with protecting their children. In a study of the Columbine High school shootings, data from the 1999 national Youth Risk Behaviour Survey (YBRS) were used to show that children in the United States interviewed after the date of the shootings were more likely to feel too unsafe to go to school, as compared to those interviewed before the shooting. This was the case 'regardless of whether the school was in an urban, suburban, or rural area, but was especially pronounced in rural areas where the likelihood of students' missing school was more than 12 times higher after Columbine'. There was no increase in any other symptoms measured in the YBRS.

The risk of imitation poses another disturbing effect of distant trauma. Kostinsky *et al* (2001) examined a database of threats of school violence reported to the Pennsylvania Emergency Management Agency, Harrisburg, during the 50 days following the Columbine incident. Threats of school violence numbered 354, far exceeding the one or two threats per year estimated by school administrators prior to 1999. The frequency of these threats demonstrated a crescendo–decrescendo pattern. In all, 56 percent of the threats were made on or before day 10 after the incident, and more than one-third occurred on days 8, 9, and 10.

War and Terrorism

The current report focuses explicitly on research relevant to potential future terrorist attacks on children in the United States. As such, prior studies examining the direct effects of war on children and adolescents are not directly relevant to the current report. Moreover, virtually no studies examine the effects of terrorism on children, though relevant data are reviewed immediately below. Among studies examining children exposed to war or terrorism as 'distant trauma,' most are fairly optimistic. Lyons' (1979) studies of the impact of the sectarian terrorism in Ireland on children in Belfast found that the main complaints were enuresis, fear of being left alone, and school refusal.

The few cases that came to clinical attention appeared to involve children of anxious parents, once again suggesting that distal effects of trauma are mediated by proximal effects on parental functioning. Among these, younger patients had significantly milder symptoms. Pfefferbaum *et al* (2003a) studied the effect of the bombing of the US embassy in Nairobi, Kenya, in which 253 people were killed and over 5000 injured. A survey of 500 children showed that, even among indirectly exposed children, reactions were more severe among those with a history of previous trauma, suggesting individual vulnerability.

This is inconsistent with Terr's observations after the Challenger disaster described above, which implicated a moderating influence of trauma experience in the other direction, more consistent with an inoculation effect. Given these inconsistencies, further research is needed to clarify the role of vulnerability *vs* protective processes that may moderate the associations between prior trauma and outcome following indirect exposure.

Some studies have noted that pre-exposure psychological characteristics of children and families moderate the impact of distant traumatic events on children's symptoms, as observed in adults as well as children directly exposed to trauma.

In Palestinian children Studies found that children with high emotional and behavioural symptoms scores at the first assessment were the most likely to have persistent PTSD a year later. Studies of children in occupied Kuwait found that social support moderated the effect on exposure on PTSD symptoms in girls, but not boys. In the United States, the three recent major terrorist events to involve children are the initial Trade Center bombing in 1993, the Oklahoma City bombing in 1995, and the 2001 Trade Center bombing. discuss all three in terms of direct *vs* indirect exposure (eg, through the media). They argue that 'Examining indirectly exposed children is important especially in terrorist events, because a goal of terrorism is to inflict fear in the broader community'.

The general conclusion is that PTSD reaction scores were relatively low in indirectly exposed samples, and that children 'reported minimal impact on functioning'. In New York, the effects of the 9/11 Trade Center disaster appears to have been quite marked even among children only indirectly affected. Prevalence of psychiatric disorders in one study was two to three times as high in New York city school students as it was in close by urban and suburban school students tested a year earlier, though it is possible that Manhattan rates were higher before the bombings as well.

In conclusion, available research on trauma exposure in children and adolescents examines diverse kinds and severity of exposure. In terms of direct exposure, a dose-response relationship with risk for psychopathology emerges in children as in adults. For indirect exposure, the impact may be weaker overall. However, for both types of exposure, outcomes are likely to be heterogeneous, with relatively few children facing high risk for adverse outcomes.

Terrorism Risk and Interventions

Preparing to minimize the immediate and long-term consequences of terror for children and adolescents requires a developmental perspective on risk, vulnerability, and resilience. Though the literature specifically addressing protective factors and recovery of children in relation to terrorism is limited, there is a more extensive literature on other adversities that provides surprisingly consistent conclusions for conceptualizing potential preventive interventions. Lessons learned to date suggest some fundamental principles for understanding, researching, and intervening to protect children in the face of terrorism.

Principle 1: The Nature of the Threat must be Considered

As noted above, children, like adults, show a dose gradient in response to direct threat. More severe reactions occur in response to events that threaten basic security (eg, a parent is killed, injured, or terrified), body and self-integrity (eg, the child is tortured, raped, or injured, or threatened with such), and to threats perpetrated by human design rather than natural disaster (for children old enough to understand). Secondary exposure via media and rumors is an increasing concern for children because of the degree of exposure to media among children in modern societies and the intensity of the live coverage that is now commonplace. Perceived exposure is important; studies find high symptom levels in children and adolescents who believed they had been exposed to a toxin but had not.

There is concern at all ages for the potential exacerbation of psychological reactions through media coverage, but children present a special case because of their immature cognitive abilities. Media is a powerful 'vector' by which terror spreads, using the model of infectious disease epidemiology. Recent survey data indicate that 36% of American children under the age of 6 have their own television in their bedroom. After Oklahoma City and 9/11, television exposure in children was associated with more post-traumatic stress symptoms, at least in the short term. Some teachers in Oklahoma City chose to forego class activities in favour of watching live reports on television in the classroom. In summary, it is clear that the degree of exposure matters and that prepared adults could influence the degree of secondary exposure. While American society values not concealing things from children, and providing opportunities for them to express their fears and anxieties, there is strong evidence that younger children, at least, do better if provided with some protection from the full intensity and repeated coverage by media of trauma and disaster.

Principle 2: Developmental Timing of the Terrorism will Influence Child and Family Reactions, Protections, and Developmental Sequelae

Normative vulnerabilities, capabilities, and protective factors for processing stress shift during development. Infants, for example, are protected from full psychological 'exposure' to terrorism by their cognitive immaturity; most adolescents, on the other hand, are capable of apprehending the full horror of such events. Yet, infants will be highly vulnerable to degradation or destruction of caregiver function as they are totally dependent on adult care. Adolescents not only are more capable of helping themselves, having more developed human capital; they also have more extensive resources outside the family in the form of friends, teachers, and other people to go to for help, representing greater social capital.

After children form attachments to caregivers, they are highly sensitive to separation and loss, particularly if frightened. Children gauge threats based on caregiver responses, a propensity termed 'social referencing.' Since terrified parents are terrifying to children, parents can moderate or mediate the propagation of terror as a vector for the spread of fear to children. Calm and functional parents, teachers, and other adults, on the other hand, can be reassuring to children.

Perceived danger and fear stimulate efforts to increase proximity to caretakers; people of all ages will seek contact with attachment figures, but this response will be intense in young children. It is also reciprocal, so that parents will seek physical contact with young children under conditions of extreme threat.

Older children may be reassured by cell phone contact, but young children will need physical contact. Separation can be more stressful to children than the traumatic event itself.

Though less emphasized in the literature, it is important to consider the impact of threats to children on the level of stress experienced by parents. The impact of such stress may explain particularly the strong effects of major disasters on mothers of young children. Efforts to prepare the general population for dealing with terrorism must consider the developmental range of responses, the possible differential sensitivity of mothers to dangers and threats to their children, and the salience of attachment figures for the psychological protection of children.

Principle 3: The Experiences and Consequences for the Children in the Context of Terrorism will be Mediated and Moderated by Family, Peer, and School Systems, and Particularly by the Quality of Relationships in these Systems

Given that many effects of terrorism on children can be indirect, interventions that improve parental functioning may reduce the transmission of effects to children. It is widely assumed that similar effects can be achieved through interventions with teachers. Generally, in the event of a terrorist attack, it may be more effective to target parents, teachers, and other adults close to children than children themselves, particularly in the case of younger children. Adults can act to buffer children, avoid worse situations, and ameliorate suffering.

In studies of naturally occurring resilience, it is clear that effective adults function as highly adaptable protective systems for children in their care; it is not well-established whether such general competence can be taught or improved through intervention, though it is likely that specific strategies for specific threats can be learned.

Principle 4: Individual Differences in Vulnerabilities and Capabilities will Influence Child Responses and Recovery Patterns

As noted earlier, children's pre-event competence and symptoms influence how they respond to trauma. Children with mental health problems may be particularly vulnerable in part because of associated inadequacies in their external protective systems (eg, their parents may be less capable and protective) and in part due to endogenous factors. Individual risk factors also can be viewed from the perspective of protective factors; that is, children who do not have the risk factor fare better through the traumatic experience. Norris *et al* delineate such risk/protective factors among all ages, including children.

Generally, the predictors of good outcomes among children following trauma bear a striking resemblance to the 'short list' of strong protective factors in the resilience literature as a whole.

Children functioning well prior to the experience and who have more resources available during the experience manage well under extenuating circumstances, reflecting fundamental human adaptive systems. Children lacking such protections may face the highest need for intervention.

Principle 5: Interventions can be directed at Different Phases of Terrorism, Different Processes, and Different Kinds of Children, in Different Situations

Interventions can focus on different systems of the child's ecology or the child him/herself. The most severely threatening situations for children may involve complex processes, unfolding over time with cumulative impact. Given this possibility, a comprehensive, 'cumulative protection' model may provide the most effective intervention across the widest group of children. Virtually no research examines the effectiveness of any intervention for large-scale disaster or terrorism. Clearly, this is a high priority for the nation and world community.

Preparation-phase (pre-event) strategies widely implemented in the United States for possible traumatic events include emergency plans in families, schools, and other community agencies. Schools are a particular focus of concern because of the proportion of time children spend in school and the relatively low adult-to-child ratio in schools.

Though research is of necessity constrained in disasters and emergent situations, available research on violent incidents (eg, school shootings, Oklahoma City bombing, 9/11, etc) generates recommendations for intervention. These include the need for:

- Emergency plans for schools, communities, families, etc, that attend to child/family issues
- Training of 'first responders' concerning child and family issues;
- Advising the public about developmentally appropriate media exposure;
- Effective risk communication and management or containment of fear/symptom contagion effects. Nevertheless, more research is needed on the

effectiveness of each of these and on the utility of assessment tools for triage and evaluation.

Principle 6: Frontline Responders need to Know Differences between Normal and Pathological Responses to Traumatic Events as well as Strategies for Prevention

Frontline responders include police, firefighters, medical personnel, emergency service providers, teachers, and day-care providers. These individuals need to recognize who is at greatest risk and how to differentiate typical from a typical reactions in children and parents. Sensitivity to separation stress is important, as is preparing the first responder for dealing with their reactions to child victims. The most important general observation about long-term recovery recognizes the resilience exhibited by most children. Children typically exhibit good recovery unless major protective systems for human development are damaged or destroyed. On the other hand, there is considerable evidence that traumatic experiences and disasters can have profound and lasting effects on some children.

While these general principles can inform initial efforts to minimize the effects of terrorism, clinicians and scientists both remain concerned that available research does not accurately capture the key aspects of children's responses to threats in the form of terrorism or other traumas. In particular, current research generates incomplete conclusions concerning factors that predict particularly good or dysfunctional outcomes. Moreover, limitations exist on knowledge of the mechanisms behind the effects of widely recognized risk or protective factors. Similarly, there are concerns about the possibility of slow-evolving, deleterious effects of gradual, but accumulating, impact on brain development. In each of these areas, recent advances in neurobiology generate hope that future studies will provide insights. Therefore, in the final section of this summary, data are reviewed on the relevance of basic science research on threat responses.

Developmental Psychobiology

Clinical research considering the potential impact of traumatic exposure on children's emotional well-being generates interest in the potential effects of stress on human brain development. As of this writing, virtually no research examines directly the impact of war or terrorism on human brain development. However, insights on the potential impact may emerge from the extensive basic science research on the developmental psychobiology of stress. Accordingly, the current section reviews research on developmental aspects of the stress response, with the goal of informing future studies examining psychobiological aspects of exposure to war or terrorism.

Research in the basic sciences has raised essential questions concerning developmental psychobiology and traumatic exposure. One key question concerns the role of specific brain systems in mediating a child's successful or unsuccessful adaptation to trauma. Another key question concerns the nature of any potential impact of traumatic events on the developing brain. While more data address the second question than the first, both questions arise in the wake of considerable basic science research documenting plasticity in brain systems engaged when mature organisms process threats.

Studies over the past 20 years precisely delineate the neural circuitry engaged in a range of mature mammalian species during the processing of a threatening stimulus or situation. While much of the initial work in this area focused on fear conditioning and learned fears, recent studies also examine stimuli and situations that produce fear in the absence of prior experiences with the stimulus. For most threatening situations, physiologic, cognitive, and behavioural responses in mature mammals are known to be regulated by a neural circuit encompassing the amygdale and prefrontal cortex (PFC), particularly ventral and medial aspects of the PFC. For some specific types of threat, other structures also are involved, such as the bed nucleus of the stria terminalis and the hippocampus.

Relatively few studies compare the degree to which the same or different neural structures mediate responses to threats at distinct stages of development. Synaptic connectivity within the primate amygdale reaches maturity earlier than afferent connections from the PFC or temporal cortex. As a result, potential developmental differences in the neural responses to threat have been presumed to reflect changes in major input pathways to the amygdale or interconnections among a circuit encompassing the amygdale, PFC, and other neocortical regions, as opposed to changes within intrinsic amygdale nuclei. However, lesion studies in non-human primates suggest that the developmental stage during which intrinsic amygdale dysfunction occurs strongly effects the degree to which fear behaviours are altered.

As a result, developmental differences in the threat response may reflect both intrinsic immaturity within specific neural structures, as well as immaturity in the connections among these structures. Regardless, the few available studies document meaningful differences across development in the role of specific neural structures in modulating responses to threats. For example, in studies of rodents, adolescent animals exhibit a higher threshold for stress-related activation of amygdala circuitry, whereas in non-human primates, amygdale lesions have been shown to produce divergent effects on threat responses among immature as opposed to mature organisms.

In contrast to the limited psychobiological data examining fear responses in juvenile mammals, a wealth of research examines the long-term effects of environmental factors operating early in development on threat response patterns exhibited by mature organisms. For example, rearing manipulations in rodents during the first two weeks of life have been shown to produce long-term alteration in physiology, cognition, and avoidant behaviour that are readily observable in mature rodents. These associations are very robust, as they emerge across a range of rearing paradigms, from many laboratories, using many outcome measures. Moreover, at least for measures of behaviour and physiology, other studies document parallel effects in non-human primates.

Finally, more recent studies in rodents document neural mediators of these developmental effects. Specifically, rearing manipulations produce long-term alterations in physiology, cognition, and behaviour through effects on a neural circuit encompassing the amygdala, PFC, and hippocampus. Neuroscientists have only begun to consider the relevance of these findings for human behaviour, due to noted cross-species differences in neurophysiology. Nevertheless, knowledge concerning plasticity in brain systems engaged by threats has heightened concerns regarding the potential long-term deleterious effects of trauma or other stressful experiences in children.

A few recent basic science findings generate specific questions about children. First, cross-fostering studies in rodents suggest that experiential effects on developmental aspects of the stress response are mediated through effects on gene regulation. These findings have generated particular interest on understanding interactions between the genetic and environmental factors in humans. Initial efforts to translate these insights to humans have heightened this interest. Two recent studies suggested that polymorphisms in genes that regulate serotonin and catecholamine function moderate the strength of the association between environmental stressors and risk for either major depression or behaviour problems, respectively. Second, gene-knockout studies suggest that genetic factors may exert different effects on stress reactivity in immature and mature organisms. For example, inactivation of the 5-HT1a receptor in a juvenile mouse produces permanent increases in stress reactivity that are not reversed by re-activation of the receptor during adulthood; conversely, inactivation of the 5HT1a receptor only after a mouse has reached maturity produces no change in stress reactivity.

As with studies of amygdale lesions in primates, findings in rodents provide evidence of developmental variation in the relationship between brain function and stress reactivity. This has raised questions on the degree to which humans exhibit developmental variation in the relationship between neural or genetic factors and stress reactivity. Behavioural genetic studies in humans note some parallels with research in developmental neurobiology. For example, genetic factors associated with anxiety or depression in adolescents or adults exhibit weaker associations with anxiety or depression in children. Finally, much of the available research in rodents examines rearing manipulation's effects on indices of hypothalamic–pituitary–adrenal (HPA) axis function and cognitive abilities instantiated in the hippocampus. While these indices provide relatively indirect measures of neural function, noninvasive measures of these indices can be acquired in humans. Thus far, data in human children document some parallels with data in rodents, non-human primates, or adult humans.

However, the inconsistencies across studies of developing humans, contrasted with non-human primates and rodents, are more marked than the consistencies. This has generated considerable interest in expanding the area of inquiry in psychobiological studies among clinical samples. More direct measures of brain function in humans may facilitate efforts to extrapolate between data in humans and rodents or non-human primates. Recent technological advances raise hopes that it will be possible to directly measure neurophysiology in children in ways that facilitate translational approaches. In particular, through advances in cognitive neuroscience, experimental paradigms have been developed that differentiate, at a behavioural or physiologic level, adult patients with PTSD from various control groups, including healthy subjects or subjects exposed to trauma who are free of PTSD symptoms.

Through advances in fMRI, similar paradigms have been used to engage specific brain regions, such as components of the medial PFC, that are involved in stress regulation among rodents and non-human primates. In neuro imaging studies, some of the most successful paradigms have used photographs of standard facial emotional expressions. For example, the viewing of faces expressing the emotion of fear consistently engages the amygdale in healthy adults, whereas the viewing of angry faces engages the ventral PFC. Moreover, differences between adults with and without PTSD have been demonstrated using such paradigms. Such findings generated initial interest in extending this line of inquiry to children. While only preliminary studies examine this issue, findings in children reveal some differences from findings in adults, increasing the need for basic developmental studies in children. Broadly conceptualized, these findings are consistent with data in non-human primates suggesting that specific neural structures play distinct roles in modulating fear at different stages of development.

For example, in some face-viewing paradigms, children exhibit greater amygdale activation to neutral as opposed to fearful faces. These differences may in turn relate to developmental differences in attention during the viewing of evocative faces. In adults, attending to emotional aspects of a face has been shown to facilitate amygdale and ventral or medial PFC engagement when fear-faces are viewed. Preliminary evidence from fMRI studies suggests that this ability to modulate amygdale and PFC activity matures relatively late. Specifically, adults, relative to adolescents, show an enhanced capacity to regulate PFC and amygdale in concert with attention demands during the viewing of fear faces. Conversely, adolescents, relative to adults, show enhanced amygdale and PFC activation to emotionally evocative facial displays under conditions when attention is not constrained. As such, these findings suggest that the circumstances for engaging relevant neural pathways differ in meaningful ways across development.

More than 50 years of research from around the world can help the United States to evaluate and prepare for the possible effects of terrorism on children. Some (hopefully few) children will be directly exposed to terrorism, and some of them (though far from all) will experience symptoms of PTSD as a consequence; most will have recovered within a year provided their environment is safe. Effects of direct exposure are likely to affect a relatively limited number of children. A much larger proportion of the child population will be indirectly exposed to terrorism, through the media and other people. Here, too, a dose–response effect is expected, which argues for adult control of the amount and content of children's exposure to the media (as well as exposure to terrified adults). Some symptoms, such as bad dreams and clinging, may occur, particularly among younger children, but these effects are unlikely to last long. A key, and potentially modifiable, predictor of children's outcomes appears to be how adults behave; parental anxieties have been found to mediate the effects of distant trauma on children's fears.

Finally, the most dangerous environments for children are those where long exposure to war and terrorism has undermined civil society, as happened in Belfast, Mozambique, and many refugee camps in the late 20th century. As in massive trauma, when all aspects of a child's ecology may have collapsed (as seen in war and natural disasters), the lives of children may be profoundly affected indirectly by the effects of the terror on the embedded systems in which they live. There is a real danger when order has disintegrated that frightened children will act to protect themselves by affiliating with terrorists, forming delinquent gangs, or emulating the violent behaviour of adults. The undermining of civil society may be more of a threat to children's mental health in the long term than the 'distant trauma' itself.

8

Terrorism and the New Security Strategy

To begin to grasp the weight of what the United States and the world now face in relation to Iraq, terrorism, and security, we must go back to the European Peace of Westphalia (1648). With that treaty European rulers established their independence from both the Roman Catholic Church and the Holy Roman Empire and laid the foundations of an international system of independent sovereign states. Implicit in the new system, however, was a potential dilemma—a dilemma that became stark by the 20th century and is now codified in the Charter of the United Nations. On the one hand, the UN system represents *international* law and procedures mutually agreed to as binding on the separate states. On the other hand, the first principle of the UN system is that each state is sovereign and thus not beholden to any superior authority.

At the core of the United Nations is the Security Council, which is supposed to promote conflict management to keep small crises from growing into a third world war. The first principle undergirding the UN Security Council, however, is state sovereignty—the right of each of its five permanent members to veto any proposed resolution. (The permanent members are the United States, Great Britain, Russia, China, and France.) As a result, when the post-World War II division between the Soviet Union and the United States quickly developed into the Cold War, the Security Council was essentially put on ice. NATO and Warsaw Pact alliances were pitted against one another for more than 40 years, determining the fate of the world and marginalizing the UN as a factor in international dispute resolution and peacekeeping.

By the end of the Cold War, the relative power of all the permanent Security Council members except the United States had declined, while U.S. power had expanded exponentially. The United States through NATO is now the primary defense department of Europe. The United States through its treaties with Japan, Korea, and Southeast Asian states is the security umbrella for the Pacific and much of Asia. The U.S. is in many ways, *de facto*, the international security regime of the world. Furthermore, between the end of World War II and the end of the Cold War more than a hundred new states—many created out of the collapsing European empires—joined the UN.

The UN today, in other words, looks very different than it did at birth. States like France, Great Britain, and Russia, still have the same Security Council authority that the United States has, despite their decline in relative power, while countries like Gabon, Qatar, Bhutan, and Togo have equal standing with every other state in the world in the United Nations General Assembly, despite their inconsequential power and authority in global affairs.The distribution of political power and authority today, I am suggesting, is in many ways incompatible with the structure and aims of the UN system, so much so that we are faced with a crisis of international law and order more profound in some respects than the crisis that emerged with World War II and the collapse of the European empires, and more profound than the crisis that gave birth to the Treaty of Westphalia. James Traub reminds us that back in 1948, U.S. Secretary of State George Marshall predicted that "should there be 'a complete lack of power equilibrium in the world, the United Nations cannot function successfully." Not only is there no power equilibrium in the world today, the UN does not even represent a consensus about the kind of political and legal systems its member states should have.

Describing the circumstances in this way helps to shed light on the problem of rogue states and states with very weak or highly unjust governments—all members of the UN—where terrorists can hide and operate underground or where governments actually support them, as the Taliban supported Al Qaeda in Afghanistan. It is one thing for the relatively stable and democratic states of the U.S., France, and Japan to cooperate in trying to stop terrorists who might circulate within and across their borders, but how do these states work with Pakistan, Indonesia, Georgia, Saudi Arabia, Sudan, Iraq, and North Korea to fight terrorism? None of these states may be supporting Al Qaeda officially, but if their governments are either too weak to fight terrorists or stand in strong opposition to the West, then what is the U.S. or any other terrorist-threatened state to do? It may no longer make sense for the United States to uphold the principle of state sovereignty for Iraq, which appears to be one of the breeding grounds of trouble for others. In fact, why should the U.S. continue to uphold an unbalanced and relatively powerless UN system at all when the U.S., on its own, has the power to try to change the political disorder of Iraq and help make the world safe for democracy?

The New National Security Strategy

The Bush administration's recently released National Security Strategy (NSS) states boldly that the time has come for the U.S. to be forthright and intentional about acting unilaterally, if necessary, to promote security and freedom in the world, even if its actions no longer square with the modes of international cooperation to which other countries have grown accustomed over the past half century. Though it does not say so, the document seems to imply that since the Cold War put the UN Security Council on ice for four decades, perhaps the new crisis of terrorism and rogue states provides a reason for the U.S. to put that system on ice again.

What is especially striking about the NSS, however, is that it does not make a standard *realist* argument, namely, that American security interests require it to act in its own defense by using its power for that purpose. Rather, the NSS reads like an *idealist* tract, calling for the U.S. to lead in building a new world order of freedom. Freedom is the active subject in many of the document's sentences. Freedom is a transnational mission, a supranational standard, and a world-historical spirit, to which the U.S. and other countries simply must subordinate themselves. As President Bush puts it in the concluding paragraph of his opening introduction to the document:

> Freedom is the non-negotiable demand of human dignity; the birthright of every person—in every civilization. Throughout history, freedom has been threatened by war and terror; it has been challenged by the clashing of wills of powerful states and the evil designs of tyrants; and it has been tested by widespread poverty and disease. Today, humanity holds in its hands the opportunity to further freedom's triumph over all these foes. The United States welcomes our responsibility to lead in this great mission.

This is freedom-idealism at its grandest. The U.S. is simply a servant of the universal cause that is now bringing about the final order of the ages. Everyone, including sovereign states, should submit to it.

But how is freedom working its will in history? Here is where the old dilemma of state sovereignty vs. transnational law and order intrudes. The NSS presents freedom as simultaneously both America's national interest and every person's and every state's birthright. The U.S. is the lead representative of freedom and therefore what America does in the world will advance the freedom of all. What is good for U.S. security is good for the world because the vanguard of freedom is leading the world to its true destiny, to its triumph over all its foes. Unlike the UN system, which allows tyrannical and unfree states to be members—all in deference to the first principle of state sovereignty—the new order must serve genuine freedom and that is what freedom's leader, the United States, intends to accomplish. Pictured this way, however, freedom's mission puts the U.S. in the lead as global policeman of last resort; as freedom's single-nation Security Council; as the vanguard of freedom's global hegemony that has not yet been fully realized.

Support and Criticism

The Bush administration's new approach is exactly right, says Tod Lindberg, writing in the Hoover Institution's *Hoover Digest*. The White House, says Lindberg, is "firmly aligning itself with Francis Fukuyama's universalist 'end of history' vision of the spread of the recognition by human beings of each other as free and equal." President Bush's speech at West Point last June, a forerunner to the NSS, "is nothing less than the founding document of a new international order with American power at its center and the spread of freedom as its aim." Lindberg even goes so far as to say that what President Bush "is now promoting with this liberty doctrine is not [just] a model. It is the answer and it is final."

On the one hand, according to Bush at West Point, "America has no empire to extend or utopia to establish. We wish for others only what we wish for ourselves—safety from violence, the rewards of liberty, and the hope for a better life." On the other hand, as Lindberg happily explains, the president made this statement from a position of military strength and with "chilling implications":

"America has, and intends to keep, military strengths beyond challenge—thereby making the destabilizing arms races of other eras pointless, and limiting rivalries to trade and other pursuits of peace."

In other words, the new world order of peace and freedom will be established and sustained by American preeminence. And this means, of course, that the way Lindberg, and perhaps the Bush administration, resolves the dilemma of state sovereignty within an international system is by establishing only one state—the United States—as the world's only true sovereign. Or to put it another way, President Bush's security strategy amounts, in some respects, to an attempt to reconstitute a pre-Westphalian international order, but in this case it will be the United States, not the Holy Roman Empire or the Roman Catholic Church, that will serve as the ultimate transnational security force and authority.

A recent Brookings Institution Policy Brief on the NSS (written by Ivo Daalder, James Lindsay, and James Steinberg) points to an inner contradiction in this vision of a new world order—a contradiction that can lead, and has already led, to charges of hypocrisy. "Which should take priority? Our [American] commitment to our ideals [like freedom]? Or a concern for our safety [national interests]? The Strategy [NSS] offers no advice on how to answer these questions, and it does not seem to recognize the possible contradiction." For the sake of our security and the fight against terrorism, for example, the U.S. cooperates with and supports states that are quite unfree and repressive of their own citizens. America is not, then, acting consistently to promote freedom but is, in some cases, "buttressing authoritarianism rather than opposing it."

John Lewis Gaddis approaches this dilemma by looking at the way the NSS conflates the fight against terrorism with the fight against a rogue state like Iraq. Since both terrorism and rogue states are the enemies of freedom, the administration aims to take on both of them with one strategy that includes preemptive military strikes if necessary. This is where Saddam Hussein fits in to the Grand Strategy, says Gaddis. "Iraq is the most feasible place where we [the U.S.] can strike the next blow. If we can topple this tyrant,... then we can accomplish a great deal. We can complete the task the Gulf War left unfinished. We can destroy whatever weapons of mass destruction Saddam Hussein may have accumulated since.

We can end whatever support he's providing for terrorists elsewhere, notably those who act against Israel. We can liberate the Iraqi people. We can ensure an ample supply of inexpensive oil. We can set in motion a process that could undermine and ultimately remove reactionary regimes elsewhere in the Middle East, thereby eliminating the principal breeding ground for terrorism."

However, if the U.S. acts to destroy Saddam Hussein's regime with the aims Gaddis articulates, few countries are likely to accept such action as legitimate American self-defense. Instead they will see it as a self-aggrandizing act of U.S. aggression with the aim of staying in control of the world. For the U.S. to appeal to a transnational ideal of freedom to justify such an attack would appear to be nothing more than a hypocritical cover for self-interested action. Instead of other states wholeheartedly joining the U.S. in its mission to serve freedom, they will be forced to recalculate how to protect their own interests in face of what they may judge to be illegitimate intervention on the part of America into another sovereign state.

The American dilemma is that the UN's means of trying to disarm a dangerous Iraq and uphold international law did not work in the 1990s. In fact, one can argue that the new UN Security Council Resolution 1441 came about only because the U.S. used its immense power to force the Security Council to act.

And that suggests that the UN remains so weak in the area of peacekeeping that it can serve as little more than a pawn in the hands of powerful states, whether Iraq or the U.S., whether France or Russia, whether Great Britain or China. What the Bush administration concludes, then, is that the U.S. had better remain the most powerful nation in the world in order to protect itself even from the UN.

By means of its new NSS, the Bush administration wants to do more than simply protect American borders. It wants to help bring about a new era of global peace and freedom. However, if the means the Bush administration uses to try to achieve this goal include unilateral, preemptive military action, then the U.S. may find that its efforts are counterproductive. The Brookings Brief quotes Henry Kissinger with approval when he says, "It cannot be in either the American national interest or the world's interest to develop principles that grant every nation an unfettered right of preemption against its own definition of threats to its security."

Hendrik Hertzberg illumines the dilemma of the Bush administration's new security strategy this way: "There's a contradiction at the heart of the Bush strategy. It implicitly recognizes that national sovereignty is in many ways an outdated and dangerous doctrine, one that must increasingly give way to other exigencies. Is the sovereignty of the Iraqi state to be valued more than the right of Iraq's neighbors and the rest of the world to be reasonably free of the fear of being vaporized or sickened unto death by Iraqi weapons of mass destruction? Of course not. So the Bush doctrine, in spite of itself, recognizes the logic of something like world government. But its idea of world government looks very much like a benevolent American dictatorship—a dictatorship of the entrepreneurial, you might say".

Building a New International System

Quite the opposite of using its position as world

hegemony to try to reorder the world toward a "freedom" that only America can police, the U.S. should, I would argue, use its current power and authority to help bring about a stronger and more just international order that elevates international and transnational governance above state sovereignty as its first principle. As a matter of principle, in other words, states ought to be acting as joint stewards of an international order of just governance that transcends but at the same time strengthens the limited territorial authority of just states.

The present UN system does not represent this kind of order and that is why, on the one hand, American hawks decry the debilitated UN and the weakness of allies and enemies alike to shape a just world. They want action, and they want to begin by having the U.S. bring down Saddam Hussein, the most evident symbol of everything that stands against freedom, democracy, and U.S. interests. But hawks haven't counted the cost of going it alone because they cling by faith to the first principle of national sovereignty and to the conviction that America is freedom's world-historical leader. Critics of the new Bush doctrine, on the other hand, decry the administration's unilateralism and its apparent movement toward imperialism. But their blind spot is in assuming that the UN system and international law as now constituted are solid and can continue to serve as a sound basis for international politics in the future, if the U.S. will only become more modest and cooperative within that system.

Neither of these approaches faces up to the new global realities of international interdependence, rising terrorism, rogue states, U.S. military preeminence throughout the world, and the crisis of the UN system. The UN, with its present structure, has not kept, and cannot keep the peace or give order to the post-Cold-War and post-9/11 world. At the moment the U.S. obviously has the greatest potential to do that, on the basis of its own sovereign power, whether or not it chooses to use the UN Security Council for its purposes. However, the U.S. cannot reorder the world entirely on its own. As the preeminent realist, Henry Kissinger, argues, "The United States must resist basing foreign policy on hegemonic power. Many of the problems affecting world order are not susceptible to solution by military means. History shows that sooner or later every powerful country calls into being countervailing forces. And at that point—and I would insist even now—the United States will not be able to sort out every international problem alone without exhausting itself physically and psychologically".

This is not to say that the U.S. should retreat from global responsibilities or lay down its power. The U.S. should not turn over its defense department to Kofi Annan or to the European Community tomorrow. An international power vacuum will not remain unfilled. However, the kind of leadership the U.S. should give must break through the contradictions of both the new NSS and the UN system. The U.S. should, quite openly, begin to direct energy and money to strengthening the principles of constitutional, representative, accountable, federal government above states as well as within them.

With the cooperation of other states that support such principles—including the rule of law, open societies, civil rights, religious freedom, and so forth—the U.S. should use its clout to draw in states that shape themselves to these standards, somewhat like the European Union sets economic and political standards for entrance into the EU.

There can be little doubt that the United States will henceforth be engaged in the world thoroughly, intricately, and almost everywhere whether its citizens want this or not. The only question is whether the U.S. will try to dictate the terms of the new world order in the name of freedom and its own preeminence, or instead will work to help define the new order as one of accountable governance under law, which can eventually transcend even American sovereignty as well as the sovereignty of every other state.

Shift toward information warfare

Information warfare tactics are being employed across the spectrum of conflict. the increasing importance of computers and their attendant networks make them primary targets for both state sponsored espionage and crime. Terrorists have recognized the value of energy distribution networks and some computer installations. At the level of insurgency and rebellion, information warfare tactics have been used to subvert state controls of the media and for communications between the rebel leadership and their worldwide support base.

The advanced information warfare techniques of computer penetration, surveillance, and exploitation developed by the following states can be utilized for terrorism as well as espionage and crime. There is a long history of state sponsorship of terrorism in the 20th century. Often the goal of computer penetrations is to provide easy access for future penetrations. In effect, foreign states are conducting information warfare espionage to have "turn key" access to U.S. systems in the future. The only difference between these acts of computer espionage and terrorism is the addition of a political motive or goal to the criminal nature of the penetration. States may, in the future, choose to provide this information to a sponsored terrorist group for use against the United States. As such, a careful examination of past and current information warfare activities at the state level is important as it may identify future terrorist targets or tactics likely to be used by state sponsored terrorist groups.

Who can perpetrate an organized "computer attack" against the United States? A study of the threat by Wayne

Madsen addresses these issues. He classifies foreign nations into one of four categories of computer advancement:

- Highly advance,
- Operationally advance,
- Basic development, and
- Initial development.

France, the United Kingdom, Japan, China, and the United States represent the first category, and their intelligence agencies are highly advanced in the science of electronic eavesdropping and computer intelligence gathering. Russia, India, Ukraine, and Colombia represent the second category. While Russia and India, arguably, have first-rate intelligence-gathering organizations, their high technology capabilities still lag behind those of the first category but are improving steadily. Libya, Ghana, and Bolivia fall into the third category. Their intelligence agencies will soon have high technology capabilities. Zaire, Ethiopia, and Tanzania represent the fourth category: their intelligence organizations lack high technology capabilities and their embryonic computer and data communications systems are vulnerable to the capabilities of the nations in the first three categories.

While this is a comprehensive list of states, the threat continues to grow. This is due to the increasing rate of computer power and technology available to sub-state actors, such as hackers." In the past, one needed to have the power and resources of a state behind them to conduct an effective worldwide SIGINT operation. Now, a few people can conduct a computer intelligence (COMPINT) effort with limited funds. Whereas access to remote sites to place antennas or military overflight of territory was a prerequisite for SIGINT, the most critical element of COMPINT is the knowledge of how to exploit a computer system. As cyberspace is a nonphysical reality, borders and geographic location of the target system are meaningless in a COMPINT effort. Since the world's computers are becoming increasingly interconnected, a modem to connect to the Internet and a desktop computer, coupled with a talented computer user, are all that is required to start intelligence gathering. With the power of desktop computers doubling every 12-18 months, the computing power that previously only a government or large corporation could afford now sits in homes across the world. While state powers have exploited these assets in the past, substate actors may exploit them easily in the future.

The first computer hacker incident to garner national attention was sponsored in part by the Soviet Union to gain access to Western technology and defense information. This incident was the subject of a book, *The Cuckoo's Egg,* by Clifford Stoll.

A group of West German Hackers, who were operating on their own, approached the KGB in East Berlin and began to sell the "product" of their hacking. Later touted as a "KGB spy ring," the hackers attempted to break into scores of military, government, and business computers to provide information to the Soviets. While the hackers thought that military items would be high on the KGB shopping list (some were), most of the requests centered on high technology computer programs and equipment design. The Soviets desired the "source code "for sophisticated and widely used computer operating systems. With this knowledge, the Soviets could create their own team of "hackers" to penetrate systems in the West.

The operating system that runs a computer exists in two forms, the "source code" which a human can read, analyze, and understand when printed, and the "compiled" version, which translates the operating system "source code" into "machine language," the actual ones and zeros that the computer understands but is completely unintelligible to humans. The process of compiling the source code is similar to encryption. The machine language can be decompiled (decrypted) with the result being only similar, not identical, to the source code. Thus, any "source code" is one of a computer programming company's most closely held secrets. Knowledge of the "source code" makes it easier for a hostile competitor or state to identify what bugs exist in the program or even insert its own bugs, recompile the code, and replace the operating system with their altered version, all without the knowledge of the end user.

In this manner, the Soviets were attempting to "get the keys to the filing cabinet rather than its contents" via their computer hackers. There are indications that the Soviet efforts to acquire this information were far more extensive than using the "amateur" hackers as their KGB contact told them that they had "competition" and may of its desires were met without the hackers providing the product. This knowledge, exploited by terrorists, could result in massive disruption of computer systems on the worldwide basis.

The computer penetration attempts by the Soviets/Russians continue. Wayne Madsen observes that "the Institute of Automated Systems (IAS) in Moscow hosts the National Center for Automated Data Exchanges with Foreign Computer Networks and Data Banks (NCADE). During Soviet rule, NCADE had a special program to broaden linkages between Soviet computer users and foreign data networks and databases to obtain valuable software programs that the Soviets could not normally obtain because of Western export restrictions." Using these channels, the Soviets penetrated a German computer and obtained production information on the Tornado fighter aircraft in 1984. As recently as 1989 a Soviet Attaché, LtCol Yuri Pakhutsov, was expelled from the U.S. for allegedly attempting to acquire information on government computer security practices and capabilities.

While the KGB of the Soviet Union was well organized and ran its "information warfare" attacks from several directorates, the current state of organized Russian computer espionage efforts is not clear. Statements made by retired Russian intelligence officers, even after the KGB-Hannover Hacker spying scandal, leave open the possibility that computer espionage efforts continue. Colonel Barkovsky was not hesitant to state that the Russian Federation has embarked on a major programme of establishing information service networks throughout the country. Not elaborated upon was whether the Russian intelligence services will take advantage of the information-gathering capabilities provided by these networks.

One can only assume that the Russians are continuing their programs to acquire and target high technology in the United States. Claire Sterling, in her book *The Terror Network,* claimed that the Soviet Union was a major sponsor of terrorism across the world. While the dissolution of the Soviet Union and the economic problem of Russia have clearly limited its ability to fund large terrorist operations, the cost involved in sponsoring cyberterrorism is significantly lower. The knowledge gained by the Soviets during Cold-War espionage efforts may (with or without the approval of the Soviet leadership) find its way into the hands of cyberterrorist organizations. This flow of information is potentially more damaging than the flow of arms and explosives to conventional terrorist organizations.

Bulgaria has been a "breeding ground" for computer viruses during and after Communist rule. In the early 1990s, the Bulgarians had developed thirty unique viruses with more than 100 different variations and were releasing them at a rate of one per week. The "Hannover hackers" of *Cuckoo's Egg* fame also identify the Bulgarians as active in computer intelligence. Madsen cites the National Intelligence Service (foreign and domestic intelligence), and Razuznavatelno Upravleniye na Ministersivoto (RUMNO) (Military intelligence) as the Bulgarian intelligence organizations most likely to be involved in computer intelligence gathering. It has also been rumored that a new "virus library" that allows anyone, not just a skilled programmer, to write a virus by "picking and choosing" among several options was first developed in Bulgaria. This system has the potential to produce thousands of new viruses to be unleashed at random or specific targets.

A cyberterrorist bent on bringing a system down could single-handedly generate a flood of viruses to infect the targeted computer. Even if virus detection software was installed, the chances are good that a virus could be created to evade detection.

France freely admits that it conducts intelligence operations against its allies and its enemies on the "economic front." As we move into the information age, the distinction between friends and enemies begins to blur. Madsen targets the Direction de la Surveillance du Territoire (DST) and the Directorate Generale de la Securite Exterieure (DGSE) as the agencies involved in COMPINT. In addition the Groupement de Communications Radio-electriques (GCR), the French NSA, maintains a close working relationship with France Telecom and, like the U.S. NSA, has strict rules on the use of encryption products within France, allegedly so that they can "break" the encryption and eavesdrop on communications within France.

Recently, the French government disclosed a document instructing the DGSE to gather intelligence on 49 U.S. aerospace and defense firms. The methods to obtain this information included bugging of Air France flights and breaking and entering of hotel rooms of visiting business executives to photocopy business materials. The Hughes Aircraft Company has been a favourite target of the French. The DGSE targeted Hughes for information on it HS 601 communication satellite, fiber optic anti-tank weapons, the Phoenix AIM-54 air to air missile, and various electro-optical sensors.

The Hughes Corporation decided (ostensibly for business reasons) to cancel its attendance at the Paris Air Show after the revelations of French targeting. Another "aviation" scheme of the French involved the collection and exploitation of telemetry signals from a Boeing test flight of its new 747-400 aircraft. A French SIGINT and technical team were sent to Washington state to intercept and analyze the test flight data for the benefit of Airbus research. While not a direct computer controlled navigation and flight control systems. The knowledge gained from Boeing's telemetry data enabled them to develop similar systems for their own aircraft. Additionally, should the detailed knowledge of computer controlled aviation systems fall into the hands of a technologically sophisticated terrorist organization, the potential to create terror is substantial. A terrorist organization would only have to convince the public that it is capable of causing the controls of a particular type of airplane to stop responding to pilot inputs to create large concern over flying in that particular type of airplane.

The Japanese place a high priority on intelligence gathering through both "official" and corporate intelligence networks. Japan's international telecom carrier, NTT "routinely cooperates with Japanese intelligence to tap the phone lines of competitors." In addition Madsen asserts that the Japanese target U.S. satellite communications stations. "A 1987 classified CIA report, *Japan: Foreign Intelligence and Security Services,* claimed that the second most important Japanese intelligence priority was the gathering (in many cases by computer) of technological and scientific developments in the United States and Western Europe."

The efforts of Japan in the "high tech" sector are not simply related to "computer break-ins" but rather to acquire design specifications in an effort similar to that of the Former Soviet Union. While the Soviets were attempting to obtain source codes and hardware that they were unable to build themselves, the Japanese were working to save money on R&D by stealing advanced U.S. technology and then bringing similar products to market simultaneously with their U.S. competition. Peter Schweizer outlines the story of a corporate spy who sold Hitachi copies of IBM's *Adirondack Workboods,* a series of books that held the secrets to future IBM technology.

Hitachi was able to use this information to develop computer hardware that was nearly identical to IBM's but cheaper since Hitachi did not bear the development costs. This case was "broken" by a Silicon Valley "sting" operation run by the FBI that initially targeted the Soviets. Japanese aggressiveness in pursuing this technology led them into the trap. The end result was an out of court settlement, reportedly for 300 million dollars between the Japanese and IBM. The information that an intelligence gathering effort obtains may be used by a sponsored terrorist organization to target a specific business or industry.

Chinese intelligence employs its large ethnic community abroad for many purposes. It is now clear that computer penetration was one of those functions. Andrew Wang, a Chinese immigrant, was arrested for stealing the source code of several programs from Ellery Systems. These programs were designed to "run" the emerging National Information Infrastructure. This source code, as previously discussed, would allow a foreign intelligence agency or terrorist group to identify and exploit loopholes in the "new information superhighway" that would carry everything from benign E-mail to national security data.

The Germans appear to have taken their cue from the success of such amateur hacker groups as the "Chaos Club" and the "Hannover Hackers" that worked with the KGB. According to Schweizer, the Germans created "Project Rahab," named after the biblical character who helped the Israelites infiltrate Jericho, in the mid 1980s to develop a "professional" hacking capability. The project was developed by the Bundes Nacrichten Dienst's (BND) Christian Stoessel, who wrote the initial "point paper" proposing hacking into foreign data bases for intelligence purposes. The project was joint effort between BND's Division I (HUMINT), Division II (SIGINT) and Division IV (HQ).

In addition to the intelligence professionals, other technical experts from a variety of outside institutions were recruited, resulting in a staff of approximately 70 people. While focused initially on retrieving information, the Project Rahab staff soon turned to offensive measures that could be of use in a time of conflict, including a variety of viruses that could be inserted in to target computers. Schweizer claims that the Project has "accessed computer systems in the Soviet Union, Japan, France, the United States, Italy, and Great Britain," Included in the "hacks" of the Rahab staff is penetration of the SWIFT network, a dedicated international banking network that carries there majority of worldwide bank transfers. The implications of this information falling into terrorist hands are clear.

Both sides waged information warfare, it appears, during the Gulf War. A Schweizer claims that a major computer penetration effort was launched during Desert Storm. A Government Accounting Office Report reinforces this claim as it outlines the efforts of Dutch hackers to penetrate U.S. unclassified military computers. The hackers exploited several well-known weaknesses and were able to penetrate a computer system that directly supported Operation Desert Storm. While the hackers did not attempt to shut down any of the penetrated systems, they did attempt to modify the software to provide easy access in the future. While the Dutch hackers have not been publicly linked to Iraqi intelligence efforts, a similar incident, involving a German citizen was detected during the GulfWar.

Lawrence Livermore Laboratories were used by "hackers" in an attempt to find information on the Patriot missile system. In this instance the actions of a third party "proxy" for Iraq had the potential to cause damage to the safety of troops on the ground, the integrity of air defenses in Israel and thus, cause a weakening of the allied coalition against Iraq. As Iraq is a known sponsor of terrorist organizations, it may turn to its proxies to carry out a cyberterror campaign against the information systems of enemy states.

The Swiss, who have a long history in cryptography, may have perpetrated an information warfare attack against other nations. The Swiss firm of Crypto AG, which sells encryption technology and hardware to nations such as Iraq, Iran, Libya and Syria, has been accused of "bugging" their crypto equipment and listening in on "encrypted" communications. Further more, it is alleged that the Swiss firm is really owned by the German BND and that the U.S. National Security Agency has played a leading role in the bugging.

While the firm has vehemently denied this charge, it raises several interesting information warfare possibilities. If supposedly "secure" crypto units were bugged without the knowledge of a client nation, the possibility exists that other computers or items of "high tech" equipment have been modified with less than possibility exists that other computers or items of "high tech" equipment have been modified with less than honorable intent. Several stories have appeared on the Internet discussing both software and hardware "flaws" distributed in products. One such flaw disabled a computer program after one month of use.

The possibility exists that a program could "lock up" a computer after a certain time period or after it received a certain activation command. Computer hardware, such as printers and circuit boards could also be shipped with "logic bombs" in their programs that would cause the equipment to cease functioning. The known cases that have been discussed have all been "benign" errors by public companies that have been rapidly fixed once identified. If, however, a foreign power were to insert its own bug in the software's source code *before* shipment and not activate the program until hostilities were imminent, a substantial portion of an affected computer network could be disabled.

The island nation of the Seychelles has undertaken a high technology campaign against enemies of its government in England. The nation was able to exploit the British telephone system and conduct wiretaps against several targets. The information obtained with these wiretaps resulted in the assassination of an exiled anti-government leader. The Seychelles demonstrate the potential threat that even a small country can pose to a superpower by using information warfare techniques. In the information age, even the smallest state or terrorist group has a chance to impact the global network.

While not responsible for the creation of the "Friday the 13th" virus, (supposedly developed by a Palestinian to protest the 40th anniversary of the end of the Palestinian mandate) the computer links between Israel's intelligence service and the United States served as a conduit for the virus to spread to the United States. The Israelis used a "low tech" solution to enter U.S. databases-they recruited Jonathan Pollard. While unable to "break DIA's computers, Israel could obtain information that Pollard retrieved from computer systems and delivered to his handlers.

This highlights the constant "human" factor in all of intelligence. Even if your computer cannot be accessed by any type of modem or network and is sitting inside a Tempest approved enclosure, an enemy agent can still physically break-in, or have an employee access the machine, copy the information from that computer onto a floppy disk and simply walk out of the building with it. Information that would have taken a wheelbarrow to get out of a secure facility now fits on a single diskette. While "hackers" may not "break into" some of their target computers, they are still able to analyze the type of information on the computer and possibly gain some information of the type of hardware and operating system that runs the computer.

While this does not help the hacker, it may allow for mare "classic" espionage action to be taken by a foreign organization, such as bribing or blackmailing someone on the "inside." As Jay Peterzell highlights, "NSA has figures that make the insider threat look soberingly real. An agency log of cases involving computer crime or computer espionage showed that up to 90% of knows security breaches are the work of corporate or government insiders." Israel was also involved in halting a second Patriot missile computer hacking operation. Israel detained an 18 year old for attacking U.S. defense computers to retrieve information on the Patriot missile system. Charges were not brought against the hacker, possibly to down play the incident and not highlight existing weaknesses in computer security.

The use of computers in revolutions highlights the importance of information control for authoritarian regimes. Without tight control of information flow, regimes cannot control the activities of dissidents. The increasing interconnection of the world provided by computers allows dissidents to "bring in "the rest of the world. They instantly broadcast atrocities and repression to a worldwide audience, with the attendant publicity often preventing a harsh crackdown by government forces.

A 1987 article in *Datamation* examined the use of computers in the Solidarity movement in Poland:

Necessity and the spread of information technology have bred a computer-savvy opposition in Poland that is capable of breaking into TV news broadcasts, producing alternative information that contradicts government data, and developing publishing and distribution systems that can spread the opposition's cause quickly and efficiently.

The Solidarity movement used information warfare tactics to get their message out to the largest possible number of Polish citizens. The actions of three astronomers and a local engineer exemplify the ability of a few individuals to influence thousands with information technology. These individuals intercepted the state-run television broadcast signal, determined the characteristics of the signal, and then used their computer equipment to time and configure their own signal. They broadcast this signal over the same frequency as the state signal, allowing 60,000 television viewers to see both signals concurrently. These viewers saw the message, "Enough price increases, lies, and repressions. It is our duty to boycott the election." the government arrested and tried the four for this action.

After being held for four months, they were convicted and ordered to pay fines ranging from $80 to $120. During their trial, the prosecutor claimed that the voting turnout was ten to 20 percent lower than average in the region that viewed the pirate television broadcast. The Solidarity movement also used computers to perform an independent prediction of the election results. This independent check ensured that the "official" government estimates were no inflated.

The struggle for the Solidarity movement was not merely to show that the official count was wrong according to Konrad Bielinski, a leader of this project. "Rather, we wanted to achieve something more, namely to take away from the state its monopoly over giving us information about ourselves." The movement also capitalized on the advantages of information technology to provide secure, reliable communication between members. Anyone can encrypt and transport a massive amount of data on disk. In addition to being easier to conceal, a computer disk is easier to destroy than a pile of paper.

The Chinese dissidents involved in the Tiananmen Square protest in 1989 did not target computer systems, but rather utilized new technology, primarily the fax machine and the Internet, to ensure that word of what was happening in China made it out of the country. Students in the United States then took the information that was flowing out of China and sent it back into the country via fax machines. Through the use of this technology, the dissidents prevented China's leadership from controlling the flow of information. While telecommunications assets were restricted in the weeks following the massacre, telecommunications connectivity facilitated its initial reporting and continuing coverage with the rest of the world.

The Zapatista uprising in southern Mexico provides another example of rebel organizations exploiting high technology. The Zapatista leadership has used the Internet to establish a worldwide organization of supporters that are beyond the control of Mexico's government. Zapatista leadership communiqués are issued via the Internet, instantly spreading their message to a worldwide audience without any interference by the Mexican authorities or news media interpretation. In the same manner as china during the Tiananmen Square uprising, Mexico lost the ability to control the flow of information both out of, and into, the country.

The information received from inside Mexico fostered extensive media coverage, limiting the repressive options open to the government. While not terrorism, the ability to form transnational networks and ensure that the message of an organization is heard on a world stage is a tool that terrorists will be exploiting the future. If there were no rapid communications channels out of the jungles of southern Mexico, it is likely that Mexican government would have been able to use much harsher methods to repress the rebellion. While the actions of rebels and dissidents are not always terrorism, these incidents highlight the fact that a small number of people can have a worldwide impact and generate international publicity of their cause without government interference. These capabilities will appeal to terrorists in the information age.

The Rise of Techno Terrorism

Electrical distribution and energy systems have been favourite targets of terrorists. The use of computers to run these networks makes them an ideal cyberterrorism target. However, as an examination of conventional terrorist and military attacks on energy systems demonstrates, these targets may be of limited value to the cyberterrorist. Statistics show that there were 240 total attacks on "Domestic Energy-related and Military Targets" from 1970 to mid 1980. The most popular of the targets were powerlines and powerstation/substations. This trend continued through 1988 with 283 recorded incidents of subnational attacks on energy systems in the United States.

A worldwide target summary shows that power pylons and power lines remained the number one target with power substations being the third most popular target. Thomas E. Griffith, in his thesis entitled *Strategic Attack of National Electrical Systems,* studies the military benefits accorded a state by attacking an enemy electrical system in a time of war. The apparent lack of utility in attacking electrical systems in war may apply to terrorists as well.

Strategic attacks on national power system can be useful in fulfilling national security aims, but only under specific conditions. First, the target country's power system should be vulnerable to destruction by being very concentrated with very few interconnections. Second, the strategy behind the attacks should be focused on stopping war production over the long term. To strike electric power to affect civilian morale, increase costs to the leadership, or impact the military will waste missions and could prove counterproductive to the political aims of the war.

The "critical node" identified by Griffith is the transformer station, where power is "stepped-up" of "stepped-down" for transmission and distribution. The components at some of these sites are custom built and could take up to eighteen months to manufacture if they are destroyed in an attack. The most recent concerted attack on energy systems in the United States was undertaken in California by a group calling itself the "Earth Night Action Group" who cut down two wooden power poles and toppled a 100-foot transmission tower in April of 1990. The result of this attack was the loss of power to 92,000 customers for up to a day.

The group struck at isolated targets rather than the transformer substations, thus lessening the impact of their action. In the late 1970s, the "New World Liberation Front" bombed a Pacific Gas and Electric transformer near San Francisco that disrupted power to 75,000 homes for approximately two hours. PG&E transformers and offices were bombed 16 times between 1975 and 1978, leading Research West, a detective agency specializing in terrorism, to call PG&E the "prime victim of terrorism in the United States." As press reports have indicated, electrical lines themselves are the most accessible targets for terrorists or criminals. In the United States, up to 300 electrical insulators can be shot off by hunters and pranksters in a single day.

These actions are not a concerted effort to bring down the electrical system by an organized group. Rather, they are random acts of vandalism for which the flexibility of the electrical system can compensate. Should an organized group simultaneously attack several critical nodes (step-up/step-down transformers) across the United States, the potential for disruption increases. Chuck Lane's statements before Congress indicate that the system is vulnerable, but it is robust enough to withstand nearly all attacks.

In summary, this investigation concluded that the networks [energy and telecommunication] of the United States are vulnerable to multisite terrorist attacks, that is, that targets are likely to be destroyed. However, the redundancy of built into the networks make them very dependable, and the real question is what level of service would be lost from such an attack. In many cases the consequences appear to be manageable. In a few cases, perhaps too many cases, the consequences are potentially catastrophic.

While the physical vulnerability of electrical system components to destruction is real, David Hinman states, "the flexibility of the system is its greatest security. Our security plans must be built upon this fact in order to have maximum effectiveness." Still, the capability exists, with relatively unsophisticated technology to disrupt power to a large portion of an electrical grid by targeting its critical nodes. While the weapons technology (firearms, explosives, etc.) are readily available to a terrorist group, some research is required to obtain the knowledge necessary to identify and target critical nodes in the energy system. Unfortunately, this information is publicly available.

The information contained in public documents mandated by the Department of Energy, Federal Communications Commission, and Department of Transportation can be used by terrorists to plan attacks on infrastructure targets. According to a Government Accounting Office report of December 1988, a mock terrorist team utilized information obtained from a public library to plan an attack on the Strategic Petroleum Reserve in 1987. While infrastructure systems in the United States remain vulnerable to physical attack, Dr. Robert K. Mullen, does not believe that these incidents will increase in the future, despite a growing terrorist presence in the United States.

That being said, there are no indicators of which I am aware, insofar as trends in the U.S. are concerned, that would suggest to me the threat to energy assets here is substantially different from what the recent historical record indicates. The presence in the U.S. of terrorist support groups does no alter this view.

While the fragility and relative open nature of electrical systems has been heralded in the press, it is the secondary effects of such attacks that concern individuals like Norman Leach.

Any terrorist group with access to moderate amounts of explosives could shut down any city in the United States simply by destroying local transformer sites. Not only would vital industries and defense programs be affected but the ensuing blackouts would cause riots in the streets that would threaten the stability of the government.

While certainly a contributing factor to the civil unrest experienced in New York City's famed blackout of 1965 and 1977, the removal of electrical power from a city is neither a necessary nor a sufficient cause for "riots that would threaten the stability of the government." The riots in the streets of Los Angeles following the Rodney King verdict as well as the riots (disguised as celebrations) after major sports championships are won show that disturbances can happen with a fully functional electrical system. The labour Day 1988 Seattle blackout, in which over 1/3 of the city was without power for 4 1/2 days, proves that a blackout does not produce riots and looting. In fact, the incidence of crime in the affected area went *down*, not up, due to an intense police presence.

The ability to cause a riot with a blackout alone is thus suspect. While a terrorist group may be able to exacerbate a crisis situation that it has fomented with the addition of a blackout, a blackout in isolation is not a fail-safe way to "ignite the masses."

While the above situation has focused primarily on the physical attack of energy systems to cause disruption, the increasing computer control of these and other infrastructure systems provides a potential target for a terrorist group.

The California Department of Water Resources recognized the risk inherent in these systems in 1991 when they implemented strict physical security control measures to protect their central computer center. The computers contained at the center were used to control the release of water from the major dams in the state. The increased security was a result of a perceived increase in the terrorist threat during Operation Desert Storm.

The possible physical risks, such as the shutdown of power plants or release of water from behind dams, will continue to increase as computerization of control systems continues. The true "critical nodes" of any system lie in its command and control network. By striking at this link to disable or control the system, a terrorist precludes the necessity to attack elements of a distributed system physically, such as transformers or pumps.

There are many parallels between energy systems and information warfare targets. Critical nodes exist in all networks that will impair the entire system. Attacking anything but these critical nodes may result in a minor degradation of service or, if the system is correctly designed, no disruption at all. Thus, the attacks on energy distribution system components such as power lines and pylons cause limited disruption for regional customers but widespread outages are very rare. While the information on the physical layout and vulnerabilities of an energy system exist, it has not been a particularly effective terrorist target.

This may be due to the lack of organizational and manpower assets a valuable to a terrorist group. In addition, those targets that are "critical nodes" may have enough security to prevent their destruction. The pattern of terrorist attacks on electrical systems may provide an insight into information age terrorism. If systems can be engineered to be redundant in some areas (and thus able to recover from attack) and defended in others (to prevent attack), it may mitigate the risks of widespread outages.

Attacks on Computer Systems

While the public has perceived buildings and airplanes as the primary targets of terrorists, attacks on computers were involved in 60% of conventional terrorist acts by 1989. the pattern of criminal computer attacks, together with terrorist activity, suggest that there may be a shift toward cyberterrorism as a physically less risky means to achieve both criminal and terrorist ends.

In the 1970s the Italian Red Brigades launched 27 attacks against companies that did business in the electronics, computer and weapons sectors. In 1980, the French organization Comite Liquidant ou Detournant les Ordinateurs (Computer Liquidation and Deterrence Committee or CLODO) undertook a series of attacks on computer companies in the Toulouse region. The organization released a statement to the press, "We are workers in the field of dp (data processing) and consequently well place to know the current and future dangers of dp and telecommunications. The computer is the favourite tool of the dominant. It is used to exploit, to put on file, to control, and to repress."

A Belgian Group, the Cellueles Communistes Combattants (Fighting Communist Cells) conducted a series of bombings in September 1984 directed against Honeywell Controls and Litton Industries. In November 1984, the same group attacked the Brussels office of Motorola. Computers were prime targets in each of these attacks.

Similar attacks have occurred in the United States. IBM's offices in White Plains N.Y. were bombed in March1984. The group claiming responsibility for the attack, the United Freedom Front, distributed a newsletter that stated "IBM is a death merchant... The computer is an integral part of the fascist South African government's policies of racist repression and control."

The CLODO group struck again in 1983 by firebombing a Sperry-Univac computer room in Toulouse to protest the U.S. invasion of Grenada. Upon putting out the fire, the message, "Reagan attacks Grenada- Sperry Multinational is an American accomplice." was found spray painted on an interior wall.

While the attacks on computer systems failed to cause any major political victory for CLODO, they did heighten the awareness that European computers are vulnerable to attack. A 1979 report by the Swedish Defense Ministry recommended that the government become involved in monitoring computer security of both public and private computers. While the proper role of the government in computer security remains open for debate, an article in the French daily *Le Figaro* states that computer attacks might be more harmful to national security than the assassination of random politicians.

In 1985 in Japan, the Middle Core Faction, a terrorist group consisting of approximately 300 individuals, attacked the commuter rail system to cause massive disruption during the height of rush hour. The group used C2W techniques to carry out its attack by first cutting strategic power and communications cables that fed the computer controls for the rail system. Secondly, the group jammed police and rescue radio frequencies in an attempt to hamper and delay response by the authorities. While no one was injured in this attack, it caused a major commuting delay affecting 6.5 million commuters and cost the Japan National Railways more than $6 million in lost ticket sales.

Rather than blowing up or tampering with the physical destruction of one rail, the group focused on the critical node (control circuits) and disabled the entire system by using technoterror, attacking physical targets to cause a disruption in cyberspace. The disruption was extensive enough that the Centralized Traffic control Office of Japan National Railways (JNR) was forced to stop operation. While the attacks were successful in creating disruption, the effects were short lived, with most of the severed cables back in full service within 24 hours. This attack, while creating problems for millions of commuters, was also linked to specific objectives.

The first was to show solidarity with the National Railways Locomotive Engineers' Union, which was on strike to protest the planned privatization of the JNR. The second goal may have been to influence the trial of Hiroko Nagata, the leader of the Extreme Leftist United Red Army. Her hearing was delayed because the rail shutdown prevented her defense lawyer from making it to court on time. The combination of computer controls and energy systems raises new possibilities for terrorists. While targeting of energy systems in the past has relied primarily on the physical destruction of key assets to disrupt service, the potential vulnerability of the control systems poses an even greater risk.

The rise of Information Warfare tactics may allow tomorrow's terrorists to focus their attacks on certain individuals to change their policies or courses of action. The increasing reliance on computers has opened new avenues for blackmail and political pressure. In 1984, a hacker penetrated TRW's credit report computers and obtained some incriminating information about a past small-claims court dispute involving then incumbent Congressional candidate Tom Lantos of California. This information was passed to his opponent who further distributed the information to the press to discredit Lantos.

In a second act of political computer crime, a hacker gained access to Representative Ed Zshau's computer system in Washington, D.C. and erased his data, including his correspondence and constituent database. These events highlight the potentially selective nature of future cyberterrorism and crime. With a skilled computed operator, a terrorist group may be able to penetrate systems to manipulate a small number of people. Instead of attacking the public to affect a target audience, cyberterrorists may choose to affect the target audience to achieve their ends directly.

While "conventional" terrorist groups have targeted computer systems in the past, "eco-terror" groups, such as Earth First, have advocated attacking computer systems. In 1987, the group published a manual that advocated both physical destruction of computer equipment (conventional terrorism) and software and data manipulation/destruction (via cyberterrorism). the manual also included techniques to reduce the risk of being caught by using advance hacking techniques. The risk of cyberterrorism exists on all fronts. It is not merely limited to the "classic" conventional terrorist group. Any group with a strong interest or agenda will be able to attempt cyberterrorism.

Criminal activity directed at, or using, computers is receiving increasing attention in the press. The expansion of the Internet to include commercial ventures has sparked a debate over the correct level of security that should be afforded individuals in cyberspace. As terrorism is often crime with different intent, several criminal acts will be explored in this section. First, the case of a Russian hacker attempting to steal more than $10 million highlights the vast amounts of money being transferred in cyberspace. Second, the attempt to use computer viruses to hold computers hostage or attack a specific company will be examined. Finally, the possible physical risks to individuals as a result of criminal cyberspace activity are addressed in the case of a Texas professor.

The use of computers and computer technology to perpetrate crimes has already occurred. Citibank recently "lost" $10.2 million electronically to a team of Russian hackers. A closer examination of the facts involved in this incident reveals some strengths and weaknesses of computer crime. First, the authorities can use the same technology employed by the cyberterrorist or criminal to track and capture him. Someone can, however, remain anonymous in cyberspace if they are not seeking financial gain, as virus writers have proven.

This incident, according to John Mohr, vice president of the New York Clearing House, is unique in that it utilized a personal computer. It appears that Vladimir L. Levin, a Russian computer expert employed by AO Saturn, a St. Petersburg trading company, broke into Citibank's computer system using stolen account identification numbers and passwords. With this information, he made 40 transfers from Citibank to accounts set up by accomplices in California and Israel. These transfers occurred from June to October 1994 and were tracked by Citibank to determine who was responsible for the crime.

While Citibank allowed the transfers to continue, the accounts into which he was transferring the money were frozen, While Levin attempted to transfer more than $10 million in this period, Citibank has recovered all but $400,000. Amy Dates of Citibank had the following answer when questioned about the level of security at Citibank:

"We move half a trillion dollars a day through the payment system. Compare that to the $400,000 they were able to withdraw. We think we have the right level of security." Despite these statements, Citibank implemented a new computer protocol to increase transaction security.

It is still unclear how Levin obtained the account numbers and their associated passwords, but an investigation is continuing into the possibility of inside help. Citibank, has implemented a new security system for its computer accounts that entails the use of "smart cards" that will generate a new password for each transaction. This technology helps to defeat password "sniffer" programs that allow criminals to capture passwords as they are transmitted across the network for future use. This may have been how Levin obtained his passwords. He appears to have had access to the network for some time before attempting his crime as he was careful to follow the patterns of routine transactions and kept his individual transfers to below $300,000 to avoid "built-in" security programs that would have highlighted the transaction as abnormal.

While the adoption of the smart card security system and the employment of encryption technology has, Citibank hopes, corrected the security weakness exploited by Levin and his friends, the amount of money lost in this crime is relatively small. The high level of publicity afforded this incident is due to its extranormality, not its dollar value. Each year, according to the American Bankers Association, the following amounts are lost due to crime: Check fraud- $10 Billion, Credit Card fraud- $712 Million, ATM fraud- $18 Million, and Online fraud (as in the Citibank case)- $5 Million.

While Citibank could use its computers to track and eventually catch Levin, computers and high technology aided in the success of a Vietnamese check fraud ring that operated undetected for seven months. The U.S. Secret

Service investigated the crime under the name, "Operation Paper Dragon" and found that the ring took in $25 Million in just over half a year. These high technology money making schemes may appeal to terrorist organizations of the future who are unable to secure, or do not desire, state sponsorship. While attractive to terrorists, the security measures put in place by the banking industry to prevent criminals will likely defeat terrorists as well.

In an apparent attempt to extort money, the computers of several universities were infected with a virus in an attempt to make them hostages. The virus demanded a ransom for the antidote to the virus.

Computer users who found the virus were told to send $2,000 to an address in Pakistan to obtain an immunity program that would rid the system of the virus. Investigation showed that the virus was written by two brothers in a computer store in Lahore, Pakistan-they had put their names, and address, and phone number in the virus! "It's like a fantasy of being a terrorist without the blood,: said Eric Corley, editor of a national hacker newsletter, 2600, whose electronic bulletin board was also infected.

The brothers' scheme did not pay well, and the virus was eradicated without their "immunity program." The "fantasy" of being a terrorist without the blood may become reality when an organization uses cyberterror weapons in an attack.

Recently, a virus was used to attack a specific business in Germany. A virus writer, known only as "The Wizard" created then released a virus that he called the "Media Market advertising virus." Media Markt is a German home-electronics group and was not involved in the virus writing or distribution. Media Markt's lawyer claims that "this is the first time that someone has distributed a virus and tied it to a company that has nothing to do with it" To stave off negative publicity, Media Markt has distributed an anti-virus program to disable the virus on affected computers.

While the true intention of the virus writer may never be known, the principle of indirect attack (attacking the general public to influence a target audience) normally utilized by terrorists was evidenced in these tactics. The virus writer, unleashed an attack on the "innocent" computer users to create negative publicity for Media Markt. In this case, Media Markt was clearly not involved in this activity. However, the anonymous and anarchic nature of cyberspace opens the possibility of creating chaos and making it appear as if someone else is responsible.

While it appears that financial gain motivated the Russian hackers in the Citibank case, the possibility exists that terrorists or criminals could perpetrate electronic attacks in the future to weaken the target company, not make money. If a terrorist group could place someone "on the inside" of a software company and infect software with a virus *before* shipment, it may call the integrity of that software company into question. While there are no reported cases of terrorists staging a concerted information warfare attack on a business, the case of Citibank might be a benchmark. Despite news that it had lost more than $10 million, Citibank stock went *up* by 1/2 a point on the day that the Russian hacker story broke.

The potential exists for terrorists to single out individuals in cyberspace. In 1994, a hacker logged into a Texas A&M professor's E-mail account and used the account to send out 20,000 racist messages. To those receiving the messages, it appeared that they had come from the professor. As a result, the professor began to receive death threats.

The Threat From Hackers Turned Terrorist

Penetration of computer systems is not difficult. The U.S. Defense Information Systems Agency undertook a penetration study of Department of Defense computers. In 1994, the agency attacked 8,932 servers and mainframes. They were able to gain access to 7,860 (88%) of these systems. Only 319 (4%) of these attacks were detected and only 19 (.2%) of the successful attacks were ever reported. The percentages suggest that even organizations that depend on computers to function rarely know when hackers have attacked them. Penetration of DOD systems has also been documented by other than DOD assets, such as the case of Defense computers being attacked by Dutch hackers during the Gulf War. While none of these penetrations were used for terrorist purposes, it is entirely possible that this may occur in the future.

Even if the hackers initially do not have terrorist intentions, they remain dangerous. A Government Accounting Office report on the Dutch hacker case states that, "the majority of the hackers' activities appeared to be aimed at gaining access to DOD computer system and then establishing methods for later entry. Should a computer hacker decide to work with terrorists, or be forced to work with terrorists via blackmail, these methods for later entry constitute a serious risk. The jump from hacker to terrorist is a small one that depends entirely on the hacker's motivation and intent. While these cases prove that hackers can penetrate systems, it does not examine the motivation for the hacker.

Several studies of the group dynamics and individual motivations for terrorists have been undertaken to help prevent terrorism. While similar studies on the "computer underground" have been undertaken, an analysis of how a terrorist organization might recruit a hacker would be worthwhile. As the world becomes more dependent on computers, understanding what makes hackers "tick" becomes as important as understanding what motivates terrorists.

The 1988 Morris Internet worm incident highlights the

incredible disruptive power of information warfare tactics for a cyberterrorist, as well as the limitations inherent in attacking computers. On November 2, 1988, Robert Tappan Morris, a Cornell University graduate student, released a "worm" onto the Internet. While Morris maintains that it was just an experiment that went terribly wrong, the Justice Department decided to prosecute Morris, who was found guilty of a felony and sentenced to three years probation, $10,000 fine and 400 hours of community service. In March of 1991, his appeal to the U.S. Count of Appeals for the second circuit was unsuccessful. In the fall of 1991, the U.S. Supreme Court refused to hear his case.

The worm program, created as an experiment by Morris, was based on three separate security flaws that Morris had discovered in the Berkeley version of the UNIX operating system. The goals of his program were: to infect three computers per network location across the Internet, to avoid slow machines and any network that was in use (to avoid detection by operators), use infected computers to find connections to other uninfected computers, steal the password files of computers and use the passwords to gain access to even more computers.

Computers had fascinated Morris his entire life. Morris' father, Bob Morris, was a computer engineer for Bell Labs, the creators of the UNIX operating system. The area of computer security had been a hobby of Robert Morris throughout his college years. His knowledge of computer systems was so extensive that both the Naval Research laboratory and the National Security Agency, NSA (where Bob Morris was serving as director of the National Computer Security Center) invited him to speak to the topic of UNIX operating system security. That this was a problem about which the NSA was deeply concerned became apparent during Morris's trial.

The presentation to the NSA was videotaped and the prosecution intended to show part of the tape concerning "how not to get caught" to show that Morris had written his program with malicious intent to break into computers. Robert's defense lawyer, Tom Guidoboni, threatened to force Robert's father to testify about the National Security Agency's interest in computer penetration, to include divulging classified material if the tape was shown. Possibly a result of NSA pressure, the tape was not used in the trial and the NSA was able to protect its secrets.

The knowledge that Robert Morris had obtained in his study of computer security was extensive. He had been aware of two flaws in the UNIX system for over a year before his worm was released. The final flaw, in the FTP, File Transfer Protocol, program (a utility in UNIX that allows individuals on different computers to transfer files back and forth between remote systems) was corrected before Morris could finish his program, so he was forced to adjust and exploit only the remaining two weaknesses.

These weaknesses were in the *sendmail* portion of the operating system and in the *finger* utility. It was a combination of these two weaknesses that allowed the worm to spread from computer to computer. The worm was originally designed to limit its growth, with each copy of the program checking to see if other copies were already running on a system before attempting to replicate. If there were other copies running, they would "negotiate" with each other to see which one would terminate. Unfortunately, the program that agreed to terminate would infect many other computers before it stopped running additionally, one in seven of the copies of the worm would not check to see if there were other copies present before infecting a machine. In effect, it refused to dies on its own. This "one in seven" system, coupled with the fact that the portion of the program controlling worm to worm communication was improperly written, led to a massive proliferation of worms on thousands of computers on the Internet, causing delay and forcing machines to be taken off the network. The battle to "beat" the worm was intense. The meeting of Berkeley UNIX experts was fortuitous in that several leading experts, including the creators of the operating system were in the same place and were able to collaborate on finding a solution to the problem. Within 24 hours, the Berkeley team had discovered how the program spread and had corrected the problems in the *sendmail* portion of the operating system. In less than 48 hours, all the weaknesses that the program attempted to exploit were corrected and the "fixes" were sent out to all users on the Internet. The attempt to understand the virus was hampered by its having been encrypted by Morris. Fortunately, the encryption scheme was extremely weak and was quickly broken, allowing the experts to unscramble the code.

The next step was to "reverse engineer" the code by decompiling it into source code to study its design and ensure that it did not have "malicious" (data altering/destroying) instructions hidden in the program. Fortunately for the users of the Internet, Morris did not write the worm to destroy data on infected computers, it would merely replicate out of control until the machine became overwhelmed with copies of the worm. Had the worm been written to destroy data, the recovery time would have been much longer with potentially massive data loss. Despite the rapid response of system experts, the publicity created by the incident was nearly as overwhelming in the media as the worm was to the infected computer systems. The worm caused so much disruption that the *New York Times* carried the story on page one for an entire week.

Additionally, both the *Wall Street Journal* and *USA Today* gave it front-page coverage. Television news and talk shows were also filled with discussion on the worm. This incident, while not malicious, highlights the power of information warfare techniques to cause massive disruption without physical harm to equipment or people. One man created a national computer crisis with a small program that received international attention and was addressed at the highest levels of the U.S. government. While appearing attractive for terrorists, this incident highlights both the positive and the negative aspects of information warfare for terrorism.

The ability of one man, in this case Robert T. Morris, to generate such an enormous amount of disruption and publicity with a small 3,000 line computer program might be very appealing to a terrorist organization attempting to achieve its aims with minimum effort and risk. Morris was eventually brought to trial for his worm, mainly because he spoke of its creation to several people. A dedicated cyberterrorist could remain anonymous in the same manner that the overwhelming majority of virus writers (such as the author of the famous Michelangelo virus - who remains unidentified) escape identification.

The personal equipment and money expenditures required for this incident were minimal as Morris had access to Cornell University's computers. While in the late 80s, Internet access was not widespread, today it is expanding at an exponential rate, with more individuals connecting to the network every day. The number of host computers connected to the Internet rose 30% from 1 July to 1 October 1994. The possible avenues of attack have expanded exponentially, as all that is required for a computer attack is a computer, a modem, and a skilled operator with the requisite information. The increasing number of host computers represents both new targets and new platforms from which to launch an attack.

As the power of computers doubles every 12-18 months, the computing power that was once reserved for major corporations and the government is now available to individuals. Since the "tools" are widely available, it is now the knowledge of how to manipulate those tools that is most important to perpetrate a computer attack. The knowledge that Morris used to attack the Internet came from extensive study of the UNIX operating system. He had known about the flaws for at least a year before writing his program to exploit their weaknesses. The correction of the FTP weakness immediately before Morris completed his worm program highlights the fragility of this information. Had that been the only weakness known to Morris, all of his work would have been for naught.

An external attack on a computer system usually occurs through weaknesses in the software that are unknown to the creators of the software. Those attempting to gain unauthorized access to a system exploit these "bugs" in programs. Once a "bug" is discovered, software developers usually rapidly distribute a "patch" that will correct the error. The flaw that took a hacker several months to find can be corrected in a matter of seconds with the installations of a software patch. The hacker or cyberterrorist is then forced to search for yet another weakness in the system. Those flaws in software exist, and are often unknown until exploited, are a double-edged sword for the potential cyberterrorist. If cyberterrorists learn of a weakness in a computer system, every day that they wait to exploit that weakness may allow a legitimate security professional or non-malicious hacker to discover and advertise the weakness, leading to the rapid distribution of a software or hardware fix to the problem.

Additionally, if cyberterrorists wish to create massive disruption, they will be forced to "show their hands" and exploit the weakness on a large number of systems or on several high value systems. If they are clever, they may be able to throw system managers off the track for a short period of time. Additionally, by using publicly available encryption techniques, they can scramble their program so that it will take years to decrypt and examine. This will exacerbate the fear of the unknown, as system managers will be unable to determine the true intent of the program. If malicious, it may require the systems to be completely shut down and all the software reloaded from a "known" clean source.

If the rouge program could not be completely understood and then removed without damage, a complete shutdown would be required for all systems that handled critical data or were used to control systems upon which human lives depend. The disruption would be far greater than that caused by the Morris worm, as it could be controlled, decrypted and safely removed from systems without damaging any of the existing software or negatively affecting the integrity of data on the machines.

The recent controversy over Netscape Corporation's use of encryption to secure Internet transactions highlights the strength and weakness of current encryption schemes. This particular encryption program was designed to allow users to send confidential information (such as credit card numbers) across the Internet securely. A French graduate student in mathematics used two supercomputers and 120 computer workstations to "brute force" decrypt (trying all possible combinations of the "key" in succession until the correct one is found) a message using this encryption program in just less than eight days.

This encryption scheme used a 40 bit key (meaning its "key" length was 40 bits-a bit is a single 0 or 1 in binary code) since it was the most powerful scheme that the U.S. government would allow to be exported. The key employed by Netscape within the United States is 128 bits. This 128 bit key, utilizing the same decryption techniques, would take 10^6 more time to break (about 2.1918 x 10^4 *years*).

In less than one month after the brute force decrypting of the 40 bit message, two graduate students at Berkeley discovered a software flaw that would allow them to decode a message encrypted with the 128 bit key in less than one minute. Netscape promptly fixed the problem and released an updated version of the encryption program within days to resecure the system.

The ability to create a program or send each other messages that would take law enforcement or government agencies 2.1918 x 10^4 years to unscramble is very appealing to cyberterrorists and common criminals. If a law enforcement agency intercepts an encrypted computer message, it is useless until it can be decrypted. This may allow cyberterrorists to move away from using the slow, but relatively secure, face-to-face method communication for potentially more secure, worldwide, and nearly instantaneous communication channel offered by encrypted E-mail.

The Institute for National Strategic Studies concluded that the communications signals themselves are becoming harder to intercept with the advent of "digital technology, frequency-hopping and spread-spectrum technologies, plus replacement of microwave with optical fiber for long-distance communication." The rise of public key encryption led the Institute to conclude that the capabilities of the codemakers are outpacing those of the codebreakers. The growing ubiquity of encryption, despite several setbacks, as in the Netscape case, has still made it difficult to obtain information that individuals desire to keep secure.

The value of encryption, and the ability of business to drive a response to crime, can be seen in the development of the GSM (Global System for Mobile communications) cellular phone standard, which uses encrypted digital signals to prevent eavesdropping and phone fraud. While in the United States, which uses an analog system, AMPS (Advanced Mobile Phone Service), a thief can steal the user ID to a cellular telephone (by intercepting its unencrypted signal) to perpetrate phone fraud. In GSM, this signal is randomly encrypted each time the phone is used, making it useless unless the correct "key" to decrypt the signal is in the possession of the interceptor. While the GSM system cuts down on cellular phone fraud, it also compounds the difficulty of intercepting the communications of known terrorists.

Unlike the physical world, in which a potential aggressor needs time and money to procure or manufacture its weapons, and time to train people to use these weapons, all of which can be observed and defenses readied by the target of aggression, the preparations of "weapons" in cyberspace is often the work of one (or several) individuals and occurs in the relative privacy and security of their own computers. With the explosion of processing power, the computers sitting in homes throughout the world are more powerful than the minicomputers, a decade ago. Unlike conventional terrorism, where the weapons of destruction are outlawed or restricted to use by the state, the weapons in cyberterrorism are available equally to the state and the terrorist organization. For a cyberspace WMD, the critical component becomes knowledge of computer systems, not the ability to procure fissionable material. The state and the terrorists operate on nearly equal footing in cyberspace.

The rapid recovery and complete eradication of the Internet worm, to include defenses against it ever occurring again, are not paralleled in the conventional world. A truck bomb manufactured from fertilizer and diesel fuel will cause damage and terror every time a terrorist parks it in or near a building and detonates it. Despite knowing the damage that car and truck bombs can cause through numerous attacks in the Middle East throughout the 1980s, authorities in the U.S. were unable to prevent the World Trade Center Bombing in New York City or the Murrah Federal Building bombing in Oklahoma City.

While improved technology and procedures allow authorities to respond more rapidly to these attacks and take some limited measures to prevent the attacks, they cannot ensure that a "copycat" crime will not occur. In cyberspace, once vulnerability is noted and a software fix is distributed, a second attack of exactly the same nature will *always* meet with defeat. What was once an open door becomes an impenetrable brick wall. If cyberterrorists were planning to exploit an identified and corrected weakness, all their effort was for naught. Their cyberspace "bomb" simply will not work. They can attempt to take his bomb elsewhere, but only if computer security administrators have shirked their duties and not installed "fixes" will they succeed.

The limited and fragile nature of weaknesses in cyberspace will force cyberterrorists to choose their targets carefully. Since an attack in cyberspace is likely to be a "one shot deal," terrorists must consider the cyberspace target to be of sufficient value to use their one-shot weapon. If a target is not sufficiently valuable, a cyberterrorists may choose to risk waiting until they can penetrate a system that will carry a substantial impact if attacked. A second factor affecting the nature of a cyberterrorist target is the likelihood that the disruption created will be temporary instead of permanent, as in the case of physical destruction of a target by a conventional or technoterrorist. The temporary nature of the disruption may cause cyberterrorists to string together numerous attacks to create disrupt of increased duration.

9

Tomorrow's Terrorist and their Expertise

As the world enters the 21st century, the information revolution will continue to propel the United States into the "third wave" of development according to Alvin and Heidi Toffler. The shift from an industrial economy and society to one focused on information and its transfer will characterize the third wave. As discussed in *The Third Wave* and their most recent work, *War and Anti-War*, the way a state wages war is similar to how it makes wealth. This idea might be applied to terrorism and revolutionary violence.

Lewis Gann's *Guerrillas in History* provides an overview of substate violence across history. Occasionally, as in the Welsh use of the longbow, substate groups possess weapons superior to those of the state. Substate actors, unless being supplied by another state, normally possess weapons that are inferior to those of the target state, they often use weapons stolen from, or discarded by, the state. As the technology, complexity, and lethality of weapons systems increased during the twentieth century, these weapons were even more tightly controlled by the state, widening the gap between state and substate "firepower." As the world shifts into the information age, this disparity in weapons decreases, with individuals and substate groups now able to control information manipulation tools that were once restricted to the state.

As the world shifts into the "third wave," where information and its control are rapidly becoming *the* most important considerations for the advancing societies of the first world, will we see a corresponding shift by terrorists and revolutionaries to using "information warfare" weapons and techniques to press their case? While terrorists and revolutionaries have "kept pace with the advance of technology, consistently exploiting new and under defended targets, (embassies, airplane hijackings, hostage taking, airplane bombing) they have done so through evolution, not innovation. Bruce Hoffman contends, "What innovation does occur is mostly in the methods used to conceal and detonate explosive devise, not in their tactics or in their use of non-conventional weapons (i.e., chemical, biological, or nuclear)." This thesis explores the implications of information age terrorism. There has already been a shift toward "information warfare" across other parts of the "conflict spectrum" with these techniques being used by criminals, agents of espionage, revolutionaries, and armies engaged in warfare. A corresponding shift in terrorist tactics has yet to occur. While some argue that it is merely a matter of time before we are faced with a major information warfare attack, there are several reason that terrorists may not actively pursue these techniques.

This onset of the information-dependent third wave provides opportunities for spectacular gains, and serious losses for individuals, corporations, and states. It is within this world that the cyberterrorist will operate. In the same manner that terrorists have exploited widely accepted technology such as dynamite and the airplane (for bombing and hijacking), they may exploit the tools of the "information age" to bring their case before the citizens of the world. The United States must prepare itself to counter this threat in an age where the old AT&T slogan, "reach out and touch someone" takes on a sinister new meaning.

To defend against a threat, one must understand its critical elements.

Cyberterrorism, like "conventional" terrorism, will strive to change the mind of its intended audience. It will be perpetrated *by* people to have an effect *on* people. However, cyberterrorism may utilize a different means to this end. A cyberterrorist will strive, not to disrupt physical reality directly (as an exploding bomb would) but rather to disrupt the normal functioning of computers and other information systems. This cyberspace disruption would cause a disruption in the physical world, The violence that is normally associated with terrorism may shift into "cyberspace" where bits and bytes, not people, are attacked. To understand the potential shift in terrorism, this thesis splits information age terrorism into three categories: conventional terrorism, Technoterrorism, and cyberterrorism.

This thesis will also analyze the costs and benefits of information warfare techniques for terrorism and the changes that they may force in the definition of terrorism. Despite the inevitable warnings that "the sky is falling," the utility of information warfare attacks may actually be lowest in the "terrorist" portion of the conflict continuum. This does not, however, obviate the need to address the threat, the information warfare threat is real; it might cause serious damage in the future. While it may not fit accepted definitions of terrorism, Neal Pollard correctly states that, "to ignore computer abuse as a political crime, simply for the sake of academic purity, is impractical, dangerous esoteric snobbery." As we will see in this examination of the "brave new world" into which we are headed, there are reasons both for and against terrorism shifting toward IW tactics in the third wave.

While the United States has yet to suffer an acknowledged cyberterrorist attack, several computer crimes and incidents reveal the power of information warfare. The trend toward information warfare appears uniform across the conflict continuum with the exception of terrorism. The cases used in this thesis were selected from unclassified literature. They were selected for their ability to highlight the potential threat posed by information warfare tactics and techniques. The ongoing information revolution, coupled with the sensitive nature of computer systems for both business and defense, ensure that this is not a comprehensive examination of all computer related incidents but it is sufficiently broad to cover the entire "low intensity" spectrum of conflict.

This thesis will examine the role of information warfare in espionage and crime using cases involving the United States. The role of telecommunications assets in the Solidarity movement in Poland, the Tiananmen Square uprising, and the Zapatista movement in Mexico will be highlighted to show the increasing value of information warfare to insurgents and rebels and the increasing importance of computer connectivity. Exploring the role computers and networks have played in terrorist actions since 1970 will identify the trend in terrorism toward infrastructure warfare, technoterrorism, and cyberterrorism. Finally, the 1988 Internet Worm incident caused by Robert Morris will be utilized as an example of both the costs and benefits information warfare tactics offer to a terrorist.

Information warfare is a concept that embraces many elements beyond simply attacking computers and communications networks. This thesis will, however, focus primarily on the portion of information warfare that deals with computers and their associated networks and only tangentially cover such topics as psychological operations. The revolutionary changes caused by computers present the possibility of revolutionary changes in the targets and conduct of terrorism.

The vulnerability of U.S. telecommunications and other infrastructure targets led to hearing before Congress, numerous reports and books, and grist for the "technothriller" novel industry. The relative weakness of U.S. infrastructure and information systems to terrorist attacks is a necessary, but not sufficient condition for information age terrorism, which this thesis has grouped into conventional terrorism, technoterrorism, and cyberterrorism. Conventional terrorism will continue to operate exclusively in the physical world. Technoterrorism will operate in the physical world to create a cyberspace disruption and cyberterrorism will operate exclusively in cyberspace. To address the level of threat posed by these types of terrorism, this thesis has examined some weaknesses in the system, and also the possible motivation for the use of information warfare by terrorism. While weaknesses and vulnerabilities may exist in the system, and the tools to exploit these weaknesses may be developed or purchased by terrorists in the future, the present concern over an "electronic Pearl Harbor" may be slightly off base.

Information warfare tactics do not create terror in the same way as conventional terrorist tactics. As such, a shift in the definition of terrorism is required to group cyberterrorism with conventional terrorism. Including cyberterrorism in the overall category of terrorism allows scholars and policy makers to place this new threat into a known framework that provides the foundation for further study and the development of prevention and response measures. Building on classic terrorism, cyberterrorism may shift toward a more "demassified" threat with shifting state sponsorship.

The purpose of this new type of terrorism may be to send a very specific message via disruption of systems as opposed to destruction of property and the killing of citizens. New technology will expand the struggle between terrorists and counter-terrorist forces into cyberspace where "classic" offense, defense, and deterrence do not exist. Instead, both sides will be forced to deal with the new opportunities and drawbacks that exist in cyberspace. The experience of both the business community and the U.S. government is valuable in determining how to combat his new threat. An effective combination of this collective experience will provide the best solution to the problem of countering cyberterrorism.

The Role of Violence in Terrorism

An examination of the elements of terror and symbolic violence highlighted the value of physical violence in the creation of terror. While not as effective in inducing terror, information warfare tactics allow tomorrow's terrorist to cause great disruption without physical harm to individuals. The violence of the cyberterrorist exists exclusively in the virtual world of cyberspace. While conventional terrorism will still involve physical destruction of property and human life, cyberterrorism will utilize cyberviolence and "virtual" destruction of data in cyberspace. While directly causing no casualties, this action will still fulfill the goals of advertising, morale building, disorientation, and response provocation. Some cyberterror actions, such as attacking safety or control systems (avionics, air traffic control, etc.) have the potential to create cascading failures that will lead to loss of life.

Cyberterrorists will in many cases, have the option of including destruction along with disruption to create terror and a more permanent result. While we have yet to see the combination of political motivation and criminal activity in cyberspace, we cannot disregard the potential of this type of terrorism.

Impact on terrorism in the future

Information warfare tactics allow a terrorist group to operate without the support of a large terrorist organization or a wealthy state sponsor. In addition, terrorists will utilize the emerging cryptography and global telecommunications system to climb out of the "dragonworld" of covert communications as described by J. Bowyer Bell and enhance their ability to communicate in a secure fashion with members scattered across the globe. These tactics may have several effects on future terrorist organizations.

First, terrorist groups may become more "demassified." In *The Third Wave,* Alvin Toffler describes how society is shifting away from large, centralized organizations to smaller, more distributed elements. The ability to steal $10 million electronically overnight, and the ability to exercise command and control utilizing "off the shelf" commercial technology may sound the death knell for state sponsored terrorism. Groups that formerly took direction and were controlled or supported by state actors, will now move into cyberspace, supporting themselves through criminal activities and removing the need for basing by becoming distributed organizations around the world. This lack of state control and funding will remove one of the key elements in present counter-terrorism planning-the punishment or coercion of the sponsoring state. The freedom from state imposed restraints will also allow terrorists to target *all* states in the future, not only those directed by the sponsor.

The lower level of support required to execute a cyberterrorist strategy may have the opposite effect, actually increasing state sponsorship. Poor states that did not have the means to support an international terrorist organization are now becoming connected to the world via the Internet and new telecommunications systems. Argentina, Iran, Peru, Egypt and the Philippines had the highest percentage growth in Internet connections from July to October of 1994. Each experienced growth ranging from 419% to 134%.

All regions of the world do not match these numbers. Africa has 35 of the world's least developed states in terms of telecommunications, an essential ingredient for connectivity with the rest of the world. Over the last 10 years, Africa has had the lowest growth in teledensity, the number of main telephone lines per 100 inhabitants. It was estimated to be.91 in 1991. States such as Sweden, with an index of 68, Switzerland, Canada, Denmark, Finland, and the United States, all with indexes in the 50s, lead the world in teledensity. The increasing numbers of connections from states that have sponsored terrorism in the past, such as Iran, as well as those that have not, is a new threat. These states may view cyberterrorism as an ideal tool with which to strike the information dependent first world. Cyberterrorism may also appeal to states as it has the added benefit of plausible deniability. There will be no large money, material, or communications "trail" to lead back to the sponsor state.

While the world (and terrorist groups) are demassifying, industry and business are pursuing more "targeted" production and advertising. This strategy attempts to focus the manufacturing and selling of products to a select audience. Technology is emerging to allow advertising to just those customers who are most likely to purchase a product. Terrorists in the information age may also mirror this trend, with new techniques and weapons that allow them to affect a target audience without resorting to violence against the general population. This technology also allows a terrorist message or action to affect many more people than was possible before. Thus, the "target" for terrorism can be as large or as small as the terrorist sees fit.

The growing, worldwide, interconnectedness of individuals and organizations may change the role played by the media in past terrorist events. While terrorists have staged many events in the last 25 years to garner maximum worldwide media attention ('72 Olympics, World Trade Center bombing, Airplane hijackings), the exponential growth of the Internet and the introduction of Direct

Broadcast Satellites with more than 500 channels and an 18" receive dish may allow terrorists to formulate, create, and distribute their own "news" to millions around the globe. The role of computers and fax machines in the Tiananmen square uprising is well documented. The Zapatista rebel organization in Mexico used the Internet and World Wide Web extensively to promote their cause and get their "message" to sympathetic audiences around the world.

The final change that information warfare tactics may bring to terrorism is a shift in terrorism itself. In the future, terrorist organizations may move toward tactics that attempt to achieve the terrorist goals without physical violence. This corresponds to the current thinking about the future of warfare. John Arquilla and David Ronfeldt have stated:

Warfare is no longer primarily a function of who puts the most capital, labor, and technology on the battlefield, but of who has the best information about the battlefield. What distinguishes the victors is their grasp of information, not only from the mundane standpoint of knowing how to find the enemy while keeping it in the dark, but also in doctrinal and organizational terms.

In the information age, shifting the definition of terrorism to include violence in cyberspace may be necessary, where electrons, not people are attacked, in the same manner as physical violence is presently included. Despite these changes, many "classical" terrorist organizations motivated by "conventional" objectives will remain viable. Terrorist groups, regardless of their level of sophistication, will adhere to the logic of symbolic violence and the creation of terror. While it is likely that conventional terrorist groups will evolve into hybrid groups employing both violence and information warfare cyberviolence, we may see the creation of new and unique terrorist organizations unlike those of the past, where close personal ties and ideology were necessary to maintain security.

The terrorist organization of the future may not have any "homeland" other than cyberspace. While it is difficult to track selected individuals in just one country or region, tracking a small number of individuals who could be anywhere on the globe, who can communicate in a secure and instantaneous fashion with each other, is likely to pose an order of magnitude increase in the problem. The "information age" provides many tools to assist in countering conventional terrorism. It also presents a host of new problems associated with countering techno and cyberterrorism.

The standard offense/defense and prevention/ preemption/disruption dynamics of counter and anti-terrorism in the physical world do not have direct counterparts in cyberspace. In the virtual world, a small number of individuals, with the right information, are as powerful as large state actors. The "balance of power" in cyberspace can shift in a matter of seconds, with the insertion or deletion of several lines of code to a program, or the installation of a new security protocol. The lessons from past conventional counter and anti-terrorism tactics are only of limited value in understanding the effectiveness of offense and defense in cyberspace.

The initiative in cyberspace does not necessarily rest with those pursuing an offensive strategy. In keeping with conventional terrorism, it is the terrorist group that normally attempts to seize the initiative by launching an offensive attack on a symbolic target. This attack is usually meant to undermine the belief that the government can protect its citizens. The government is then forced to reexamine and often change the way it attempts to maintain security. In cyberspace, no government has promised to guarantee "safety and security" as they have in the physical world. In the anarchic world of cyberspace, each individual serves as their own sovereign state. The government has addressed the security of individuals only in limited form, with passage of several laws concerning computer security. The commercial sector has attempted to defend the individual with the introduction of virus detection and encryption programs.

Neither business nor government has advocated an offensive posture against computer hackers and potential cyberterrorists. The focus has, out of necessity, been directed toward defense. The use of offensive tactics would work well if the enemy could be unambiguously identified. A skilled cyberterrorist can make the identification of those responsible, a cornerstone of conventional U.S. counterterrorism policy, exponentially more difficult in cyberspace. Even if an attacker in cyberspace can be identified, the range of responses open to the defender is somewhat limited. In the case of an unsophisticated hacker or criminal, access to the network can be denied.

The problems posed by the emergence of cyberterrorism mirrors many of the problems presented by information warfare between states. What is the correct balance between U.S. government protection and commercial sector protection? The possible solutions run the gamut from a completely government to a completely commercial protection of information. The best solution will likely lie somewhere between these two poles.

The U.S. government, through a variety of agencies is responsible for the vast majority of counter and anti-terrorism activities and policies in the United States. Governments meet with other states to negotiate cooperative agreements concerning the prosecution of terrorists and their sponsor states. The U.S. military has been utilized on several occasions to respond to terrorism and signal the resolve of the United States to counter terrorism by force if necessary. This situation is not mirrored in cyberspace, where borders are meaningless and international standards are generally set by multinational technical committees with little government input. The nature of cyberspace creates several fundamental questions.

While the government is committed to defending the rights of U.S. citizens in the physical world, with force if necessary, it has not made the same sweeping commitment to its citizens in cyberspace. The concept of being an "American" in cyberspace rapidly loses any meaning with the explosion of international connections to the Internet. While a computer may be physically located in the United States, the majority of its users may reside in another country. Should the U.S. government defend the rights of these individuals in cyberspace in the same manner as "official" U.S. citizens?

Commercial Response to the Problem

The actions taken by individuals and industry to combat the "hacker threat" are, at present, the best response to a portion of the terrorist information warfare threat. As we have seen, the confidentiality, integrity, and availability of data are critical in the information age. The growing ubiquity of encryption, with products such as Netscape offering 128 bit encryption of U.S. transactions raises the threshold to a level where it is not remotely cost effective to attempt to "brute force" decrypt a message for its contents. With the further introduction of smart cards and random password authentication, plus the addition of new communication protocols that prevent "spoofing" or fooling the network into thinking you are someone else, the confidentiality of data is becoming a reality.

The new protocols, used with encryption and "digital signatures" will ensure the integrity of data as well. The availability of data remains a lucrative target for cyberterrorists at present. This target is rapidly disappearing with the growing redundancy of communications paths that are becoming available to data. The loss of one ATM network did not cause a shutdown of all the ATMs in the United States, rather, it only affected about 2% of ATM users. In several years, with the addition of global cellular communications equipment, the paths that data will have from point A to B will be redundant to a point where a terrorist could not disable all of them at once.

All of the above actions were driven by the commercial sector, not by the government. We have entered an age where the military and the government no longer have the capability to develop technology and give the "spin-offs" to the commercial sector. Rather, the commercial sector has taken the lead in innovation and development of technology and the government and military are constantly trying to "spin-on" this technology by adapting civilian products to military use. This has leveled the playing field in cyberspace, for a cyberterrorist has the same access to this technology as the government.

A composite Government/commercial response may be the most beneficial in protecting against a cyberterrorist threat. The networks of the United States can be viewed in much of the same manner as postal routes. There are laws that protect the individual from unauthorized tampering with mail while it is in transit to its recipient regardless of the carrier (U.S. Postal Service, Federal Express, United Parcel Post, etc.). Senders of an authorized package have every right to assume that the government will ensure that their package is delivered intact and unopened to its final destination. In extreme cases, such as letter bombs and illegal materials being sent, the government becomes involved in tracking and prosecuting those who abuse the system at the expense of public safety or in violation of the law. Materials that are detrimental to the national security of the United States naturally receive much attention from

Federal authorities. It is up to the sender of each package to ensure that they properly wrap it for shipment. If it is information that is unimportant, they can send it on a postcard, with the writing openly visible to anyone who may see the card.

The more sensitive the information, the more tightly wrapped the package becomes. Encryption serves as the "wrapping" on the message sent out via public networks. The more sensitive or important the information, the higher the level of encryption required to ensure that the message will be authentic and intact when it reaches its destination. While unencrypted E-mail may be adequate for some matters, other correspondence will require increasingly higher levels of classification for protection. With the diffusion of encryption technology, it will become increasingly easy to ensure confidentiality of all messages. In the postal analogy, the government does not guarantee service by all companies in the delivery service.

Rather, it maintains a level of general safety in which all can operate. Thus, both public and private utilities and telecommunications carriers can expect the government to become involved when a major problem occurs. While each company is responsible for "low level" problems, such as routine security at warehouses and the collection of overdue bills, the government will assist in correcting "high level" problems where lives are at stake due to the content of the material being shipped. The government, in effect, protects the individual from the carrier and the carrier from the individual.

The difficulty in the age of information is determining what constitutes a cyberspace letter bomb and how it is different from a benign cyber-postcard. Where is the level between "low level" and "high level" problems to be drawn? The anarchic nature of cyberspace has prevented any attempts at close regulation abbey the government. Every individual must take a certain level of responsibility for their own "safety" in cyberspace. While U.S. citizens have a reasonable expectation of security within the borders of the United States, the ability of the U.S. government to protect them decreases as they venture further abroad. The same is true in cyberspace, where a user in a closed network had a reasonable expectation of security.

As soon as users connect that network to the Internet, it is open for attack by anyone. It is up to the user to prevent low level attacks by "locking his doors" and following good computer security practices. In so doing, a computer user can defeat all but the most advanced opponents in cyberspace. In cases where in the information is deemed to be sufficiently important, the government can be called in to assist in defense of that information and its associated network. While the government may be called upon to assist in the defense of cyberspace, the doctrinal and organizational foundations have not yet been established to allow for this involvement. Further study of this problem is necessary to ensure that any government involvement is proportional and effective.

While cyberspace can place individuals and states on equal footing, the state clearly retains an advantage in the physical world. This advantage may provide a useful tool in the prosecution of cyberterrorism. While the doctrine of asymmetric response was utilized during the Cold War to deter a nuclear exchange, a cyberspace equivalent of this doctrine may prove useful in the information age. If a state commits to defending cyberspace, the first course of action is likely to be the securing of systems to prevent unauthorized access. By raising the threshold of skill and technology required to penetrate a system, amateurs and unskilled cyberterrorists may be deterred from pursuing an offensive in cyberspace. By securing systems from "low level" attacks, the various government agencies involved in counter and anti-terrorism will be free to pursue the "high level" threats that are sure to exist in cyberspace.

It remains to be seen if an offensive response, such as a military strike against a computer center or selected organizations, will be tolerated by the citizens of the United States. Will people be willing to launch an air strike against computer terrorists in the same fashion as they were launched against terrorists training bases in Libya? The implications of an offensive, asymmetric response to the terrorist problem must be explored, as a response that exists exclusively in cyberspace may not be sufficient to deter, or even slow down a cyberterrorist. At the dawn of the information age, the borders of the United States are no longer secure. We must recognize the potential threat and adjust our thinking to formulate an effective individual and state response.

One of the distinctive characteristics of the times we live in is the overwhelming presence of violence in our societies. Whether it is a bomb going off in a market place, or the hijacking of an aircraft where innocent people are held at ransom to achieve political ends, we live in an age, where the manipulation and loss of innocent lives has become commonplace. Such is the all-pervasive nature of indiscriminate violence, that "terrorism" is considered as one of the prime threats to peace and security in our societies.

The word terrorism came into wide usage only a few decades ago. One of the unfortunate results of this new terminology is that it limits the definition of terrorism to that perpetrated by small groups or individuals. Terrorism, in fact, spans the entire world, and manifests itself in various forms. Its perpetrators do not fit any stereotype. Those who hold human lives cheap, and have the power to expend human lives, appear at different levels in our societies. The frustrated employee who kills his colleagues in cold-blood or the oppressed citizen of an occupied land who vents his anger by blowing up a school bus are terrorists who provoke our anger and revulsion.

Ironically however, the politician who uses age-old ethnic animosities between peoples to consolidate his position, the head of state who orders "carpet bombing" of entire cities, the exalted councils that choke millions of civilians to death by wielding the insidious weapon of sanctions, are rarely punished for their crimes against humanity. It is this narrow definition of terrorism that implicates only individuals and groups, that has caused Muslims to be associated with acts of destruction and terror, and as a result, to become victims of hate violence and terror themselves. Sometimes the religion of Islam is held responsible for the acts of a handful of Muslims, and often for the acts of non-Muslims!

Could it be possible that Islam, whose light ended the Dark Ages in Europe, now propound the advent of an age of terror? Could a faith that has over 1.2 billion followers the world over, and over 7 million in America, actually advocate the killing and maiming of innocent people? Could Islam, whose name itself stands for "peace" and "submission to God", encourage its adherents to work for death and destruction? For too long, have we relied on popular images in the media and in Hollywood films, for answers to these pertinent questions. It is now time to look at the sources of Islam, and its history to determine whether Islam does indeed advocate violence.

The Glorious Qur'an says:

"...take not life, which God hath made sacred, except by way of justice and law: thus doth He command you, that ye may learn wisdom." [Al-Qur'an 6:151]

Islam considers all life forms as sacred. However, the sanctity of human life is accorded a special place. The first and the foremost basic right of a human being is the right to live. The Glorious Qur'an says:

"...if any one slew a person - unless it be for murder or for spreading mischief in the land - it would be as if he slew the whole people: and if any one saved a life, it would be as if he saved the life of the whole people."

[Al-Qur'an 5:32]

Such is the value of a single human life, that the Qur'an equates the taking of even one human life unjustly, with killing all of humanity. Thus, the Qur'an prohibits homicide in clear terms. The taking of a criminal's life by the state in order to administer justice is required to uphold the rule of law, and the peace and security of the society. Only a proper and competent court can decide whether an individual has forfeited his right to life by disregarding the right to life and peace of other human beings.

Ethics of War

Even in a state of war, Islam enjoins that one deals with the enemy nobly on the battlefield. Islam has drawn a clear line of distinction between the combatants and the non-combatants of the enemy country. As far as the non-combatant population is concerned such as women, children, the old and the infirm, etc., the instructions of the Prophet are as follows: "Do not kill any old person, any child or any woman". "Do not kill the monks in monasteries" or "Do not kill the people who are sitting in places of worship." During a war, the Prophet saw the corpse of a woman lying on the ground and observed: "She was not fighting. How then she came to be killed?" Thus non-combatants are guaranteed security of life even if their state is at war with an Islamic state.

While Islam in general is misunderstood in the western world, perhaps no other Islamic term evokes such strong reactions as the word 'jihad'. The term 'jihad' has been much abused, to conjure up bizarre images of violent Muslims, forcing people to submit at the point of the sword. This myth was perpetuated throughout the centuries of mistrust during and after the Crusades. Unfortunately, it survives to this day. The word Jihad comes from the root word jahada, which means to struggle. So jihad is literally an act of struggling.

The Prophet Muhammad (peace be upon him) said that the greatest jihad is to struggle with the insidious suggestions of one's own soul. Thus jihad primarily refers to the inner struggle of being a person of virtue and submission to God in all aspects of life. Secondarily, jihad refers to struggle against injustice. Islam, like many other religions, allows for armed self-defense, or retribution against tyranny, exploitation, and oppression. The Glorious Qur'an says:

"And why should ye not fight in the cause of God and of those who, being weak, are ill-treated (and oppressed)? - Men, women, and children, whose cry is: "Our Lord! Rescue us from this town, whose people are oppressors; and raise for us from thee one who will protect; and raise for us from thee one who will help!"

[Al-Qur'an 4:75]

Thus Islam enjoins upon its believers to strive utmost, in purifying themselves, as well as in establishing peace and justice in the society. A Muslim can never be at rest when he sees injustice and oppression around him. As Martin Luther King Jr. said:

"We will have to repent in this generation not merely for the hateful words and actions of the bad people but for the appalling silence of the good people."

Islam enjoins upon all Muslims to work actively to maintain the balance in which God created everything. However, regardless of how legitimate the cause may be, the Glorious Qur'an never condones the killing of innocent people. Terrorizing the civilian population can never be termed as jihad and can never be reconciled with the teachings of Islam.

History of Tolerance

Even Western scholars have repudiated the myth of Muslims coercing others to convert. The great historian De Lacy O'Leary wrote:

"History makes it clear, however, that the legend of fanatical Muslims, sweeping through the world and forcing Islam at the point of sword upon conquered races is one of the most fantastically absurd myths that historians have ever repeated."

Muslims ruled Spain for roughly 800 years. During this time, and up until they were finally forced out, the non-Muslims there were alive and flourishing. Additionally, Christian and Jewish minorities have survived in the Muslim lands of the Middle East for centuries. Countries such as Egypt, Morocco, Palestine, Lebanon, Syria, and Jordan all have significant Christian and/or Jewish populations.

This is not surprising to a Muslim, for his faith prohibits him from forcing others to see his point of view. The Glorious Qur'an says:

"Let there be no compulsion in religion: Truth stands out clear from Error: whoever rejects evil and believes in God hath grasped the most trustworthy hand-hold, that never breaks. And God heareth and knoweth all things."

[Al-Qur'an 2:256]

Far from being a militant dogma, Islam is a way of life that transcends race and ethnicity. The Glorious Qur'an repeatedly reminds us of our common origin:

"O mankind! We created you from a single (pair) of a male and a female, and made you into nations and tribes, that ye may know each other (not that ye may despise (each other). Verily the most honored of you in the sight of God is (he who is) the most righteous of you. And God has full knowledge and is well acquainted (with all things)." [Al-Qur'an 49:13]

Thus, it is the universality of its teachings that makes Islam the fastest growing religion in the world. In a world full of conflicts and deep schisms between human beings, a world that is threatened with terrorism, perpetrated by individuals and states, Islam is a beacon of light that offers hope for the future.

Cracks in the System

Three flights up a scruffy building in central Moscow, a small paper sign pasted on the wall directs visitors to Directorate R of the Moscow police. R stands for nothing: it was just the next code letter available in 1986 when the police decided to set up their own communications-security branch. These days the Directorate's bread-and-butter work is computer and mobile-phone fraud. But their biggest nightmare — and that of their counterparts in Western Europe and the U.S. — is digital attack. "This, unfortunately, is the future face of terrorism," says Dmitri Chepchugov, head of Directorate R.

So far, politically motivated computer attacks have been irritations or embarrassments rather than full-blown catastrophes. Chinese hackers attacked some 1,200 sites, including the White House, the Department of Energy and the Air Force, defacing some sites and putting others temporarily out of service, during a standoff with Washington over a spy plane last year. Russians and Eastern Europeans did the same during the war in Kosovo, and Pakistani and Indian hackers are doing it right now. Over a period of several years, U.S. investigators believe hackers — probably from Russia — tunneled into department of Defense sites and illegally downloaded large quantities of technical defense research, all unclassified, according to the Pentagon. The leap from this kind of sporadic hacking to virtual terrorism is only a matter of time, specialists believe.

"After every terrorist attack, security is tightened up and improved," Chepchugov remarks. "But these days you don't need to get a truck bomb into, say, a chemical plant or crash a plane into it. All you need is a group of hackers who get into the computerized control system, knock it out, and trigger a disaster." Michael Vatis — a former head of the FBI's National Infrastructure Protection Center, the lead U.S. federal agency for computer crime, cyberterrorism and cyberespionage — agrees. "We have seen a clear decision by terrorist groups like al-Qaeda to focus on critical infrastructures, financial networks and power grids," says Vatis, now director of the Institute for Security Technology Studies at Dartmouth College. "And they have developed expertise with computer systems for secure communications and planning attacks. The next step is to put the two together."

The likely targets would be a country's power or water supply, gas and oil production or storage facilities, telecommunications or banking networks and transport or emergency services. Attackers could try to disrupt these systems during a conventional assault or, even worse, attempt to trigger a disaster by destroying them outright. Most government and many commercial organizations insulate the sensitive parts of their computer systems from the Internet. But it is harder to protect computerized systems from an inside job. This is what happened a little over two years ago in Russia, in an incident that briefly surfaced in the press and was quickly hushed up. In early 2000, officials say, a disgruntled employee of Gazprom, the oil and natural gas monopoly, helped a group of hackers seize for several hours the corporation's computer systems — including that regulating gas flow through the firm's pipelines. Gazprom subsequently denied press reports of the break-in.

And, officials add, the politically powerful corporation was furious when the information was made public. "Heads rolled in the Interior Ministry after the newspaper report came out," says another senior official. But, this person adds, "We were very close to a major natural disaster." Chepchugov says there are some indications that at least one radical fundamentalist is showing interest in computers. The imam of Finsbury Park mosque in north London, Abu Hamza al-Masri (also known as Mustafa Kemal) "has gathered around himself a group of computer specialists," Chepchugov says.

"This is indirect proof that Muslim extremists understand the potential of computer-based terrorism." Meanwhile, another Russian specialist in computer crime remarks, "I think our American friends are very interested in the Pakistan Hackerz Club [a pro-Pakistan hacker group]," which they apparently suspect of having contacts with radical groups. Al-Qaeda works like any other criminal group in the world of computers, says Anatoly Platonov of the Interior Ministry's Directorate K, which also deals with cybercrime. "They have the money and are looking for the brains." Sooner or later, specialists believe, they will find them.

10

The Truth about Terrorism

Prophets are always unpopular, because they say hard things. They speak for God – usually indicating God's displeasure with what the people and their political and religious leaders were doing. Boy, do we need some strong prophesying today. There is plenty going on that I'm quite sure God is very displeased about: immorality and deceit in high places, for example. And no, I'm not talking about Monica Lewinsky. God would probably not have gotten Nathan involved in chastising David if adultery and deceit were all that was involved. But David went beyond that. He was responsible for the death of Bathsheba's husband. It was this premeditated murder, brought on by greed, selfishness, envy, and passion, that got God and Nathan into the act.

Similarly today, it is not infidelity, but murder and violence that stir the heart of God. I am talking about the bombing of our embassies in Africa and about our cruise missile attacks on Afghanistan and Sudan. And it is not Clinton's dissembling about his sexual pecadillos, but his lying to the American people about the roots of terrorism that calls out for repentance.

First, terrorism is wrong. Whether it is in the Middle East or Northern Ireland or Oklahoma City, it is wrong. There are always reasons for such violence. But there is never justification. It is always wrong. It is always displeasing to God. It is always a sin. What is terrorism? It is the use of fear, violence, and intimidation to achieve an end. We usually think of it as a tool of small, frustrated groups unable to achieve their ends by other means. But the dictionary doesn't limit it to that. Mine says that one meaning of the word "terrorism" is a system of government that uses fear to rule.

We usually think of it as violence by the weak against the strong. But according to the dictionary, it is just as likely to be violence by the strong against the weak. So the use of death squads by the military government of El Salvador or Honduras or Guatemala or Argentina against impoverished peasants is terrorism. The use by the government of China of tanks against students in Tiananmen Square is terrorism. The bombing of buses in Tel Aviv by Hamas is terrorism. But so is the bulldozing of Palestinian houses by Israel. The bombing of U.S. embassies is terrorism. But so was the mining of the harbor in Nicaragua by Ronald Reagan, the bombing of Baghdad by George Bush, and in all probability the cruise missile attacks by Bill Clinton against targets inAfghanistan and Sudan. The atomic bombing of Hiroshima and Nagasaki was terrorism; and so is the possession of nuclear weapons and the threat to use them.

It is not *my* job to pronounce God's displeasure with the violent acts of terrorists in Arab countries halfway around the world. That's for *their* prophets to do. Our job is to speak truth to power right here in our own country. As one committed to a consistent pro-life ethic, I do not believe that the use of deadly force is *ever* the correct response to a problem. With Cardinal Mahony of Los Angeles, the late Cardinal Bernardin of Chicago, and many others, I oppose terrorism, war, the death penalty, euthanasia, abortion, the denial of the necessities of life (food, shelter, water, basic health care, and dignity) to the powerless, and all other violations of life. This is what we call a "seamless garment."

This is not dogma. We do not condemn those who do not agree with us. But we believe that it is in accord with the will of God as revealed in Jesus of Nazareth, and we maintain our right to attempt to convince others that this is truth.

I therefore condemn our recent cruise missile attacks as violations of the will of God. Were they also violations of international law? I think probably so, but that's for international lawyers to debate. Was that "pharmaceutical plant" making chemical weapons, as our government claims, or medicines as the Sudanese claim? I don't know. I haven't seen the evidence or the intelligence data. We may *never* know. Was the bombing of our embassies worse, causing more death and injury? Of course. Hopefully, some Muslim prophet will preach against that. I am not attempting to judge the military appropriateness or political justification for the cruise missile attack. I am merely saying that it was a use of deadly violence, against the consistent pro-life ethic which I proclaim, and (according to my belief) against the will of God.

But there is another matter which concerns me even more, because it bears on the future direction of this country. President Clinton did not tell the American people the truth of why we are the targets of terrorism. He said that we are the target because we stand for democracy, freedom, and human rights in the world. Nonsense! We are the target of terrorists because we stand for dictatorship, bondage, and human exploitation in the world. We are the target of terrorists because we are hated. And we are hated because we have done hateful things.

In how many countries have agents of our government deposed popularly-elected leaders and replaced them with puppet military dictators who were willing to sell out their own people to American multinational corporations?

We did it in Iran when the U.S. Marines and the CIA

deposed Mossadegh because he wanted to nationalize the oil industry. We replaced him with the Shah, and trained, armed, and paid his hated Savak national guard, which enslaved and brutalized the people of Iran... all to protect the financial interests of our oil companies. Is it any wonder there are people in Iran who hate us?

We did it in Chile when we deposed Allende, democratically elected by the people to introduce communism. We replaced him with the brutal right-wing military dictator, General Pinochet. Chile has still not recovered. We did it in Vietnam when we thwarted democratic elections in the South which would have united the country under Ho Chi Minh. We replaced him with a series of ineffectual puppet crooks who invited us to come in and slaughter their people. We did it in Iraq, where we killed a quarter of a million civilians in a failed attempt to topple Saddam Hussein, and where we have killed a million since then with our sanctions. About half of these innocent victims have been children under the age of five.

And, of course, how many times have we done it in Nicaragua and all the other banana republics of Latin America? Time after time we have ousted popular leaders who wanted the riches of the land to be shared by the people who worked it. We replaced them with murderous tyrants who would sell out and control their own people so that the wealth of the land could be taken out by the likes of Domino sugar, the United Fruit Company, Folgers, and Chiquita Banana.

In country after country, we have thwarted democracy, stifled freedom, and trampled human rights. *That's* why we are hated around the world. And that's why we are the target of terrorists. People in Canada enjoy better democracy, more freedom, and greater human rights than we do. So do the people of Norway and Sweden. Have you heard of Canadian embassies being bombed? Or Norwegian embassies? Or Swedish embassies. No.

We are not hated because we practice democracy, freedom, and human rights. We are hated because we deny these things to people in third world countries whose resources are coveted by our multinational corporations. Tell people the truth, Mr. President... about terrorism, not about poor Monica. You and your mid-life libido and zippergate will fade from memory with your presidency. But if the lies about terrorism go unchallenged, then the terror war now unleashed will likely continue until it destroys us.

The threat of nuclear terrorism is closing in upon us. Chemical terrorism is close at hand, and biological terrorism is a future danger. None of our thousands of nuclear weapons can protect us from these threats. These idols of plutonium, titanium, and steel are impotent. No "Star Wars" system... no matter how technically advanced, no matter how many trillions of dollars is poured into it... can protect us from even a single terrorist bomb. Not one weapon in our vast arsenal can shield us from a nuclear weapon delivered in a sailboat or a Cessna or a suitcase or a Ryder rental truck. Not a penny of the 273 billion dollars a year we spend on so-called defense can actually defend us against a terrorist bomb. Nothing in our enormous military establishment can actually give us one whit of real security.

That is a military fact. It reminds me of God's message to us in psalm 33: "A king is not saved by his mighty army. A warrior is not saved by his great strength. A war horse is a vain hope for victory, and with its might it cannot save."

As a retired lieutenant colonel and a frequent lecturer on national security issues, I often quoted that psalm. And the obvious reaction to it is, "Then what can we do? How can we be secure? Is there nothing we can do to provide security for our people?

There is. It is found just a page or two later in the book of Psalms, in psalm 37: "Trust in the Lord and do good, that you may dwell in the land and have security." That's it. It's so simple.

Back in the Cold War, it wasn't easy to sell this approach to security. Faced with another nuclear superpower (or at least, so we were told), it was tempting to hold onto our weapon idolatry. It was easy to think that only our armed forces and their superior technology kept us safe. Even I found it difficult to give up the concept of nuclear deterrence. But now things are different. The Roman Catholic bishops of the United States are retreating from their conditional acceptance of deterrence. Seventy of them have signed a letter saying that even the possession of nuclear weapons is no longer moral. Sixty retired generals have said that our security will be enhanced by nuclear abolition.

And the "Colonel Bowman" part of me now agrees with the "Bishop Bowman" part of me that psalm 37 is our best path to security. Getting rid of our nuclear weapons — unilaterally if necessary — will enhance our security. Drastically altering our foreign policy in line with psalm 37 will ensure it. In short, we must change our ways. We no longer face another nuclear superpower. We have run out of real enemies. Our defense budget is 26 times as much as that of all our potential adversaries combined. The only real threat we face is that of terrorism. And if we understand the reason that threat exists (and this is why it is so crucial that the American people be told the truth), then the way to protect against that threat becomes clear. We change our ways.

Instead of sending our sons and daughters around the world to kill Arabs so we can have the oil under their sand, we send them to rebuild their infrastructure, supply clean water, and feed starving children. Instead of continuing to kill thousands of Iraqi children every day with our sanctions, we help Iraqis rebuild their electric powerplants, their water treatment facilities, their hospitals — all the things we destroyed in our war against them and prevented them from rebuilding with our sanctions. Instead of seeking to be king of the hill, we become a responsible member of the family of nations. Instead of stationing hundreds of thousands of troops around the world to protect the financial interests of our multinational corporations (they prefer the term "national interests"), we bring them home and expand the Peace Corps.

Instead of training terrorists and death squads in the techniques of torture and assassination, we close the School of the Americas. Instead of supporting military dictatorships, we support true democracy — the right of the people to choose their own leaders. Instead of supporting insurrection, destabilization, assassination, and terror around the world, we abolish the CIA and give the money to relief agencies.

In short, we do good instead of evil. We become the good guys, once again. If we abolished our armed forces and used our resources to feed the hungry, cure the sick, and care for the needy — both at home and around the world — who would try to stop us? Who would hate us? Who would want to bomb us? The threat of terrorism would vanish. "Trust in the Lord and do good, that you may dwell in the land and have security."

That is the truth, Mr. President. That is what the American people need to hear. We are good people. We only need to be told the truth and given the vision. You can do it, Mr. President. The big money people from the multinational corporations and banks paid for your election. But they have given up on you. Forget them. Divorce yourself from the greed which has caused such an unjust division of the fruits of creation. Seek to end the injustice rather than perpetuating it with violence and intimidation.

Refrain from terrorism, even in response to the same. Stop the killing. Stop the justifying. Stop the retaliating. Put people first. Tell them the truth, and lead them in God's way.

Sept. 11, 2001, was not "the day everything changed," but the day that revealed how much had already changed. On Sept. 10, how many journalists had the Council of American-Islamic Relations or the Canadian Islamic Congress or the Muslim Council of Britain in their Rolodexes? If you'd said that whether something does or does not cause offence to Muslims would be the early 21st century's principal political dynamic in Denmark, Sweden, the Netherlands, Belgium, France and the United Kingdom, most folks would have thought you were crazy. Yet on that Tuesday morning the top of the iceberg bobbed up and toppled the Twin Towers.

This is about the seven-eighths below the surface — the larger forces at play in the developed world that have left Europe too enfeebled to resist its remorseless transformation into Eurabia and that call into question the future of much of the rest of the world. The key factors are: demographic decline; the unsustainability of the social democratic state; and civilizational exhaustion.

Let's start with demography, because everything does: If your school has 200 guys and you're playing a school with 2,000 pupils, it doesn't mean your baseball team is definitely going to lose but it certainly gives the other fellows a big starting advantage. Likewise, if you want to launch a revolution, it's not very likely if you've only got seven revolutionaries. And they're all over 80. But, if you've got two million and seven revolutionaries and they're all under 30 you're in business.

For example, I wonder how many pontificators on the "Middle East peace process" ever run this number:

- The median age in the Gaza Strip is 15.8 years.

Once you know that, all the rest is details. If you were a "moderate Palestinian" leader, would you want to try to persuade a nation — or pseudo-nation — of unemployed poorly educated teenage boys raised in a UN-supervised European-funded death cult to see sense? Any analysis of the "Palestinian problem" that doesn't take into account the most important determinant on the ground is a waste of time.

Likewise, the salient feature of Europe, Canada, Japan and Russia is that they're running out of babies. What's happening in the developed world is one of the fastest demographic evolutions in history: most of us have seen a gazillion heartwarming ethnic comedies — *My Big Fat Greek Wedding* and its ilk — in which some uptight WASPy type starts dating a gal from a vast loving fecund Mediterranean family, so abundantly endowed with sisters and cousins and uncles that you can barely get in the room. It is, in fact, the inversion of the truth. Greece has a fertility rate hovering just below 1.3 births per couple, which is what demographers call the point of "lowest-low" fertility from which no human society has ever recovered.

And Greece's fertility is the healthiest in Mediterranean Europe: Italy has a fertility rate of 1.2, Spain 1.1. Insofar as any citizens of the developed world have "big" families these days, it's the anglo democracies: America's fertility rate is 2.1, New Zealand a little below. Hollywood should be making *My Big Fat Uptight Protestant Wedding* in which some sad Greek only child marries into a big heartwarming New Zealand family where the spouse actually has a sibling. As I say, this isn't a projection: it's happening now. There's no need to extrapolate, and if you do it gets a little freaky, but, just for fun, here goes: by 2050, 60 per cent of Italians will have no brothers, no sisters, no cousins, no aunts, no uncles.

The big Italian family, with papa pouring the vino and mama spooning out the pasta down an endless table of grandparents and nieces and nephews, will be gone, no more, dead as the dinosaurs. As Noel Coward once remarked in another context, "Funiculi, funicula, funic yourself." By mid-century, Italians will have no choice in the matter. Experts talk about root causes. But demography is the most basic root of all. A people that won't multiply can't go forth or go anywhere. Those who do will shape the age we live in.

Demographic decline and the unsustainability of the social democratic state are closely related. In America, politicians upset about the federal deficit like to complain that we're piling up debts our children and grandchildren will have to pay off. But in Europe the unaffordable entitlements are in even worse shape: there are no kids or grandkids to stick it to.

You might formulate it like this:

Age + Welfare = Disaster for you;

Youth + Will = Disaster for whoever gets in your way.

By "will," I mean the metaphorical spine of a culture. Africa, to take another example, also has plenty of young people, but it's riddled with AIDS and, for the most part, Africans don't think of themselves as Africans: as we saw in Rwanda, their primary identity is tribal, and most tribes have no global ambitions. Islam, however, has serious global ambitions, and it forms the primal, core identity of most of its adherents — in the Middle East, South Asia and elsewhere.

Islam has youth and will, Europe have age and welfare.

We are witnessing the end of the late 20th century progressive welfare democracy. Its fiscal bankruptcy is merely a symptom of a more fundamental bankruptcy: its insufficiency as an animating principle for society. The children and grandchildren of those fascists and republicans who waged a bitter civil war for the future of Spain now shrug when a bunch of foreigners blow up their capital. Too sedated even to sue for terms, they capitulate instantly. Over on the other side of the equation, the modern multicultural state is too watery a concept to bind huge numbers of immigrants to the land of their nominal citizenship. So they look elsewhere and find the jihad. The Western Muslim's pan-Islamic identity is merely the first great cause in a world where globalized pathologies are taking the place of old-school nationalism.

For states in demographic decline with ever more lavish social programs, the question is a simple one: can they get real? Can they grow up before they grow old? If not, then they'll end their days in societies dominated by people with a very different world view.

Which brings us to the third factor — the enervated state of the Western world, the sense of civilizational ennui, of nations too mired in cultural relativism to understand what's at stake? As it happens, that third point is closely related to the first two. To Americans, it doesn't always seem obvious that there's any connection between the "war on terror" and the so-called "pocketbook issues" of domestic politics. But there is a correlation between the structural weaknesses of the social democratic state and the rise of a globalized Islam. The state has gradually annexed all the responsibilities of adulthood — health care, child care, care of the elderly — to the point where it's effectively severed its citizens from humanity's primal instincts, not least the survival instinct. In the American context, the federal "deficit" isn't the problem; it's the government programs that cause the deficit.

These programs would still be wrong even if Bill Gates wrote a cheque to cover them each month. They corrode the citizen's sense of self-reliance to a potentially fatal degree. Big government is a national security threat: it increases your vulnerability to threats like Islamism, and makes it less likely you'll be able to summon the will to rebuff it.

We should have learned that lesson on Sept. 11, 2001, when big government flopped big-time and the only good news of the day came from the ad hoc citizen militia of Flight 93.

There were two forces at play in the late 20th century: in the Eastern bloc, the collapse of Communism; in the West, the collapse of confidence. One of the most obvious refutations of Francis Fukuyama's famous thesis *The End Of History* — written at the victory of liberal pluralist democracy over Soviet Communism — is that the victors didn't see it as such. Americans — or at least non-Democrat-voting Americans — may talk about "winning" the Cold War but the French and the Belgians and Germans and Canadians don't. Very few British do. These are all formal NATO allies — they were, technically, on the winning side against a horrible tyranny few would wish to live under themselves.

In Europe, there was an initial moment of euphoria: it was hard not be moved by the crowds sweeping through the Berlin Wall, especially as so many of them were hot-looking Red babes eager to enjoy a Carlsberg or Stella Artois with even the nerdiest running dog of imperialism. But, when the moment faded, *pace* Fukuyama, there was no sense on the Continent that our Big Idea had beaten their Big Idea. With the best will in the world, it's hard to credit the citizens of France or Italy as having made any serious contribution to the defeat of Communism. *Au contraire,* millions of them voted for it, year in, year out. And, with the end of the Soviet existential threat, the enervation of the West only accelerated.

In Thomas P. M. Barnett's book *Blueprint for Action,* Robert D. Kaplan, a very shrewd observer of global affairs, is quoted referring to the lawless fringes of the map as "Indian territory." It's a droll joke but a misleading one. The difference between the old Indian Territory and the new is this: no one had to worry about the Sioux riding down Fifth Avenue. Today, with a few hundred bucks on his ATM card, the fellow from the badlands can be in the heart of the metropolis within hours.

Here's another difference: in the old days, the white man settled the Indian territory. Now the followers of the badland's radical imams settle the metropolis. And another difference: technology. In the old days, the Injuns had bows and arrows and the cavalry had rifles. In today's Indian Territory, countries that can't feed their own people have nuclear weapons.

But beyond that the very phrase "Indian territory" presumes that inevitably these badlands will be brought within the bounds of the ordered world. In fact, a lot of today's "Indian territory" was relatively ordered a generation or two back — West Africa, Pakistan, Bosnia. Though Eastern Europe and Latin America and parts of Asia are freer now than they were in the seventies, other swaths of the map have spiralled backwards. Which is more likely? That the parts of the world under pressure will turn into post-Communist Poland or post-Communist Yugoslavia? In Europe, the demographic pressures favour the latter.

The enemies we face in the future will look a lot like al-Qaeda: transnational, globalized, locally franchised, extensively outsourced — but tied together through a powerful identity that leaps frontiers and continents. They won't be nation-states and they'll have no interest in becoming nation-states, though they might use the husks thereof, as they did in Afghanistan and then Somalia. The jihad may be the first, but other transnational deformities will embrace similar techniques. Sept. 10 institutions like the UN and the EU will be unlikely to provide effective responses.

We can argue about what consequences these demographic trends will have, but to say blithely they have none is ridiculous. The basic demography explains, for example, the critical difference between the "war on terror" for Americans and Europeans: in the U.S., the war is something to be fought in the treacherous sands of the Sunni Triangle and the caves of the Hindu Kush; you go to faraway places and kill foreigners. But, in Europe, it's a civil war. Neville Chamberlain dismissed Czechoslovakia as "a faraway country of which we know little." This time round, for much of Western Europe it turned out the faraway country of which they knew little was their own.

Four years into the "war on terror," the Bush administration began promoting a new formulation: "the long war." Not a good sign. In a short war, put your money on tanks and bombs. In a long war, the better bet is will and manpower. The longer the long war gets, the harder it will be, because it's a race against time, against lengthening demographic, economic and geopolitical odds. By "demographic," I mean the Muslim world's high birth rate, which by mid-century will give tiny Yemen a higher population than vast empty Russia. By "economic," I mean the perfect storm the Europeans will face within this decade, because their lavish welfare states are unsustainable on their post-Christian birth rates. By "geopolitical," I mean that, if you think the United Nations and other international organizations are antipathetic to America now, wait a few years and see what kind of support you get from a semi-Islamified Europe.

Almost every geopolitical challenge in the years ahead has its roots in demography, but not every demographic crisis will play out the same way. That's what makes doing anything about it even more problematic — because different countries' reactions to their own particular domestic circumstances are likely to play out in destabilizing ways on the international scene. In Japan, the demographic crisis exists virtually in laboratory conditions — no complicating factors; in Russia, it will be determined by the country's relationship with a cramped neighbour —

China; and in Europe, the new owners are already in place — like a tenant with a right-to-buy agreement.

Let's start in the most geriatric jurisdiction on the planet. In Japan, the rising sun has already passed into the next phase of its long sunset: net population loss. 2005 was the first year since records began in which the country had more deaths than births. Japan offers the chance to observe the demographic death spiral in its purest form. It's a country with no immigration, no significant minorities and no desire for any: just the Japanese, aging and dwindling. At first it doesn't sound too bad: compared with the United States, most advanced societies are very crowded. If you're in a cramped apartment in a noisy congested city, losing a couple hundred thousand seems a fine trade-off.

The difficulty, in a modern social democratic state, is managing which people to lose: already, according to the *Japan Times*, depopulation is "presenting the government with pressing challenges on the social and economic front, including ensuring provision of social security services and securing the labour force." For one thing, the shortage of children has led to a shortage of obstetricians. Why would any talented ambitious med school student want to go into a field in such precipitous decline? As a result, if you live in certain parts of Japan, childbirth is all in the timing. On Oki Island, try to time the contractions for Monday morning. That's when the maternity ward is open — first day of the week, 10 a.m., when an obstetrician flies in to attend to any pregnant mothers who happen to be around. And at 5.30 p.m. she flies out.

So, if you've been careless enough to time your childbirth for Tuesday through Sunday, you'll have to climb into a helicopter and zip off to give birth alone in a strange hospital unsurrounded by tiresome loved ones. Do Lamaze classes on Oki now teach you to time your breathing to the whirring of the chopper blades? The last local obstetrician left the island in 2006 and the health service isn't expecting any more. Doubtless most of us can recall reading similar stories over the years from remote rural districts in America, Canada, Australia. After all, why would a village of a few hundred people have a great medical system? But Oki has a population of 17,000, and there are still no obstetricians: birthing is a dying business.

So what will happen? There are a couple of scenarios: whatever Japanese feelings on immigration, a country with great infrastructure won't empty out for long, any more than a state-of-the-art factory that goes belly up stays empty for long. At some point, someone else will move in to Japan's plant.

And the alternative? In *The Children Of Men*, P. D. James' dystopian fantasy about a barren world, there are special dolls for women whose maternal instinct has gone unfulfilled: pretend mothers take their artificial children for walks on the street or to the swings in the park. In Japan, that's no longer the stuff of dystopian fantasy. At the beginning of the century, the country's toy makers noticed they had a problem: toys are for children and Japan doesn't have many. What to do? In 2005, Tomy began marketing a new doll called Yumel — a baby boy with a range of 1,200 phrases designed to serve as companions for the elderly.

He says not just the usual things — "I wuv you" — but also asks the questions your grandchildren would ask if you had any: "Why do elephants have long noses?" Yumel joins his friend, the Snuggling Ifbot, a toy designed to have the conversation of a five-year old child which its makers, with the usual Japanese efficiency, have determined is just enough chit-chat to prevent the old folks going senile. It seems an appropriate final comment on the social democratic state: in a childish infantilized self-absorbed society where adults have been stripped of all responsibility, you need never stop playing with toys. We are the children we never had.

And why leave it at that? Is it likely an ever smaller number of young people will want to spend their active years looking after an ever greater number of old people? Or will it be simpler to put all that cutting-edge Japanese technology to good use and take a flier on Mister Roboto and the post-human future? After all, what's easier for the governing class? Weaning a pampered population off the good life and re-teaching them the lost biological impulse or giving the Sony Corporation a licence to become the Cloney Corporation? If you need to justify it to yourself, you'd grab the graphs and say, well, demographic decline is universal. It's like industrialization a couple of centuries back; everyone will get to it eventually, but the first to do so will have huge advantages: the relevant comparison is not with England's early 19th century population surge but with England's Industrial Revolution.

In the industrial age, manpower was critical. In the new technological age, manpower will be optional — and indeed, if most of the available manpower's Muslim, it's actually a disadvantage. As the most advanced society with the most advanced demographic crisis, Japan seems likely to be the first jurisdiction to embrace robots and cloning and embark on the slippery slope to trans-humanism. Demographic origin need not be the final word. In 1775, Benjamin Franklin wrote a letter to Joseph Priestly suggesting a mutual English friend might like to apply his mind to the conundrum the Crown faced:

Britain, at the expense of three millions, has killed 150 Yankees this campaign, which is £20000 a head... During the same time, 60000 children have been born in America. From these data his mathematical head will easily calculate the time and the expense necessary to kill us all.

Obviously, Franklin was oversimplifying. Not every American colonist identified himself as a rebel. After the revolution, there were massive population displacements:

as United Empire Loyalists well know, large numbers of New Yorkers left the colony to resettle in what's now Ontario. Some American Negroes were so anxious to remain subjects of King George III they resettled as far as Sierra Leone. For these people, their primary identity was not as American colonists but as British subjects. For others, their new identity as Americans had supplanted their formal allegiance to the Crown. The question for today's Europe is whether the primary identity of their fastest-growing demographic is Muslim or Belgian, Muslim or Dutch, Muslim or French.

That's where civilizational confidence comes in: if "Dutchness" or "Frenchness" seems a weak attenuated thing, then the stronger identity will prevail. One notes other similarities between revolutionary America and contemporary Europe, the United Empire Loyalists were older and wealthier; the rebels were younger and poorer. In the end, the former simply lacked the latter's strength of will.

Europe, like Japan, has catastrophic birth rates and a swollen pampered elderly class determined to live in defiance of economic reality. But the difference is that on the Continent the successor population is already in place and the only question is how bloody the transfer of real estate will be.

If America's "allies" failed to grasp the significance of 9/11, it's because Europe's home-grown terrorism problems had all taken place among notably static populations, such as Ulster and the Basque country. One could make generally safe extrapolations about the likelihood of holding Northern Ireland to what cynical strategists in Her Majesty's Government used to call an "acceptable level of violence." But in the same three decades as Ulster's "Troubles," the hitherto moderate Muslim populations of south Asia were radicalized by a politicized form of Islam; previously formally un-Islamic societies such as Nigeria became semi-Islamist; and large Muslim populations settled in parts of Europe that had little or no experience of mass immigration.

On the Continent and elsewhere in the West, native populations are aging and fading and being supplanted remorselessly by a young Muslim demographic. Time for the obligatory "of courses", *of course,* not all Muslims are terrorists — though enough are hot for jihad to provide an impressive support network of mosques from Vienna to Stockholm to Toronto to Seattle. *Of course,* not all Muslims support terrorists — though enough of them share their basic objectives (the wish to live under Islamic law in Europe and North America) to function wittingly or otherwise as the "good cop" end of an Islamic good cop/bad cop routine. But, at the very minimum, this fast-moving demographic transformation provides a huge comfort zone for the jihad to move around in. And in a more profound way it rationalizes what would otherwise be the nuttiness of the terrorists' demands.

An IRA man blows up a pub in defiance of democratic reality — because he knows that at the ballot box the Ulster Loyalists win the elections and the Irish Republicans lose. When a European jihadist blows something up, that's not in defiance of democratic reality but merely a portent of democratic reality to come. He's jumping the gun, but in every respect things are moving his way.

You may vaguely remember seeing some flaming cars on the evening news toward the end of 2005. Something going on in France, apparently. Something to do with — what's the word? — "youths." When I pointed out the media's strange reluctance to use the M-word vis-à-vis the rioting "youths," I received a ton of emails arguing there's no Islamist component, they're not the *madrasa* crowd, they may be Muslim but they're secular and Westernized and into drugs and rap and meaningless sex with no emotional commitment, and rioting and looting and torching and trashing, just like any normal healthy Western teenagers. These guys have economic concerns, it's the lack of jobs, it's conditions peculiar to France, etc. As one correspondent wrote, "You right-wing shit-for-brains think everything's about jihad."

Actually, I don't think everything's about jihad. But I do think, as I said, that a good 90 per cent of everything's about demography. Take that media characterization of those French rioters: "youths." What's the salient point about youths? They're youthful. Very few octogenarians want to go torching Renaults every night. It's not easy lobbing a Molotov cocktail into a police station and then hobbling back with your walker across the street before the searing heat of the explosion melts your hip replacement. Civil disobedience is a young man's game.

In June 2006, a 54-year-old Flemish train conductor called Guido Demoor got on the Number 23 bus in Antwerp to go to work. Six — what's that word again? — "youths" boarded the bus and commenced intimidating the other riders. There were some 40 passengers aboard. But the "youths" were youthful and the other passengers less so. Nonetheless, Mr. Demoor asked the lads to cut it out and so they turned on him, thumping and kicking him. Of those 40 other passengers, none intervened to help the man under attack. Instead, at the next stop, 30 of the 40 scrammed, leaving Mr. Demoor to be beaten to death. Three "youths" were arrested, and proved to be — *quelle surprise!* — of Moroccan origin. The ringleader escaped and, despite police assurances of complete confidentiality, of those 40 passengers only four came forward to speak to investigators. "You see what happens if you intervene," a fellow rail worker told the Belgian newspaper *De Morgen*. "If Guido had not opened his mouth he would still be alive."

No, he wouldn't. He would be as dead as those 40 passengers are, as the Belgian state is, keeping his head down, trying not to make eye contact, cowering behind his newspaper in the corner seat and hoping just to be left alone. What future in "their" country do Mr. Demoor's two children have? My mother and grandparents came from Sint-Niklaas, a town I remember well from many childhood visits. When we stayed with great-aunts and other relatives, the upstairs floors of the row houses had no bathrooms, just chamber pots. My sister and I were left to mooch around cobbled streets with our little cousin for hours on end, wandering aimlessly past smoke-wreathed bars and cafes, occasionally buying *frites* with mayonnaise. With hindsight it seemed as parochially Flemish as could be imagined. Not anymore. The week before Mr. Demoor was murdered in plain sight, bus drivers in Sint-Niklaas walked off the job to protest the thuggery of the — here it comes again — "youths." In little more than a generation, a town has been transformed.

Of the ethnic Belgian population, some 17 per cent are under 18 years old. Of the country's Turkish and Moroccan population, 35 per cent are under 18 years old. The "youths" get ever more numerous, the non-youths get older. To avoid the ruthless arithmetic posited by Benjamin Franklin, it is necessary for those "youths" to feel more Belgian. Is that likely? Colonel Gadhafi doesn't think so:

There are signs that Allah will grant Islam victory in Europe — without swords, without guns, without conquests. The fifty million Muslims of Europe will turn it into a Muslim continent within a few decades.

On Sept. 11, 2001, the American mainland was attacked for the first time since the War of 1812. The perpetrators were foreign — Saudis and Egyptians. Since 9/11, Europe has seen the London Tube bombings, the French riots, Dutch murders of nationalist politicians. The perpetrators are their own citizens — British subjects, *citoyens de la République française*. In Linz, Austria, Muslims are demanding that all female teachers, believers or infidels, wear head scarves in class. The Muslim Council of Britain wants Holocaust Day abolished because it focuses "only" on the Nazis'(alleged)Holocaust of the Jews and not the Israelis' ongoing Holocaust of the Palestinians.

How does the state react? In Seville, King Ferdinand III is no longer patron saint of the annual fiesta because his splendid record in fighting for Spanish independence from the Moors was felt to be insensitive to Muslims. In London, a judge agreed to the removal of Jews and Hindus from a trial jury because the Muslim defendant's counsel argued he couldn't get a fair verdict from them. The Church of England is considering removing St. George as the country's patron saint on the grounds that, according to various Anglican clergy, he's too "militaristic" and "offensive to Muslims." They wish to replace him with St. Alban, and replace St. George's cross on the revamped Union Flag, which would instead show St. Alban's cross as a thin yellow streak.

In a few years, as millions of Muslim teenagers are entering their voting booths, some European countries will not be living formally under sharia, but — as much as parts of Nigeria, they will have reached an accommodation with their radicalized Islamic compatriots, who like many intolerant types are expert at exploiting the "tolerance" of pluralist societies. In other Continental countries, things are likely to play out in more traditional fashion, though without a significantly different ending. Wherever one's sympathies lie on Islam's multiple battle fronts the fact is the jihad has held out a long time against very tough enemies. If you're not shy about taking on the Israelis and Russians, why wouldn't you fancy your chances against the Belgians and Spaniards?

"We're the ones who will change you," the Norwegian imam Mullah Krekar told the Oslo newspaper *Dagbladet* in 2006. "Just look at the development within Europe, where the number of Muslims is expanding like mosquitoes. Every Western woman in the EU is producing an average of 1.4 children. Every Muslim woman in the same countries is producing 3.5 children." As he summed it up: "Our way of thinking will prove more powerful than yours."

A few years ago, terrorists destroyed two U.S. embassies. President Clinton retaliated against suspected facilities of Osama bin Laden. In his television address, the President told the American people that we were the targets of terrorism because we stood for democracy, freedom, and human rights in the world.

On that occasion, I wrote: "Tell people the truth, Mr. President... about terrorism, not about poor Monica. If your lies about terrorism go unchallenged, then the terror war you have unleashed will likely continue until it destroys us.

"The threat of nuclear terrorism is closing in upon us. Chemical terrorism is at hand, and biological terrorism is a future danger. None of our thousands of nuclear weapons can protect us from these threats. These idols of plutonium, titanium, and steel are impotent. Our worship of them for over five decades has not brought us security, only greater danger. No 'Star Wars' system... no matter how technically advanced, no matter how many trillions of dollars was poured into it... can protect us from even a single terrorist bomb. Not one weapon in our vast arsenal can shield us from a nuclear weapon delivered in a sailboat or a Piper Cub or a suitcase or a Ryder rental truck. Not a penny of the 273 billion dollars a year we spend on so-called defense can actually defend us against a terrorist bomb. Nothing in our enormous military establishment can actually give us one whit of security. That is a military fact.

"Mr. President, you did not tell the American people the truth about why we are the targets of terrorism. You said that we are the target because we stand for democracy, freedom, and human rights in the world. Baloney! We are the target of terrorists because we stand for dictatorship, bondage, and human exploitation in the world. We are the target of terrorists because we are hated. And we are hated because our government has done hateful things.

"In how many countries have we deposed popularly elected leaders and replaced them with puppet military dictators who were willing to sell out their own people to American multinational corporations?

"We did it in Iran when we deposed Mossadegh because he wanted to nationalize the oil industry. We replaced him with the Shah, and trained, armed, and paid his hated Savak national guard, which enslaved and brutalized the people of Iran. All to protect the financial interests of our oil companies. Is it any wonder there are people in Iran who hate us?

"We did it in Chile when we deposed Allende, democratically elected by the people to introduce socialism. We replaced him with the brutal right-wing military dictator, General Pinochet. Chile has still not recovered.

"We did it in Vietnam when we thwarted democratic elections in the South which would have united the country under Ho Chi Minh. We replaced him with a series of ineffectual puppet crooks who invited us to come in and slaughter their people — and we did. (I flew 101 combat missions in that war which you properly opposed.)

"We did it in Iraq, where we killed a quarter of a million civilians in a failed attempt to topple Saddam Hussein, and where we have killed a million since then with our sanctions. About half of these innocent victims have been children under the age of five.

"And, of course, how many times have we done it in Nicaragua and all the other banana republics of Latin America? Time after time we have ousted popular leaders who wanted the riches of the land to be shared by the people who worked it. We replaced them with murderous tyrants who would sell out and control their own people so that the wealth of the land could be taken out by Domino Sugar, the United Fruit Company, Folgers, and Chiquita Banana.

"In country after country, our government has thwarted democracy, stifled freedom, and trampled human rights. *That's* why we are hated around the world. And that's why we are the target of terrorists.

"People in Canada enjoy better democracy, more freedom, and greater human rights than we do. So do the people of Norway and Sweden. Have you heard of Canadian embassies being bombed? Or Norwegian embassies? Or Swedish embassies. No.

"We are not hated because we practice democracy, freedom, and human rights. We are hated because our government denies these things to people in third world countries whose resources are coveted by our multinational corporations. And that hatred we have sown has come back to haunt us in the form of terrorism — and in the future, nuclear terrorism.

"Once the truth about why the threat exists is understood, the solution becomes obvious. We must change our government's ways.

"Instead of sending our sons and daughters around the world to kill Arabs so the oil companies can sell the oil under their sand, we must send them to rebuild their infrastructure, supply clean water, and feed starving children.

"Instead of continuing to kill thousands of Iraqi children every day with our sanctions, we must help them rebuild their electric power plants, their water treatment facilities, their hospitals — all the things we destroyed in our war against them and prevented them from rebuilding with our sanctions.

"Instead of seeking to be king of the hill, we must become a responsible member of the family of nations. Instead of stationing hundreds of thousands of troops around the world to protect the financial interests of our multinational corporations, we must bring them home and expand the Peace Corps.

"Instead of training terrorists and death squads in the techniques of torture and assassination, we must close the School of the Americas (no matter what name they use). Instead of supporting military dictatorships, we must support true democracy — the right of the people to choose their own leaders. Instead of supporting insurrection, destabilization, assassination, and terror around the world, we must abolish the CIA and give the money to relief agencies.

"In short, we do good instead of evil. We become the good guys, once again. The threat of terrorism would vanish. That is the truth, Mr. President. That is what the American people need to hear. We are good people. We only need to be told the truth and given the vision. You can do it, Mr. President. Stop the killing. Stop the justifying. Stop the retaliating. Put people first. Tell them the truth."

Needless to say, he didn't... and neither has George W. Bush. Well, the seeds our policies have planted have borne their bitter fruit. The World Trade Center is gone. The Pentagon is damaged. And thousands of Americans have died. Almost every TV pundit is crying for massive military retaliation against whoever might have done it (assumedly the same Osama bin Laden) and against whoever harbors or aids the terrorists (most notably the Taliban government of Afghanistan). Steve Dunleavy of the New York Post screams "Kill the bastards! Train assassins, hire mercenaries, put a couple of million bucks up for bounty hunters to get them dead or alive, preferably dead. As for cities or countries that host these worms, bomb them into basketball courts." It's tempting to agree. I have no sympathy for the psychopaths that killed thousands of our people. There is no excuse for such acts. If I was recalled to active duty, I would go in a heartbeat. At the same time, all my military experience and knowledge tells me that retaliation hasn't rid us of the problem in the past, and won't this time. By far the world's best anti-terrorist apparatus is Israel's. Measured in military terms, it has been phenomenally successful. Yet Israel still suffers more attacks than all other nations combined.

If retaliation worked, Israelis would be the world's most secure people. Only one thing has ever ended a terrorist campaign — denying the terrorist organization the support of the larger community it represents. And the only way to do that is to listen to and alleviate the legitimate grievances of the people. If indeed Osama bin Laden was behind the four hijackings and subsequent carnage, that means addressing the concerns of the Arabs and Muslims in general and of the Palestinians in particular. It does NOT mean abandoning Israel. But it may very well mean withdrawing financial and military support until they abandon the settlements in occupied territory and return to 1967 borders. It may also mean allowing Arab countries to have leaders of their own choosing, not hand-picked, CIA-installed dictators willing to cooperate with Western oil companies.

Chester Gillings has said it very well: "How do we fight back against bin Laden? The first thing we must ask ourselves is what is it we hope to achieve — security or revenge? The two are mutually exclusive; seek revenge and we WILL reduce our security. If it is security we seek, then we must begin to answer the tough questions — what are the grievances of the Palestinians and the Arab world against the United States, and what is our real culpability for those grievances? Where we find legitimate culpability, we must be prepared to cure the grievance wherever possible. Where we cannot find culpability or a cure, we must communicate honestly our positions directly to the Arab people. In short, our best course of action is to remove ourselves as a combatant in the disputes of the region."

To kill bin Laden now would be to make him an eternal martyr. Thousands would rise up to take his place. In another year, we would face another round of terrorism, probably much worse even than this one. Yet there is another way. In the short term, we must protect ourselves from those who already hate us. This means increased security and better intelligence.

I proposed to members of Congress in March that we should deny any funds for "Star Wars" until such time as the Executive Branch could show that they are doing all possible research on the detection and interception of weapons of mass destruction entering the country clandestinely (a far greater threat than ballistic missiles). There are lots of steps which can be taken to increase security without detracting from civil rights. But in the long term, we must change our policies to stop causing the fear and hatred which creates *new* terrorists.

Becoming independent of foreign oil through conservation, energy efficiency, production of energy from renewable sources, and a transition to non-polluting transportation will allow us to adopt a more rational policy toward the Middle East. The vast majority of Arabs and Muslims are good, peaceful people. But enough of them, in their desperation and anger and fear, have turned first to Arafat and now to bin Laden to relieve their misery. Remove the desperation, give them some hope, and support for terrorism will evaporate. At that point bin Laden will be forced to abandon terrorism (as has Arafat) or be treated like a common criminal. Either way, he and his money cease to be a threat. We CAN have security... or we can have revenge. We cannot have both.

Change and Continuity in Terrorism

Terrorism today reflects both change and continuity. New adversaries with new motivations and new rationales have appeared in recent years to challenge some of our most basic assumptions about terrorists and terrorism. Their emergence, however, has not produced the anticipated changes in either terrorist weaponry or tactics that were predicted to follow in the wake of the Aum Shinrikyo's 1995 nerve gas attack on the Tokyo subway. Instead, as has been the case for more than a century, the gun and the bomb remain the terrorists' main weapons of choice. Thus, as fanatical or irrational as even this new breed of terrorists may seem, like their more traditional counterparts, they too have remained remarkably conservative operationally: adhering to the same familiar and narrow tactical repertoire that they both have mastered and equally importantly believe maximizes their likelihood of success.

For this reason, future terrorist use of chemical, biological, radiological or nuclear (CBRN) weapons may be far less certain than is now commonly assumed and therefore current efforts to address this threat may prove as ineffective as they are misplaced. In the past, terrorism was practiced by a group of individuals belonging to an identifiable organization with a clear command and control apparatus who had a defined set of political, social or economic objectives. Radical leftist organizations such as the Japanese Red Army, Germany's Red Army Faction, Italy's Red Brigades as well as ethno-nationalist terrorist movements like the Abu Nidal Organization, the IRA, and the Basque separatist group, ETA, reflected this stereotype of the traditional terrorist group.

They issued communiqués taking credit for—and explaining—their actions and however disagreeable or distasteful their aims and motivations were, their ideology and intentions were at least comprehensible. Most significantly, however, these familiar terrorist groups engaged in highly selective and mostly discriminate acts of violence. They bombed various "symbolic" targets representing the source of their animus (embassies, banks, national airline carriers, etc.) or kidnapped and assassinated specific persons whom they blamed for economic exploitation or political repression generally in order to attract attention to themselves and their causes. Finally, these groups were often numerically constrained. They mostly comprised relatively small numbers of persons.

Neither the Japanese Red Army nor the Red Army Faction, for example, ever numbered more than 20 to 30 hard-core members. The Red Brigades were hardly larger, with a total of fewer than 50 to 75 dedicated terrorists. Even the Provisional Irish Republican Army and the Basque separatist group ETA could only call on the violent services of perhaps some 200-400 activists while the feared Abu Nidal Organization was limited to in excess of some 500 men-at-arms at any given time. In contrast to the stereotypical terrorist group of the past, this new generation of terrorists evidence several important organizational changes which in turn have affected their operations, decision-making and targeting. Rather than the pyramidal, hierarchical organizational structures that were dominant among terrorist organizations during the 1970s and 1980s, terrorists are now increasingly part of far more amorphous, indistinct, and broader movements.

These movements also tend to operate on a linear rather than hierarchical basis. Hence, instead of the classic cellular structure that was common to previous generations of terrorist organizations, some contemporary groups are more loosely connected or indirectly linked through networks comprised of both professional— i.e., full-time—terrorists and amateurs—i.e., mostly, hangers-on, supporters, sympathizers and would-be terrorists who may lack the expertise or experience of their more established counterparts. The absence of any existing, publicly identified central command authority is significant in that it may remove previous inhibitions on the terrorists' desire to inflict widespread, indiscriminate casualties. In some instances, individual networks therefore may have greater freedom and independence in tactical decisions than traditional terrorist cells of the past given the absence of some central command structure or actual functioning headquarters.

Accordingly, this particular trend in terrorism may represent a very different and potentially far more lethal one than that posed by more familiar, traditional, terrorist adversaries. Further, the anonymity intrinsic to this type of operation coupled with the lack of a discernible organizational structure with a distinguishable command chain behind the attackers is deliberately designed to prevent easy identification, facilitate the perpetrators' escape and evasion, and also hopefully avoid retaliation by the victim states' military forces. Finally, many terrorist movements today are also seen to have less easily defined aims or identified objectives. Some are motivated by unswerving hostility towards the West in general and the United States in particular or a desire for revenge and retaliation that is frequently fuelled by compelling religious imperatives and justifications rather than abstract political ideologies.

Thus in contrast to the intelligible demands of past familiar, predominantly secular terrorist groups who mostly claimed credit for and explained their violent acts; the most heinous and lethal attacks perpetrated by terrorists over the past decade—mostly those directed against civilians—have gone unclaimed. By maintaining their anonymity, terrorists may believe that are able to capitalize further on the fear and alarm intrinsically generated by their violence. This array of changes has in turn raised serious concern about the continued relevance of much of the conventional wisdom on terrorism—particularly as it pertains to potential future terrorist use of CBRN weapons. In the past, most analyses of the possibility of mass indiscriminate killing involving chemical, biological, radiological or nuclear terrorism tended to discount it.

Few terrorists, it was argued, know anything about the technical intricacies of either developing or then dispersing such weapons. Political, moral, and practical considerations were also perceived as important restraints on terrorist use of such weapons of mass destruction. Finally and most significantly, we assured ourselves that terrorists wanted more people watching than dead. Therefore we believed that terrorists arguably had little interest and still less to gain from killing wantonly and indiscriminately. While some of these arguments perhaps were still pertinent to most secular terrorists, incidents like the 1995 nerve gas attack on the Tokyo subway by an apocalyptic Japanese religious sect, the bombing of New York City's World Trade Center Islamic extremists two years before and the bombing of a government office building in Oklahoma City by an American Christian white supremacist just a month after the Tokyo incident—coupled with other attacks perpetrated by religious-inspired terrorists throughout the world during the 1990s—appeared to have rendered these arguments dangerously anachronistic. Upon closer examination, however, this has not proven to be so—despite fears, arguments and spending to the contrary.

First, this new era of terrorism—supposedly more lethal and bloody than before—that the new terrorists were thought surely to wreck has yet to materialize. Indeed, despite the overall rise in terrorism's lethality reported by such authoritative sources, as the U.S. State Department's annual *Global Patterns of Terrorism* publications, a total of 87 Americans were killed in 40 attacks perpetrated by terrorists overseas between 1990 and 1999. Terrorism, of course, remains a threat to Americans traveling or working abroad, and whatever the total number, it is incontestably tragic that any American should lose his or her life to violence or be wantonly harmed and injured simply because of the nationality of the passport they carry, the uniform they wear, or the job that they perform.

Nonetheless, the fact remains that despite the so-called appearance of the "new face of terrorism" heralded by many, the streets of the world hardly run red with American blood. In fact, approximately six times as many Americans were killed by terrorists in the 1980s as compared with the 1990s. Nor is the situation terribly different in the U.S. itself. Admittedly, a total of 176 persons were killed by terrorists in this country during the 1990s—more than twice the international figure. At the same time, however, this tragic death toll is the result of three out of a total of only 25 terrorist incidents reported to have occurred in the U.S. between 1990 and 1997 (the last year for which figures have been published) according to the Federal Bureau of Investigation (FBI). And of the three incidents, it was one especially heinous act—the 1995 bombing of the Alfred P. Murrah Federal office building in Oklahoma City—that accounts for the overwhelming majority of fatalities (168 deaths).

Again, there is no doubt that terrorism remains a threat to the lives and well-being of Americans in our own country, but the *actual* number of terrorist incidents (as opposed to the hundreds of CBRN hoaxes that the FBI and other law enforcement and public safety agencies now routinely respond to), remains remarkably few and those that cause fatalities still less. None of the above, it should be emphasized, is meant to suggest that the U.S. should become complacent about the threat of terrorism (domestic or international) or in any way relax our vigilance either at home or abroad. Terrorism poses—and will likely to continue to pose—a serious threat to Americans and American interests both in this country and overseas.

Nonetheless, it is equally clear that there has been a tendency to exaggerate the dimensions of the threat and the *strategic* impact that terrorist violence has actually wrought. And by overreacting and falling prey to a sense of acute fear and intimidation, we also disproportionately inflate the terrorists' power in ways that are both counterproductive and often completely divorced from reality. America's current preoccupation with Osama bin Laden and attendant—however inadvertent—lionization of his stature and power is arguably such a case in point. Despite his vast wealth and alleged legions of minions, it is hardly likely that bin Laden could ever hope to vanquish the U.S. military, overthrow our government or achieve any fundamental political changes in American foreign or domestic policy.

Yet, this single individual is held in fear and accorded a stature far in excess of his specific capabilities and unique accumulation of financial resources or even what one human being could conceivably wield over a long established nation-state, much less the globe's sole super power. Terrorism is fundamentally the use (or threatened use) of violence in order to achieve psychological effects in a particular target audience. The fomenting of widespread fear and intimidation is therefore ineluctably the terrorists' intent.

Accordingly, by succumbing to terrorist threats and braggadocio and, failing to distinguish their inflated rhetoric from genuine intentions, much less actual capabilities, we risk making hard policy choices and budgetary allocations based mostly on misperception and misunderstanding rather than on hard analysis built on empirical evidence. Indeed, the incorrect lessons derived from the Aum experience in general and the 1995 nerve gas attack in particular illustrate the dangers of responding emotionally and viscerally rather than soberly and calmly to such terrorist threats.

Even if the motives of terrorists are changing in such a way that they are becoming more lethal and even if this in turn may cause them to contemplate ever more bloody and heinous acts that might lead to CBRN weapons use, these trends do not necessarily imply that terrorists *currently* possess (as it is frequently portrayed) either the requisite scientific knowledge or technical capabilities to implement their violent ambitions. In this respect, as easy as some argue that it may be for terrorists to culture anthrax spores or brew up a concoction of deadly nerve gas, the effective dissemination or dispersal of these viruses and poisons still presents serious technological hurdles that greatly inhibit their effective use. Indeed, the same Japanese religious sect that is most directly responsible for precipitating our current obsession with terrorism and CBRN weapons is precisely a case in point.

The Aum Shinrikyo, it must be said, was by no means a typical terrorist group. Rather than the handful of men and women, with limited training, technical capabilities and resources that has dominated our conception of the archetypal terrorist organization, Aum was unique. It was a religious movement with upwards of fifty thousand members and offices in New York, Germany, Australia and Sri Lanka in addition to Japan and Russia. Aum had assets estimated to be in the neighborhood of $1 billion—and at least certainly in the hundred millions. It specifically recruited graduates with scientific and engineering degrees from Japan's leading universities and provided them with state of the art laboratories and lavish budgets with which to fund the group's variegated weapons R&D programs. Indeed, when police raided the sect's laboratories following the nerve gas attack, for example, they found enough Sarin to kill an estimated 4.2 million persons.

In addition, Aum had either already produced or had plans to develop other powerful nerve agents such as VX, tabun and soman; chemical weapons such as mustard gas and sodium cyanide; and deadly biological warfare pathogens that included anthrax, the highly contagious disease known as Q-fever—and possibly the deadly Ebola virus as well. Aum's most ambitious project, however, was doubtless its efforts to develop a nuclear capability. To this end, the group had purchased a 500,000-acre sheep station in a remote part of Western Australia. There, they hoped to mine uranium that was to be shipped back to Aum's laboratories in Japan where scientists using laser enrichment technology would convert it into weapons-grade nuclear material.

The group had also assembled impressive panoply of conventional weaponry. Aum is believed to have purchased large quantities of small arms from Russian sources and to have been in the market for advanced weaponry such as tanks, jet fighters, surface-to-surface rocket launchers, and even a tactical nuclear weapon. What is known is that Aum succeeded in obtaining a surplus twin-turbine Mi-117 helicopter—complete with chemical spray dispersal devices. The group also planned— —and had gone as far as to acquire sophisticated robotic manufacturing devices—to produce at least a 1,000 knock-off versions of Russia's world-famous AK-47 assault rifle along with one million bullets. Finally, the sect had determined how to the manufacture TNT and the central component of plastic explosives, RDX.

As the above inventory of armaments and technological and engineering accomplishments suggests, Aum was no ordinary terrorist group. Rather than the handful of men and women, with limited training, technical capabilities and resources that has long colored our conception of the archetypal terrorist organization, Aum was—by any measure—unique. It was a religious movement with upwards of sixty thousand members and offices in New York, Germany, Australia, and Sri Lanka—in addition to Japan and Russia. Aum had assets estimated to be in the neighborhood of $1 billion—and at least certainly in the hundred millions.

It specifically recruited graduates with scientific and engineering degrees from Japan's leading universities and provided them with state-of-the-art laboratories and lavish budgets with which to fund the group's variegated weapons R&D programs. Indeed, as many as 80 scientific personnel were specifically detailed to work on the group's chemical weapons programs, according to one estimate; it's biological weapons research, however, never employed more than perhaps 20 persons at most. However, despite Aum's considerable financial wealth, the technical expertise that it could call upon from its well-educated members and the vast resources and state-of-the-art equipment at their disposal; the group could not effect even a single truly successful chemical or biological attack.

On at least nine occasions the group attempted to disseminate botulinum toxin (*Clostridium botulinum*) or anthrax (*Bacillus anthracis*) using aerosol means: each time they failed either because the botulinum agents they grew and enriched were not toxic or the mechanical sprayers used to disseminate the anthrax spores became clogged and hence inoperative. Even the more successful Sarin attack on the Tokyo subway would be laughable if not for the tragic deaths of 12 persons and the physical and psychological harm caused to many more victims. For all its sophisticated research and development, the best means the group could find to disseminate the nerve gas was in plastic trash bags that had to be poked open with sharpened umbrella tips in order to release the noxious mixture.

Finally, the group's distinct lack of success in actually wrecking the mass destruction or mass casualties ascribed to these types of weapons, despite the considerable resources at its disposal, speaks volumes about the challenges facing any lesser-endowed terrorist organization. Indeed, neither was mass destruction achieved nor mass casualties even inflicted. New research has revealed that of the five thousand persons who received medical treatment in the aftermath of the subway attack, the vast majority (73.9 percent) was suffering from shock, emotional upset or evidenced some psychosomatic symptom. Accordingly, even the number of persons physically injured or affected by the attack is much lower than previously reported.

In sum, upon further examination and analysis, Aum's experience suggests—however counter-intuitively or contrary to popular belief—the immense technological difficulties faced by any non-state entity in attempting to weaponize and effectively disseminate chemical and biological weapons. It also provides striking refutation of the argument voiced with increasing frequency in recent years of the ease with which such weapons can be fabricated and made operational.

Public officials, journalists and analysts, for example, have repeatedly alleged that biological attacks in particular are relatively easy for terrorists to undertake. According to one state emergency management official, for example, biological weapons "are available—and easy to make....One does not need a degree in microbiology to make this work, being able to read is enough.... It's not like enriching uranium."

Similarly, both the White House and senior FBI officials have argued that the information needed to develop chemical and biological weapons can be readily obtained from the Internet and other open sources. Such claims do not square with the facts, given Aum's experience and its concerted, years-long R&D activities or indeed of subsequent research that has examined this question of ease of alleged fabrication and dissemination. Indeed, in the words of the national intelligence officer responsible for non proliferation issues and thus the country's senior intelligence analyst on this issue: "while popular culture can explore the potential BW threat, actually developing and using an effective biological weapon poses certain technological challenges."

Future Possible CBRN Terrorism

The above analysis is not to suggest, however, that there either is no threat of terrorist use of CBRN or that it is one that should be dismissed or discounted. Indeed, the difficulties now facing a terrorist, who may seek to use a CBRN weapon to achieve mass effects, could of course change dramatically, because of new discoveries, further advances in technology, or other material factors. What this speech has argued is that some public pronouncements and media depictions concerning the ease with which terrorists might wreak genuine mass destruction or inflict widespread casualties, do not always reflect the significant hurdles currently confronting any non-state entity seeking to employ such weapons.

In this respect, it should be stressed that a limited terrorist attack involving not a WMD per se, but an unconventional chemical, biological, or radiological weapon on a deliberately small scale—either alone or as part of a series of smaller incidents occurring either simultaneously or sequentially in a given location—could have disproportionately enormous consequences, generating unprecedented fear and alarm, and thus serving the terrorists' purpose just as well as a larger weapon or more ambitious attack with massive casualties could have. Hence, the issue here may not be as much a ruthless terrorist's use of some WMD designed to achieve mass casualties, as the calculated terrorist's use of some unconventional weapon to achieve far-reaching psychological effects in a particular target audience.

To focus on weapons of truly "mass destruction" may, therefore, be missing the point and sidestepping the potential, credible threats posed by terrorists in this regard. The most salient terrorist threat involving an unconventional weapon, accordingly, will likely not involve or even attempt the destruction of an entire city (as often proclaimed by fictional thriller writers and some government officials), but the far more deliberate and delicately planned use of a chemical, biological, or radiological agent for more discrete purposes. Yet despite the empirical evidence regarding terrorism trends and patterns of activity (both domestic and international) and the correct lessons that should be drawn from the case of Aum, the U.S. remains singularly preoccupied with the threat of mass casualty terrorism based on planning for worst-case scenarios.

This is largely a result of a mindset that took root in the immediate aftermath of both the 1995 Tokyo nerve gas attack and the large number of casualties inflicted at Oklahoma City and which has fundamentally shaped our thinking and perceptions of the terrorist threat ever since. Despite the evidence to the contrary that has emerged regarding Aum and its implications for subsequent terrorist CBRN ambitions and indeed the overall pattern of terrorist activity in the five years since the 1995 subway attack, no significant reassessment, reconsideration or revision of the CBRN terrorism threat profile established during the 1995-1996 time frame has yet to be undertaken. Thus, a critical first step in assessing the threat as it exists today and is likely to evolve in the future should be to perform a new overall, net assessment of the terrorist threat not only internationally but domestically as well.

Based on that assessment—which will address conditions, circumstances and vulnerabilities of today and not from five years ago—a determination can be made whether the worst-case scenario threat assessment approach that has dominated current domestic planning and preparedness for potential acts of CBRN terrorism—is still appropriate, much less relevant. The current narrow policy focus lower-probability/higher-consequence threats, which in turn posit virtually limitless vulnerabilities, does not reflect the realities of contemporary terrorist behaviour and operations. "This kind of analysis," Brian Jenkins recently warned in testimony before Congress, "can degenerate into a fact-free scaffold of anxieties and arguments—dramatic, emotionally powerful, but analytically feeble." Similarly, at the same congressional hearing, another expert, John Parachini, counseled that the "apparent over reliance on worst-case scenarios shaped primarily by vulnerability assessment rather than an assessment that factors in the technical complexities, motivations of terrorists and their patterns of behaviour seems to be precisely the sort of approach we should avoid."

The main weakness in such an approach is in the axiomatic assumption that any less serious incident can be addressed equally well by planning for the most catastrophic threat—ignoring the fact that the higher-probability/lower-consequence attacks might present unique challenges of their own. Finally, this approach may be the least efficacious means of setting budgetary priorities and allocating resources and indeed assuring the security of our country. This was precisely the point made by Henry L. Hinton, Jr., the Assistant Comptroller General, National Security and International Affairs Division, U.S. General Accounting Office, when he testified before Congress in March 1999.

"The [most] daunting task before the nation," he argued, "is to assess—to the best of its ability—the emerging threat with the best available knowledge and expertise across the many disciplines involved. The United States cannot fund all the possibilities that have dire consequences. By focusing investments on worst-case possibilities, the government may be missing the more likely threats the country will face. With the right threat and risk assessment process, participants, inputs, and methodology, the nation can have greater confidence that it is investing in the right items in the right amounts. Even within the lower end of the threat spectrum—where the biological and chemical terrorist threat currently lies—the threats can still be ranked and prioritized in terms of their likelihood and severity of consequences. A sound threat and risk assessment could provide a cohesive roadmap to justify and target spending...."

Moreover, at a time when the U.S. is especially preoccupied with these "high-end" terrorist threats involving mass destruction CBRN weapons, the series of apartment building bombings that occurred in Russia and Dagestan during August and September 1999 is a salutary reminder of how terrorists can still achieve their dual aim of fear and intimidation through entirely conventional means and traditional methods: using bombs to blow things up. This fact has important implications for America's—and indeed also other countries'—counter-terrorism preparedness. Given the limited resources and constrained capabilities typical of most terrorists, they perhaps reflexively shun weapons and tactics that either cannot be relied upon completely or that pose such enormous complexities in terms of their employment (e.g., achieving effective dispersal or dissemination) as to border on the unappealing, if not useless. For this reason, it can be said that terrorists remain essentially content with the limited killing potential of their handguns and machine-guns and the slightly higher rates that their bombs can achieve.

In other words, they seem to prefer the assurance of the modest success provided by their more conventional weapons and traditional tactics to the risk of failure inherent in more complex and complicated operations involving CBRN weapons. Indeed, of the more than 9,000 incidents recorded in The RAND Chronology of International Terrorism since 1968, fewer than 100 evidence *any* indication of terrorists plotting to attempting to use chemical, biological or radiological weapons or to steal, or otherwise fabricate on their own, nuclear devices—much less actually to carry out such attacks. As one critic has observed in connection with the current concern over terrorist use of biological agents: "Nasty people and the ingredients for bioterrorism were all in place over a decade ago. Why now the drumbeating?" Indeed, since the beginning of the century little more than a dozen terrorist incidents in fact have occurred that resulted in the deaths of more than a 100 persons at one time: an arguably infinitesimal number given the total volume of terrorism that has occurred worldwide within past quarter century, much less one hundred years.

There is another relevant paradox affecting terrorist behaviour. Terrorists have long been seen as far more imitative as they are innovative. However, to date, no similar or copycat act of terrorism, which at the time was thought might likely follow in the wake of the 1995 Sarin nerve gas on the Tokyo subway, has materialized. In this respect, the Tokyo incident has been the exception rather than the rule in terms of terrorist behaviour. "This fact gains significance," Brian Jenkins recently observed, "when we note that past terrorist and criminal innovations—airline hijackings, political kidnappings, malicious product tampering—were promptly imitated. And terrorist attacks involving chemical and biological agents, if they do occur, are likely to remain rare events—they will not become the truck bomb of the next decade."

Hence, the real issue and the most likely threat may not be the ruthless terrorist using some weapon of mass destruction as proclaimed by many, but calculated terrorist using some CBRN weapon to achieve far-reaching psychological effects. We may therefore be missing the point and sidestepping the real threat posed by terrorists in this regard. When and if a CBRN terrorist attack does occur in the U.S., it will not be the destruction of an entire city depicted by fictional thriller-writers and government officials alike: but the far more deliberate and delicately planned use of a chemical, biological or radiological agent for more discreet purposes. In this respect, even a limited terrorist attack involving not a chemical, biological or radiological weapon on a deliberately small scale could have disproportionately enormous consequences, generating unprecedented fear and alarm and thus serving the terrorists' purpose just as well as a larger weapon or more ambitious attack with massive casualties could.

Given this mixed picture of terrorist patterns and trends and the inherent uncertainty in attempting to predict future terrorist behaviour, what should we do or, perhaps more apposite, what can we do to counter effectively the terrorist threat today and in the future? Hard issues require hard questions. It may therefore appropriate now to pause, to take stock of the situation and to assess where terrorism is going, where precisely our countermeasures are in response to that trajectory and thereby reexamine some of the fundamental conclusions about terrorism reached five years ago—in the wake of the Tokyo and Oklahoma incidents—to determine their relevance to both contemporary and likely future trends and developments in this area.

We need to begin this reexamination by focusing on the entire CBRN terrorism issue. In this respect, even if one concedes the cogency of these perceived threats today, two critical questions need to be asked. One is whether we are drawing the correct lessons from the defining terrorist events of the past decade and the other is "how much is enough" to prepare the U.S. to adequately respond to this challenge and, equally important, upon what basis will the success or effectiveness of these measures be made? The second question we need to ask is how do we effectively counter the threat posed by transnational, stateless terrorist groups? In the past, we have relied on the use of military force and economic sanctions, but these options were directed almost exclusively against state-sponsors of terrorism.

The issue that thus arises is whether these measures are still relevant and useful to the challenges posed by transnational terrorist movements such as the one associated with bin Laden. Hand-in-glove with this reexamination should be increased attention paid to the role of psychological operations directed against both terrorist organizations and generally towards shaping public opinion against terrorism in countries or regions of the world susceptible to terrorist manipulation. Third, we need to ask whether key U.S. government policies to combat terrorism are working and being enforced. Included among these is the very positive development three years ago when the State Department established a list of Foreign Terrorist Organizations that are proscribed by the Secretary of State from engaging in fundraising and other support activities in the U.S. But we need to be confident that this important measure is both adequate to counter the financing of terrorism and also that it is in fact being rigorously enforced against the nearly 30 designated groups who have operated in this country in the past and may still be doing so.

Fourth, are death penalty statutes as applied to terrorists genuinely useful in deterring or preventing future acts of terrorism? This is not meant to kindle a broader debate over capital punishment in this country, but to ask whether there is a demonstrable, empirical value to putting convicted terrorists to death or might not such a policy in fact prove counterproductive: inspiring new acts of revenge and retaliation against the U.S., creating martyrs and political heroes out of murderers and thugs and also, not incidentally, possibly reducing international cooperation over the extradition of terrorists to the U.S. because of foreign opposition to our death penalty statutes?

Fifth, is the American intelligence community correctly configured to counter the terrorist threats of today and tomorrow? The U.S. intelligence community is essentially a cold war-era artifice, created more than half a century ago to counter a specific threat from a specific country and a specific ideology. Is that architecture, which has largely remained unchanged since the immediate post-World War II period, still relevant to today's challenges? An estimated 60% of the community's focus, for example, remains on military intelligence pertaining to the standing armed forces of established nation-states. Given the emergence of transnational, non-state adversaries, however, is this balance still the appropriate one? There are no easy answers to the intelligence and terrorism issue, but without debate and discussion, there can be no assurances that we are in fact on the right track.

Sixth, should there be a domestic terrorism net assessment as there is a foreign terrorist net assessment? If so, how should it be done and who should conduct it? Also, as previously noted, should there not now also be a new foreign terrorist net assessment that takes into account the *overall* pattern of terrorist activity and trends since 1995 and does not remain fixated solely on the signal events of that specific time period? Seventh, are our efforts directed against terrorism in this country oriented too much towards response and recovery rather than on preemption and prevention? In recent years, crisis management and emergency response have dominated our thinking in the U.S. about terrorism countermeasures. Is this approach the correct one and has the right balance been struck between these equally critical sides of the scale?

Eighth, as our concern with terrorism and terrorism threats grow alongside the array of countermeasures brought to bear against this threat, what are the implications for the continued protection of our fundamental constitutional rights and civil liberties? Here, any new measures strengthening preemption and prevention of terrorism need to be balanced with appropriate and effective oversight. Previous instances of abuse and transgression must serve as critical signposts to ward off the repetition of past mistakes if we are to ensure both the confidence of the public and these measures' long-term effectiveness. Finally, one of the most striking aspects of the current debate over the terrorism and counterterrorist policy is how wide the intellectual chasm separating the academic and policymaking communities over this issue has grown.

The position of most academic terrorism analysts has been far more restrained and skeptical concerning the CBRN terrorist threat, for example, than many of their counterparts in government, the military, and law enforcement. Yet, their cautionary appraisals are either dismissed or have long ago been superseded by a policy process that is already plowing full-steam ahead. Further thought might therefore profitably be devoted to understanding why this bifurcation of views has emerged and indeed how these differences of opinion might be bridged and effectively harnessed to enhance future policy formulation on this issue. In conclusion, it should be noted as serious and potentially catastrophic as a terrorist CBRN attack might prove, it is highly unlikely that it could ever completely undermine the national security, much less threaten the survival of a nation like the U.S. or indeed most other Western countries.

This point should be self-evident, but given the rhetoric and hyperbole with which the threat of CBRN terrorism is frequently couched, it requires reiteration. Even Israel, a comparatively small country in terms of population and landmass, who throughout its existence has often been isolated and surrounded by enemy states, and subjected to unrelenting terrorist attack and provocation, as the renowned French scholar Gérard Chaliand cogently points out, has never regarded terrorism as a paramount threat to its national security and longevity, worthy of profligate budgets or the diversion of disproportionate resources and attention. In addition it should be noted that even in the wake of the intense and fear concern that followed the 1995 Tokyo nerve gas attack, the Japanese government did not fall, widespread disorder did not ensue throughout the country nor did society collapse.

There is no reason to assume that the outcome would be any different in the U.S. or in any other Western democratic state in the event of a similar terrorist attack involving a chemical or biological weapon. To take any other position risks surrendering to the fear and intimidation that is precisely the terrorists' timeless stock and trade. There is a thin line between prudence and panic. The challenge, therefore, in responding to the threat of terrorists' is to craft a defense that is not only both cost effective and appropriate, but that is also sober and practical.

11

Future of Suicide Terrorism

Suicide attack is an ancient practice with a modern history. Its use by the Jewish sects of Zealots and Sicarii ("daggers") in Roman-occupied Judea and by the Islamic Order of Assassins (*hashashin*) during the early Crusader times is legendary examples. The concept of "terror" as systematic use of violence to attain political ends was first codified by Maximilien Robespierre during the French Revolution. He deemed it an "emanation of virtue" that delivers "prompt, severe, and inflexible" justice, as "a consequence of the general principle of democracy applied to our country's most pressing needs". The Reign of Terror, during which the ruling Jacobin faction exterminated thousands of potential enemies, of whatever sex, age, or condition, lasted until Robespierre's fall (July 1794). Similar justification for state-sponsored terror was common to 20th century revolutions, as in Russia (Lenin), Cambodia (Pol Pot), and Iran (Khomeini).

Whether subnational (e.g., Russian anarchists) or state-supported (e.g., Japanese *kamikaze*), suicide attack as a weapon of terror is usually chosen by weaker parties against materially stronger foes when fighting methods of lesser cost seem unlikely to succeed. Choice is often voluntary, but typically under conditions of group pressure and charismatic leadership. Thus, the kamikaze ("divine wind") first used in the battle of the Philippines (November 1944) were young, fairly well educated pilots who understood that pursuing conventional warfare would likely end in defeat. Many of these young men were well read in Western philosophy and literature, some were Marxists or Christians.

Few believed they were dying for the emperor as a war leader or for military purposes. Rather, the state was apparently able to manipulate a deep intellectual and aesthetic tradition of painful beauty to convince the pilots that it was their honor to "die like beautiful falling cherry petals" for their real and fictive families, including parents, fellow pilots and the emperor and people of Japan. When collectively asked by Adm. Takijiro Onishi to volunteer for "special attack" (*tokkotai*) "transcending life and death", all stepped forward, despite assurances that refusal would carry no shame or punishment. In the Battle of Okinawa (April 1945) some 2000 kamikaze rammed fully fueled fighter planes into more than 300 ships, killing 5000 Americans in the most costly naval battle in U.S. history. Because of such losses, there was support for using the atomic bomb to end World War II.

The first major contemporary suicide terrorist attack in the Middle East was the December 1981 destruction of the Iraqi embassy in Beirut (27 dead, over 100 wounded). Its precise authors are still unknown, although it is likely that Ayatollah Khomeini approved its use by parties sponsored by Iranian intelligence. With the assassination of pro-Israeli Lebanese President Bashir Gemayel in September 1982, suicide bombing became a strategic political weapon. Under the pro-Iranian Lebanese Party of God (Hezbollah), this strategy soon achieved geopolitical effect with the October 1983 truck-bomb killing of nearly 300 American and French servicemen. American and France abandoned the multinational force policing Lebanon. By 1985, these attacks arguably led Israel to cede most of the gains made during its 1982 invasion of Lebanon.

In Israel-Palestine, suicide terrorism began in 1992, becoming part of a systematic campaign in late 1993 with attacks by Hezbollah trained members of the Islamic Resistance Movement (Hamas) and Palestine Islamic Jihad (PIJ) aimed at derailing the Oslo Peace Accords. As early as 1988, however, PIJ founder Fathi Shiqaqi established guidelines for "exceptional" martyrdom operations involving human bombs. He followed Hezbollah in stressing that God extols martyrdom but abhors suicide: "Allah may cause to be known those who believe and may make some of you martyrs, and Allah may purify those who believe and may utterly destroy the disbelievers"; however, "no one can die except by Allah's leave".

The recent radicalization and networking through Al-Qaeda of militant Islamic groups from North Africa, Arabia, and Central and Southeast Asia stems from the Soviet-Afghan War (1979–1989. With financial backing from the United States, members of these various groups were provided opportunities to pool and to unify doctrine, aim, training, equipment, and methods, including suicide attack. Through its multifaceted association with regional groups (by way of finance, personnel, and logistics), Al-Qaeda aims to realize flexibly its global ambition of destroying Western dominance through local initiatives to expel Western influences. According to Jane's Intelligence Review: "All the suicide terrorist groups have support infrastructures in Europe and North America".

Calling the current wave of radical Islam "fundamentalism" (in the sense of "traditionalism") is misleading, approaching an oxymoron. Present-day radicals, whether Shi'ite (Iran, Hezbollah) or Sunni (Taliban, Al-Qaeda), are much closer in spirit and action to Europe's post-Renaissance Counter-Reformation than to any traditional aspect of Moslem history. The idea of a ruling ecclesiastical authority, a state or national council of clergy, and a religious police devoted to physically rooting out heretics and blasphemers has its clearest historical model in the Holy Inquisition. The idea that religion must struggle to assert control over politics is radically new to Islam.

Dubious Public Perceptions

Recent treatments of Homeland Security research concentrate on how to spend billions to protect sensitive installations from attack. But this last line of defense is probably easiest to breach because of the multitude of vulnerable and likely targets (including discotheques, restaurants, and malls), the abundance of would-be attackers (needing little supervision once embarked on a mission), the relatively low costs of attack (hardware store ingredients, no escape needs), the difficulty of detection (little use of electronics), and the unlikelihood that attackers would divulge sensitive information (being unaware of connections beyond their operational cells).

Exhortations to put duct tape on windows may assuage (or incite) fear, but will not prevent massive loss of life, and public realization of such paltry defense can undermine trust. Security agencies also attend to prior lines of defense, such as penetrating agent-handling networks of terrorist groups, with only intermittent success. A first line of defense is to prevent people from becoming terrorists. Here, success appears doubtful—should current government and media opinions about why people become human bombs translate into policy.

Suicide terrorists often are labeled crazed cowards bent on senseless destruction who thrive in the midst of poverty and ignorance. The obvious course becomes to hunt down terrorists while simultaneously transforming their supporting cultural and economic environment from despair to hope. What research there is, however, indicates that suicide terrorists have no appreciable psychopathology and are at least as educated and economically well off as their surrounding populations.

A Fundamental Attribution Error

U.S. President George W. Bush initially branded 9/11 hijackers "evil cowards." For U.S. Senator John Warner, preemptive assaults on terrorists and those supporting terrorism are justified because: "Those who would commit suicide in their assaults on the free world are not rational and are not deterred by rational concepts". In attempting to counter anti-Moslem sentiment, some groups advised their members to respond that "terrorists are extremist maniacs who don't represent Islam at all".

Social psychologists have investigated the "fundamental attribution error," a tendency for people to explain behaviour in terms of individual personality traits, even when significant situational factors in the larger society are at work. U.S. government and media characterizations of Middle East suicide bombers as craven homicidal lunatics may suffer from a fundamental attribution error. No instances of religious or political suicide terrorism stem from lone actions of cowering or unstable bombers. Psychologist Stanley Milgram found that ordinary Americans also readily obey destructive orders under the right circumstances.

When told by a "teacher" to administer potentially life-threatening electric shocks to "learners" who fail to memorize word pairs, most comply. Even when subjects stressfully protest as victims plead and scream, use of extreme violence continues—not because of murderous tendencies but from a sense of obligation in situations of authority, no matter how trite. A legitimate hypothesis is that apparently extreme behaviours may be elicited and rendered commonplace by particular historical, political, social, and ideological contexts.

With suicide terrorism, the attribution problem is to understand why nonpathological individuals respond to novel situational factors in numbers sufficient for recruiting organizations to implement policies. In the Middle East, perceived contexts in which suicide bombers and supporters express themselves include a collective sense of historical injustice, political subservience, and social humiliation vis-a'-vis global powers and allies, as well as countervailing religious hope. Addressing such perceptions does not entail accepting them as simple reality; however, ignoring the causes of these perceptions risks misidentifying causes and solutions for suicide bombing. There is also evidence that people tend to believe that their behaviour speaks for itself, that they see the world objectively, and that only other people are biased and misconstrue events.

Moreover, individuals tend to misperceive differences between group norms as more extreme than they really are. Resulting misunderstandings —encouraged by religious and ideological propaganda—lead antagonistic groups to interpret each other's views of events, such as terrorism/freedom-fighting, as wrong, radical, and/or irrational. Mutual demonization and warfare readily ensue. The problem is to stop this spiral from escalating in opposing camps.

Across our society, there is wide consensus that ridding society of poverty rids it of crime. According to President Bush, "We fight poverty because hope is the answer to terror... We will challenge the poverty and hopelessness and lack of education and failed governments that too often allow conditions that terrorists can seize". At a gathering of Nobel Peace Prize laureates, South Africa's Desmond Tutu and South Korea's Kim Dae Jong opined, "at the bottom of terrorism is poverty"; Elie Wiesel and the Dalai Lama concluded, "education is the way to eliminate terrorism".

Support for this comes from research pioneered by economist Gary Becker showing that property crimes are predicted by poverty and lack of education. In his incentive-based model, criminals are rational individuals acting on self-interest. Individuals choose illegal activity if rewards exceed probability of detection and incarceration together with expected loss of income from legal activity ("opportunity costs"). Insofar as criminals lack skill and education, as in much bluecollar crime, opportunity costs may be minimal; so crime pays.

Such rational-choice theories based on economic opportunities do not reliably account for some types of violent crimes (domestic homicide, hate killings). These calculations make even less sense for suicide terrorism. Suicide terrorists generally are not lacking in legitimate life opportunities relative to their general population. As the Arab press emphasizes, if martyrs had nothing to lose, sacrifice would be senseless: "He who commits suicide kills himself for his own benefit, he who commits martyrdom sacrifices himself for the sake of his religion and his nation... The Mujahed is full of hope".

Research by Krueger and Maleckova suggests that education may be uncorrelated, or even positively correlated, with supporting terrorism. In a December 2001 poll of 1357 West Bank and Gaza Palestinians 18 years of age or older, those having 12 or more years of schooling supported armed attacks by 68 points, those with up to 11 years of schooling by 63 points, and illiterates by 46 points. Only 40% of persons with advanced degrees supported dialogue with Israel versus 53% with college degrees and 60% with 9 years or less of schooling.

In a comparison of Hezbollah militants who died in action with a random sample of Lebanese from the same age group and region, militants were less likely to come from poor homes and more likely to have had secondary school education. More recently, Krueger and colleagues found that although one third of Palestinians live in poverty, only 13 percent of Palestinian suicide bombers do; 57 percent of bombers have education beyond high school versus 15 percent of the population of comparable age.

Nevertheless, relative loss of economic or social advantage by educated persons might encourage support for terrorism. In the period leading to the first Intifada (1982–1988), the number of Palestinian men with 12 years or more of schooling more than doubled; those with less schooling increased only 30%. This coincided with a sharp increase in unemployment for college graduates relative to high school graduates. Real daily wages of college graduates fell some 30%; wages for those with only secondary schooling held steady. Underemployment also seems to be a factor among those recruited to Al-Qaeda and its allies from the Arabian Peninsula.

The Institutional Factor

Although humiliation and despair may help account for susceptibility to martyrdom in some situations, this is neither a complete explanation nor one applicable to other circumstances. Studies by psychologist Ariel Merari point to the importance of institutions in suicide terrorism. His team interviewed 32 of 34 bomber families in Palestine/Israel (before 1998), surviving attackers,and captured recruiters.

Suicide terrorists apparently span their population's normal distribution in terms of education, socioeconomic status, and personality type (introvert vs. extrovert). Mean age for bombers was early twenties. Almost all were unmarried and expressed religious belief before recruitment (but no more than did the general population). Except for being young, unattached males, suicide bombers differ from members of violent racist organizations with whom they are often compared.

Overall, suicide terrorists exhibit no socially dysfunctional attributes (fatherless, friendless, or jobless) or suicidal symptoms. They do not vent fear of enemies or express "hopelessness" or a sense of "nothing to lose" for lack of life alternatives that would be consistent with economic rationality. Merari attributes primary responsibility for attacks to recruiting organizations, which enlist prospective candidates from this youthful and relatively unattached population. Charismatic trainers then intensely cultivate mutual commitment to die within small cells of three to six members. The final step before a martyrdom operation is a formal social contract, usually in the form of a video testament.

From 1996 to 1999 Nasra Hassan, a Pakistani relief worker, interviewed nearly 250 Palestinian recruiters and trainers, failed suicide bombers, and relatives of deceased bombers. Bombers were men aged 18 to 38: "None were uneducated, desperately poor, simple-minded, or depressed... They all seemed to be entirely normal members of their families". Yet "all were deeply religious," believing their actions "sanctioned by the divinely revealed religion of Islam." Leaders of sponsoring organizations complained, "Our biggest problem is the hordes of young men who beat on our doors."

Psychologist Brian Barber surveyed 900 Moslem adolescents during Gaza's first Intifada (1987–1993). Results show high levels of participation in and victimization from violence. For males, 81% reported throwing stones, 66% suffered physical assault, and 63% were shot at (versus 51%, 38%, and 20% for females). Involvement in violence was not strongly correlated with depression or antisocial behaviour. Adolescents most involved displayed strong individual pride and social cohesion.

This was reflected in activities: for males, 87% delivered supplies to activists, 83% visited martyred families, and 71% tended the wounded (57, 46, and 37% for females). A follow-up during the second Intifada (2000 –2002) indicates that those still unmarried act in ways considered personally more dangerous but socially more meaningful. Increasingly, many view martyr acts as most meaningful. By summer 2002, 70 to 80% of Palestinians endorsed martyr operations.

Previously, recruiters scouted mosques, schools, and refugee camps for candidates deemed susceptible to intense religious indoctrination and logistical training. During the second Intifada, there has been a surfeit of volunteers and increasing involvement of secular organizations (allowing women). The frequency and violence of suicide attacks have escalated (more bombings since February 2002 than during 1993--2000); planning has been less painstaking. Despite these changes, there is little to indicate overall change in bomber profiles (mostly unmarried, average socioeconomic status, moderately religious).

In contrast to Palestinians, surveys with a control group of Bosnian Moslem adolescents from the same time period reveal markedly weaker expressions of self-esteem, hope for the future, and prosocial behaviour. A key difference is that Palestinians routinely invoke religion to invest personal trauma with proactive social meaning that takes injury as a badge of honor. Bosnian Moslems typically report not considering religious affiliation a significant part of personal or collective identity until seemingly arbitrary violence forced awareness upon them.

Thus, a critical factor determining suicide terrorism behaviour is arguably loyalty to intimate cohorts of peers, which recruiting organizations often promote through religious communion.

Consider data on 39 recruits to Harkat al-Ansar, a Pakistani-based ally of Al-Qaeda. All were unmarried males, most had studied the Quran. All believed that by sacrificing themselves they would help secure the future of their "family" of fictive kin: "Each [martyr] has a special place—among them are brothers, just as there are sons and those even more dear". A Singapore Parliamentary report on 31 captured operatives from Jemaah Islamiyah and other Al-Qaeda allies in Southeast Asia underscores the pattern: "These men were not ignorant, destitute or disenfranchised.

All 31 had received secular education... Like many of their counterparts in militant Islamic organizations in the region, they held normal, respectable jobs... As a group, most of the detainees regarded religion as their most important personal value... secrecy over the true knowledge of jihad, helped create a sense of sharing and empowerment vis-a`-vis others".

Such sentiments characterize institutional manipulation of emotionally driven commitments that may have emerged under natural selection's influence to refine or override short-term rational calculations that would otherwise preclude achieving goals against long odds. Most typically, such emotionally driven commitments serve as survival mechanisms to inspire action in otherwise paralyzing circumstances, as when a weaker person convincingly menaces a stronger person into thinking twice before attempting to take advantage. In religiously inspired suicide terrorism, however, these emotions are purposely manipulated by organizational leaders, recruiters, and trainers to benefit the organization rather than the individual.

Little tangible benefit (in terms of rational choice theories) accrues to the suicide bomber, certainly not enough to make the likely gain one of maximized "expected utility." Heightened social recognition occurs only after death, obviating personal material benefit. But for leaders who almost never consider killing themselves (despite declarations of readiness to die), material benefits more likely outweigh losses in martyrdom operations. Hassan cites one Palestinian official's prescription for a successful mission: "a willing young man... nails, gunpowder, a light switch and a short cable, mercury (readily obtainable from thermometers), acetone... The most expensive item is transportation to an Israeli town". The total cost is about $150.

For the sponsoring organization, suicide bombers are expendable assets whose losses generate more assets by expanding public support and pools of potential recruits. Shortly after 9/11, an intelligence survey of educated Saudis (ages 25 to 41) concluded that 95% supported Al-Qaeda. In a December 2002 Pew Research Center survey on growing anti-Americanism, only 6% of Egyptians viewed America and its "War on Terror" favourably. Money flows from those willing to let others die, easily offsetting operational costs (training, supporting personnel, safe houses, explosives and other arms, transportation, and communication). After a Jerusalem supermarket bombing by an 18-year-old Palestinian female, a Saudi telethon raised more than $100 million for "the Al-Quds Intifada"

Massive retaliation further increases people's sense of victimization and readiness to behave according to organizational doctrines and policies structured to take advantage of such feelings. In a poll of 1179 West Bank and Gaza Palestinians in spring 2002, 66% said army operations increased their backing for suicide bombings. By year's end, 73% of Lebanese Moslems considered suicide bombings justifiable. This radicalization of opinion increases both demand and supply for martyrdom operations. A December 2002 UN report credited volunteers with swelling a reviving Al-Qaeda in 40 countries. The organization's influence in the larger society—most significantly its directing elites—increases in turn.

The last line of defense against suicide terrorism — preventing bombers from reaching targets—may be the most expensive and least likely to succeed. Random bag or body searches cannot be very effective against people willing to die, although this may provide some semblance of security and hence psychological defense against suicide terrorism's psychological warfare. A middle line of defense, penetrating and destroying recruiting organizations and isolating their leaders, may be successful in the near term, but even more resistant organizations could emerge instead.

The first line of defense is to drastically reduce receptivity of potential recruits to recruiting organizations. But how? It is important to know what probably will not work. Raising literacy rates may have no effect and could be counterproductive should greater literacy translate into greater exposure to terrorist propaganda (in Pakistan, literacy and dislike for the United States increased as the number of religious madrasa schools increased from 3000 to 39,000 since 1978). Lessening poverty may have no effect, and could be counterproductive if poverty reduction for the entire population amounted to a downward redistribution of wealth that left those initially better off with fewer opportunities than before.

Ending occupation or reducing perceived humiliation may help, but not if the population believes this to be a victory inspired by terror (e.g., Israel's apparently forced withdrawal from Lebanon). If suicide-bombing is crucially (though not exclusively) an institution-level phenomenon, it may require finding the right mix of pressure and inducements to get the communities themselves to abandon support for institutions that recruit suicide attackers. One way is to damage the community's social and political fabric so that any support by the local population or authorities for sponsors of suicide attacks collapses, as happened regarding the kamikaze as a by-product of the nuclear destruction of Hiroshima and Nagasaki.

In the present world, however, such a strategy would neither be morally justifiable nor practical to implement, given the dispersed and distributed organization of terrorist institutions among distantly separated populations that collectively number in the hundreds of millions. Likewise, retaliation in kind ("tit-for-tat") is not morally acceptable if allies are sought. Even in more localized settings, such as the Israeli-Palestinian conflict, coercive policies alone may not achieve lasting relief from attack and can exacerbate the problem over time. On the inducement side, social psychology research indicates that people who identify with antagonistic groups use conflicting information from the other group to reinforce antagonism. Thus, simply trying to persuade others, without bombarding them with more self-serving information, may only increase hostility.

Other research suggests that most people have more moderate views than what they consider their group norm to be. Inciting and empowering moderates from within to confront inadequacies and inconsistencies in their own knowledge (of others as evil), values (respect for life), and behaviour (support for killing), and other members of their group, can produce emotional dissatisfaction leading to lasting change and influence on the part of these individuals. Funding for civic education and debate may help, also interfaith confidence-building through intercommunity interaction initiatives (as Singapore's government proposes). Ethnic profiling, isolation, and preemptive attack on potential (but not yet actual) supporters of terrorism probably will not help.

Another strategy is for the United States and its allies to change behaviour by directly addressing and lessening sentiments of grievance and humiliation, especially in Palestine (where images of daily violence have made it the global focus of Moslem attention). For no evidence (historical or otherwise) indicates that support for suicide terrorism will evaporate without complicity in achieving at least some fundamental goals that suicide bombers and supporting communities share. Of course, this does not mean negotiating over all goals, such as Al-Qaeda's quest to replace the Western-inspired system of nation-states with a global caliphate, first in Moslem lands and then everywhere. Unlike other groups, Al-Qaeda publicizes no specific demands after martyr actions. As with an avenging army, it seeks no compromise. But most people who currently sympathize with it might.

Perhaps to stop the bombing we need research to understand which configurations of psychological and cultural relationships are luring and binding thousands, possibly millions, of mostly ordinary people into the terrorist organization's martyr-making web. Study is needed on how terrorist institutions form and on similarities and differences across organizational structures, recruiting practices, and populations recruited. Are there reliable differences between religious and secular groups, or between ideologically driven and grievance-driven terrorism? Interviews with surviving Hamas bombers and captured Al-Qaeda operatives suggest that ideology and grievance are factors for both groups but relative weights and consequences may differ.

We also need to investigate any significant causal relations between our society's policies and actions and those of terrorist organizations and supporters. We may find that the global economic, political, and cultural agenda of our own society has a catalyzing role in moves to retreat from our world view (Taliban) or to create a global counterweight (Al-Qaeda). Funding such research may be difficult. As with the somewhat tendentious and self-serving use of "terror" as a policy concept, to reduce dissonance our governments and media may wish to ignore these relations as legitimate topics for inquiry into what terrorism is all about and why it exists. This call for research may demand more patience than any administration could politically tolerate during times of crisis. In the long run, however, our society can ill afford to ignore either the consequences of its own actions or the causes behind the actions of others. Potential costs of such ignorance are terrible to contemplate. The comparatively minor expense of research into such consequences and causes could have inestimable benefit.

Two important documents crucial to the War on Terrorism were recently released in the United States. On May 23, the U.S. General Accounting Office delivered its final report to Congress on "Combating Terrorism". On June 3, the Pew Research Center published the latest installment of a multiyear survey on global attitudes to political policies and social values. The GAO report does not evaluate the effectiveness of anti-terrorist programs, and the Pew survey of 15,000 people in 21 nations does not inquire into reasons for global attitudes. Nevertheless, the Pew findings, together with recent research on the socio-economic backgrounds of terrorists and their supporters, seriously undermine the rationale and prognosis for the War on Terrorism.

According to GAO, funding to combat overseas terrorism increased 133 percent from 2001 to $11.4 billion for fiscal 2004. In addition, the Department of Defense spent $30 billion on military operations against terrorism in 2002 alone (considerably more in 2003, including 78.7 billion voted for a war against Iraq primarily billed as depriving terrorists of weapons of mass destruction). Despite detailed review of actions related to billions spent by dozens of federal civilian and military agencies there is little mention of funding or efforts to understand or prevent people becoming terrorists in the first place.

Moreover, the fact that the number of suicide attacks by Al-Qaeda (or its allies) and by Palestinian bombers one month after Baghdad's fall (5 in Israel, 3 in Saudi Arabia, 5 in Morocco) was higher than for every month in the preceding year suggests that, contrary to earlier claims by President Bush and others in the U.S. Administration and media, the war on terrorism has not appreciably diminished the scourge of suicide attack – the most devastating form of terrorism. GAO describes interagency efforts to "defeat and prevent terrorism". Prevention focuses on the goal of "diminishing the underlying conditions that terrorists seek to exploit", as presented in the President's National Strategy for Combating Terrorism (released in February to elaborate Section III of the new National Security Strategy of the United States).

NSCT is prefaced by "an understanding of the terrorist threat" as outlined in the President's Address to Congress on September 20, 2001: America was attacked because the 9/11 plotters "hate our freedoms" and democracy, and they incite hatred among their supporters by exploiting "conditions of poverty, deprivation, social disenfranchisement". Accordingly, a U.S. State Department report issued on the first anniversary of 9/11 said that development aid should be based on "the belief that poverty provides a breeding ground for terrorism". But the Pew findings indicate that populations supporting terrorist actions are actually disposed favourably to American forms of government, education, economy and personal liberty, despite these people's trust in Osama Bin Laden and support for suicide actions.

Studies by Palestinian political scientist Khalil Shikaki suggest that upwards of 80% of Palestinians consider Israel to have the most admirable form of government, with America next, although numerous polls indicate that 60-70% of Palestinians also express support for suicide attack. An earlier Zogby poll of Arab impressions of America shows the same pattern of support for America's freedoms and democracy but rejection of its dealings with others – a pattern that undercuts the thesis of a "clash of civilizations" or NSCT's conclusion of "a clash between civilization and those who would destroy it".

Newer studies also confirm earlier reports showing that suicide terrorists and their supporters are not impoverished, uneducated, spiteful, or socially disfavoured. Palestinian economist Basel Saleh compiled information on 171 militants killed in action (nearly all during the Second

Intifada, 2000-2003) from Hamas and Palestinian Islamic Jihad (PIJ) news services, including 87 suicide attackers.

Majorities of militants were unmarried males (20-29 yrs.), from families with both parents living and 6-10 siblings, and who completed secondary school or attended college. Suicide attackers, which included bombers and shooters, had more pronounced tendencies in these directions. A majority of Hamas bombers attended college; PIJ had more shooters aged 14-19. Majorities of bombers, but few shooters, had prior histories of arrest or injury by Israel's army; however, most shooters had one or more family members with such histories. This underscores the earlier speculation that personal grievance could be a greater factor in Palestinian cases than for Al-Qaeda and its ideological allies.

Sources with the U.S. Army Defense Intelligence Agency provided summaries of interrogations with detainees at Guantanamo, Cuba. Saudi-born operatives, especially those in leadership positions, are often "educated above reasonable employment level... a surprising number have graduate degrees and come from high-status families." Motivation and commitment are evident in the willingness to sacrifice material and emotional comforts (families, jobs, physical security), and to pay their own way from their homes to travel long distances. Many told interrogators that if released from detention they would return to Jihad. Detainees evince little history of personal grievance, but frequently cite older relatives and respected community members who participated in earlier Jihads as influencing decisions to join the fight.

Yemenis have more modest education and social status, and are often recruited and financed through mosques in Yemen and abroad (especially England). As with Hamas and PIJ, religious indoctrination by Al-Qaeda and allies (of recruits who initially express only moderate religiosity) appears crucial to creating intimate cells of fictive kin whose members commit to willingly die for one another. All 9/11 attackers, including 15 Saudis and 4 others of Middle Eastern origin, were young, single males from middle class families. All were recruited in Europe by religious organizations connected with Al-Qaeda, when most were enrolled in a secular higher education curriculum. No "personality" defects were evident before the attack, and none discovered in hindsight (despite intense scrutiny).

Social psychologists have long documented what they call "the fundamental attribution error". This interpretation bias seems to be especially prevalent in "individualistic" cultures, such as those of the United States and Western Europe. In contrast, many cultures (in Africa and Asia) in which a "collectivist" ethic is more prevalent show less susceptibility to such judgments. U.S. government and media characterizations of Middle East suicide bombers as homicidal maniacs may also suffer from a fundamental attribution error: there is no instance of religious or political suicide terrorism resulting from the lone action of a mentally unstable bomber (e.g., a suicidal Unabomber) or even of someone acting entirely under his own authority and responsibility (e.g., a suicidal Timothy McVeigh).

What leads a normal person to suicide terrorism? Part of the answer may lie in philosopher Hannah Arendt's notion of the "banality of evil", which she used to describe the fact that mostly ordinary Germans were recruited to man Nazi extermination camps, not sadistic lunatics. (Milgram interpreted his experiments on obedience to authority among American adults as confirming Arendt's thesis). The primacy of situational over personality factors suggests the futility of attempts to psychologically profile the suicide terrorist. A Federal Interagency report on "The Sociology and Psychology of Terrorism" in current use by the CIA, and which includes detailed literature reviews and psychological profiles of Al-Qaeda, Hamas and other suicide-sponsoring organization leaders, states: "People who have joined terrorist groups have come from a wide variety of cultures, nationalities and ideological causes, all strata of society, and diverse populations. Their personalities and characteristics are as diverse as those of people in the general population. There seems to be a general agreement among psychologists that there is no particular psychological attribute that can be used to describe the terrorist or any 'personality' that is distinctive of terrorists". Months – sometimes years – of intense indoctrination can lead to "blind obedience" no matter who the individual, as indicated in research on people who become torturers for their governments.

It is the particular genius of institutions, like Al-Qaeda, Hamas or Hezbollah, that takes ordinary people into a mind-set of historical, political and religious grievance and turns them into human bombs. Intense indoctrination often lasting 18 months or more causes recruits to identify emotionally with their small cell (typically 3-8 members), viewing it as a family of fictive kin for whom they are as willing to die as a mother for her child or a soldier for his buddies. Like good advertisers, the charismatic leaders of martyr-sponsoring organizations turn ordinary desires for family and religion into cravings for what they're pitching, to the benefit of the manipulating organization rather than the individual being manipulated (much as the pornography industry turns universal and innate desires for sexual mates into lust for paper or electronic images to ends that reduce personal fitness but benefit the manipulators).

Despite numerous studies of individual behaviour in group contexts that show situation to be a much better predictor than personality, the Pew survey finds that Americans overwhelmingly believe that personal decision, success and failure depend upon individual choice, responsibility and personality. Most of the world disagrees. This is plausibly one reason for which Americans tend to think of terrorists as "homicidal maniacs", whereas the rest of the world tends not to.

Whether because of a fundamental attribution error, or willful blindness to avoid dissonance with one's own worldview, Americans mostly view attempts to understand what motivates terrorism as at best a waste of time, at worst pandering to terrorism. But countering terrorism also requires facing problems with our own society's appraisals and actions. Such considerations are wholly absent from the GAO report and the NSCT. What these people dislike is not America's internal liberties or culture, but its external actions and foreign policy. A 1997 U.S. Department of Defense Science Board report surmises (in response to the suicide bombing of U.S. Air Force housing at Khobar Towers in Saudia Arabia): "Historical data show a strong correlation between U.S. involvement in international situations and an increase in terrorist attacks against the United States".

There seems to be a direct correlation between U.S. military and counterinsurgency aid, human rights abuses by the governments aided, and rise in terrorism. Amnesty International and Human Rights Watch regularly document "horrific" and "massive" humans rights abuses occurring in those countries that receive the most U.S. aid in absolute terms. Thus, the U.S. State Dept. 2003 budget for Foreign Military Financing is $4.107 billion. The FMF budget includes as its top receivers: $2.1 billion for Israel, $1.3 billion for Egypt, $98 million for Colombia, $50 million for Pakistan.

Special Economic Support Funds were also budgeted as part of emergency supplemental bills: $600 million for Pakistan; $40.5 million in economic and law enforcement assistance for Uzbekistan; $45 million in FMF for Turkey and Uzbekistan; $42.2 million for training and equipment for border security forces in the Central Asian Republics (Uzbekistan, Tajikistan, Turkmenistan, Turkey, Kyrgyzstan,

Azerbaijan, Kazakhstan); and additional millions in special Defense Department funds for counterterrorism training and operations in the Central Asian Republics and Georgia. A recent National Research Council report, "Discouraging Terrorism," finds that: "With respect to political context, terrorism and its supporting audiences appear to be fostered by policies of extreme political repression and discouraged by policies of incorporating both dissident and moderate groups responsibly into civil society and the political process".

The situation may be critical in Central Asia, one area of intensified U.S. intervention where anti-American and pro-Radical Islamic sentiment is rapidly rising, and where Al-Qaeda appears to be relocating. The GAO report highlights two key objectives in realizing the NSCT goal of diminishing support for terrorism: strengthening the "Partnership Initiative" and winning the "War of Ideas." The NSCT's Partnership Initiative involves counterterrorism aid, including law enforcement training and military assistance, "intended to promote U.S. national security interests by contributing to global and regional stability, strengthening military support for democratically-elected governments" and fostering "democratic values including respect for internationally recognized civil and human rights" (GAO, pp. 119-120). Winning the "War of Ideas" involves foreign aid programs and media broadcasts to promote democratic values "to kindle the hopes and aspirations of freedom." (NSCT, p. 14)

The "new partners in the war on terrorism" cited in the GAO report are the Eurasian Republics of Kazakhistan, Kyrgystan, Tajikistan, Turkmenistan, Uzbekistan, Georgia. (GAO, p. 24) All but one of them is run by a former Communist Party leader-turned-nationalist, whose rule – like Saddam's – involves a brutal personality cult. All have been condemned by Amnesty International and Human Rights Watch for increasing human rights abuses. As for winning the War of Ideas about democracy and personal freedoms, the Pew survey strongly suggests that Muslim opinion in favour of these values means that war was already won. This raises suspicion that the call to battle against haters of democracy and freedom – like the alarms about Iraq's imminent use of weapons of mass destruction and its ties to Al-Qaeda - was cynically designed to rally the home front for a strategic push into South and Central Asia. The Pew survey intimates that much of the world – apart from America – thinks so.

12

Future of Terrorism

In order to assess the future threat posed by terrorism one must bear in mind the changes which have made terrorism a new force in analyses of world order. The main areas in these changes are transport and communication, weaponry, the effects on society of concentration of vital functions on a decreasing number of critical nodes, and changes in social structure and attitudes. With the advancement of science and technology, developments in these areas have made terrorism a different and more sinister threat than it has been in the past. The question for the future is will these developments continue and will they magnify the threat which we already recognise is posed by terrorism?

The transport and communications sectors are unlikely to see significant improvements, at least in the near future, which may have major implications for the scope and incidence of terrorism.

Whilst particular targets in these areas may become more attractive, the changes which gave terrorism greater impact have already taken place. The ease of movement around the world made possible by the expansion of the airline industry, in particular, and the spread of ideas and ease of relaying news of terrorist incidents made possible by communications advances are now everyday features of our existence. There are no foreseeable changes in these areas of a sort, such as, will enable a quantum leap in the leverage terrorism can exert or the ease with which operations can be conducted.

Availability of Weapons

The same cannot be said, however, in the case of the development and availability of weapons. The rate of turnover of conventional weapons by the world's military forces has increased dramatically in recent times and many of these weapons are finding their way into the open market. It is inevitable that in the future any group which is determined to do so will be able to purchase or steal powerful, conventional weapons. Given the rate at which weapons now become obsolescent, the arms which will find their way into the hands of a large number of terrorist outfits will be very sophisticated by past standards capable of operation at a considerable distance from the target and with significantly increased destructive power.

The fact that states are more involved in backing terrorist groups than in the past also means that it is easier for the latter to gain access to sophisticated arms in significant quantities. The increasing involvement of states with terrorist groups means increasing availability of various forms of high explosives which are extremely powerful in relation to their bulk and which can be moulded to fit any shape or cavity, thus making them easy to conceal, and are difficult to detect by conventional screening methods.

Some counter-measures are now available or being developed to counter this particular threat. However, though more sophisticated detection devices are being evaluated, the reality is that as detection capability becomes more refined, so the composition of explosives is altered with the consequence that totally successful screening will never be possible.

Similarly, while there is a strong case to be made for responsible governments to legislate to mandate the inclusion of microtaggants (tiny chips conveying information about the type, manufacturer, batch, seller, etc.) in explosives at the time of manufacture which would facilitate their detection, tracing and identification, the reality again is that many countries will continue to supply explosives not so treated to those who use terrorist tactics.

Frightening Prospect

To many people, the most frightening prospect for the future is that terrorist groups might gain access to and use weapons of mass destruction, specifically, nuclear, biological or biochemical weapons. Most attention to date has been directed to the possibility of some form of nuclear material falling into terrorist hands. There are a number of readily conceivable scenarios. One would involve the terrorist seizure of a nuclear facility under threat of having the facility sabotaged, thus releasing radioactive material over a large area. Given the level of security that has been shown to exist at some nuclear power plants in the past, it is not inconceivable that a determined group of well-equipped and well-organised terrorists could assault and take over a nuclear facility. If Al Qaeda could make an assault on the Pentagon, seizure of a nuclear power plant is comparatively a much easier job.

Other scenarios involve the acquisition of a nuclear weapon by a terrorist group. A number of possibilities exist here. One is that a nuclear weapon state may supply a terrorist group with such a weapon. Theoretically more likely is the theft of a nuclear device from a military storage point. The fact that a U.S. rocket could be smuggled out of West Germany, as occurred some years ago, indicates that subterfuge sometimes may also be successful. Probably the most controversial possibility is that of terrorists being able to construct their own crude nuclear device. Experts differ as to the feasibility of such a project.

However, much of the data needed to design a nuclear bomb are now freely available, as was documented by a highly publicized television science programme which in March 1975 featured a 20-year-old undergraduate from Massachusetts Institute of Technology who had designed a technically conceivable nuclear bomb. It would appear, then, that a sufficiently dedicated terrorist group could overcome the technical difficulties and construct a credible nuclear bomb. In all probability the capability already exists.

There can be little doubt, then, that it will be soon possible (if not already) to mount a credible terrorist attack involving nuclear, biological or biochemical agents. The one factor which holds this eventuality in abeyance would appear to be a rational calculation concerning what would be achieved by such an act. It is generally conceded that terrorists make rational calculations and that these show the use of mass destruction weapons to be counter-productive. Will this be so in the future?

The future looks bleak as far as forms of political violence in general, and terrorism as a specific technique, are concerned. Many of the factors that have led to the elevation of terrorism as a serious threat to open societies will be exacerbated in the future. To fail to respond firmly to the threat would be to give up a cherished way of life without fighting for it.

Paying For the War on Terrorism

Shortly after the terrorist attacks of September 11, 2001, President Bush pledged to prosecute a war against terrorism along multiple fronts, using every tool available. He promised not only to engage the U.S. military, but to pursue diplomatic efforts, intelligence measures, law enforcement actions, economic measures, media outreach activities, financial measures, security measures and preparations to respond to disasters should the other measures fail.

Since September 2001, the Bush administration and Congress have added hundreds of billions of dollars to federal budgets for national defense, homeland security, and international affairs. Most Americans would agree that some new spending was warranted, given the nature of the threat and America's evident lack of preparedness for it. Such added spending comes at the expense of other federal priorities, however. Thus, it is important to ensure that every dollar spent on national security, homeland security, recovery, or combating terrorism is spent wisely.

This chapter considers three fundamental alternatives for securing the nation: offense, defense, and prevention. After a discussion of terms it examines federal levels of spending since 9/11/2001 for the three main alternatives and asks how resources might be reallocated to provide more real security.

Three Ways to Improve Security

To illuminate the main tradeoffs involved among the options for improving national security in an era of global mass-casualty terrorism, it is helpful to group those options into three broad categories: offense, defense, and prevention. By offensive measures, generally mean military ones, including everything from raising and maintaining a strong force to conducting military operations like those in Iraq and Afghanistan. In addition, include U.S. efforts to collect, process, and disseminate intelligence upon which the military effort relies.

By defensive options, we mean those related to homeland security. They include, for example, law enforcement measures aimed at tracking down terrorists and bringing them to justice, border and aviation security, physical and cyber protection of critical facilities and systems, improvements to the public health infrastructure, and preparations to respond to and mitigate the consequences of attacks should they occur.

By preventive measures, we mean the non-military international measures aimed at reducing the likelihood of future acts of terrorism. They include assisting and rewarding foreign governments and individuals for their cooperation in the fight against terrorism, conducting diplomacy, helping other governments to secure their nuclear materials and weapons of mass destruction, reaching out to audiences abroad with positive messages about the United States, providing humanitarian assistance to populations affected by the fight, working to prevent failed states, and improving the economic conditions that might allow terrorists to gain a foothold in poor or failing states.

Experts agree that no strategy can completely insure the United States against future terrorist attacks. Moreover, it may not be possible to say with any assurance which specific activities will be the most effective in preventing future acts of terrorism, protecting against them, or mitigating their consequences. Nevertheless, the categories described here suggest a framework that can be useful in setting and articulating priorities and in assessing whether plans are balanced.

Since the autumn of 2001, the United States has added about $340 billion in new money to federal budgets for the military, homeland security, and international affairs. The large infusion of cash into national security budgets since September 11, 2001, is heavily weighted toward the offense. Of the new money, about $240 billion goes to the Department of Defense, about $60 billion pays for homeland security, and about $40 billion goes toward international affairs. In other words, since September 11, 2001, the United States has added four times as much money for offense as for defense, and six times as much for offense as for prevention.

When compared on an annual basis, the combined rise in spending for offense, defense, and prevention is enormous. For fiscal year 2004, budget authority in those three categories is nearly $160 billion higher (after accounting for inflation) than it was in the regular appropriation for 2001. That represents a real increase of more than 40 percent in those categories in just three years. To put the figure in perspective, the $160 billion rise in annual spending in those security-related accounts is about the same as the total federal bill for Medicaid this year.

Unfortunately, most of the $160 billion post-9/11 real increase in the annual budget for the three security categories will go not toward improving real security, but to operations in Iraq and business as usual in the Pentagon. The lion's share—more than $85 billion—goes for the occupation in Iraq. Of that money, $64 billion goes toward military operations there, while some $18.5 billion will pay for development and reconstruction of the occupied country.

The Bush administration argues that the war in Iraq is a necessary element of the fight against terrorism. Yet prewar links between Iraq and terrorists of global reach have not been clearly demonstrated. More troubling, current indications are that the war and its aftermath may be turning Iraq into a magnet and a breeding ground for terrorists, making the expense of the war there appear not only unnecessary to combating terrorism, but counterproductive to the fight.

Another fraction of the $160 billion will go toward countries that aid the United States in the Iraq occupation or in the fight against terrorism. About $1.5 billion goes toward a new foreign aid program targeted toward nations that embrace economic, legal, and political reforms. About $20 billion of the real increase in annual spending is devoted to homeland security, the defensive component of national security.

Outside of the spending for operations in Iraq, the Defense Department gained another $55 billion in its annual appropriation between 2001 and 2004, most of it for business as usual. Of the $55 billion, less than $15 billion goes to homeland security or combating terrorism, largely by beefing up physical security at U.S. military installations at home and abroad. Instead, several billion dollars go to new entitlements for military retirees - not the nation's 25 million living veterans, but the 1.7 million among them who served in the military for 20 years or more.

Most of the entitlement increase goes for a new health care benefit for retirees of Medicare age. While valued by those individuals, it does virtually nothing to help the military compete as an employer in American labor markets, and therefore will not help the nation in the fight against terrorism. A few billion dollars will go to work off backlogs in maintenance and repair of military buildings and equipment. But most of the military increase goes to develop and procure military hardware that has little or nothing to do with fighting terrorism: for ballistic missile defense, the Air Force F-22 air-to-air fighter, the Marine Corps V-22 tilt-rotor aircraft, the Army's Comanche helicopter and new Stryker combat vehicle, and the future F-35 Joint Strike Fighter. Thus, while the nation added a substantial amount of money across the three security categories after the autumn of 2001, there is good reason to doubt the contribution that spending will make toward real security.

As one might expect from the Bush administration's announced strategy of "taking the war to the enemy," this year's total spending for the three categories of security measures is also very heavily weighted toward the offense. Under current plans, the federal government will spend about $520 billion for offense, defense, and prevention in fiscal year 2004. Of that sum, about $440 billion will go to the military for non-homeland security functions. About $40 billion will pay for homeland security, and the remaining $40 billion will go toward international affairs, including reconstruction in Iraq. In other words, the United States will pay about eleven times as much for offense as for either defense or prevention this year.

Of course, no formula can prescribe the ideal weight of effort among offense, defense, and prevention. To the extent that preventive actions can keep terrorists from gaining a foothold in poor countries or avert terrorist acts from occurring, they would seem to be more important than either defensive or offensive measures. They may also be cheaper, however, making it inappropriate to judge their value based upon their cost. Yet it is not difficult to see that reallocating even relatively small amounts of the money devoted to offense this year could go a long way toward bolstering either prevention or defense.

For example, in 2003, the Council on Foreign Relations nonpartisan Task Force on Emergency Responders found that the United States is still "dangerously ill prepared to handle a catastrophic attack on American soil." The task force identified nearly $100 billion in funds needed over a five-year period to prepare local fire services, search and rescue teams, hospitals, public health systems, and other emergency responders to handle the types of disasters that could be caused by terrorism. If reallocated from offensive measures to first-responder preparedness, an annual expenditure of $20 billion would provide substantially more real security than spending the same amount on business-as-usual programs in the Defense Department.

Alternatively, for just $5 billion of the $64 billion the Defense Department received in the 2004 supplemental appropriation for the occupation in Iraq, we could inspect ten times as many containers at U.S. ports. For $4 billion, we could quadruple efforts to secure nuclear materials from the former Soviet Union. For about $12 billion, we could double our foreign aid spending. Any of those alternatives would provide substantially more bang for the buck in combating terrorism and providing real security for

Americans than the Iraq war. The administration touts a multi-faceted campaign to disrupt and destroy terrorism worldwide, one that balances military measures with diplomatic and economic efforts, law enforcement, financial measures, information, and intelligence. Looking at the problem of combating terrorism using the three categories suggested (offense, defense, and prevention) can help in thinking through the tradeoffs involved among the many choices.

Unfortunately, the changes in spending and plans since September 11 reflect far more of "business as usual" than one would hope. Too much of the enormous increase in defense spending between 2001 and 2004 goes to support Cold War forces and new military entitlements that will do little to improve the military's competitiveness as an employer. As a result, its contribution toward the war on terrorism will be far lower than it could be.

More troubling, except for less than $20 billion for nation-building in occupied Iraq, the share of new spending devoted to international programs that could prevent terrorism is pitifully small when compared with the enormous boost in spending for military solutions or the costs of military operations in Iraq. And despite a significant infusion of money since 9/11, homeland security appears to remain badly underfunded.

Responding to Terrorism

The number and lethality of international terrorist incidents directed against U.S. interests increased last year. The Riyadh and Al Khobar bombings in Saudi Arabia resulted in the largest number of U.S. fatalities at the hands of international terrorists since the December 1988 downing of Par. Am 103 over Lockerbie, Scotland. Terrorist violence represents a serious threat to U.S. personnel, facilities, and interests around the world.

Terrorism remains a complex phenomenon spawned by a mix of factors and motivations. Loosely organized groups of radical Islamics, such as those that carried out the bombing of the World Trade Center, pose a growing challenge. Established entrenched ethnic, nationalist, and religiously motivated terrorist movements continue to operate and have been joined by groups that espouse new causes and ideologies. Despite the collapse of the Soviet Union and international communism, leftist ideologically-based terrorists continue to operate. State sponsors of terrorism, particularly Iran, pose a significant continuing threat. Other state sponsors such as Syria, Libya, Iraq, and Sudan, although more cautious, provide safe haven and other forms of support to a variety of terrorist movements.

The world is in a period of transition and flux as it moves from the relative stability of the bipolar model to a new political order which has yet to be defined. The disintegration of the Soviet Union and the collapse of the East European communist regimes produced a power vacuum that has enabled nationalist, ethnic, and religious forces long thought dormant to reassert themselves and contribute to the volatility of the post-Cold War era. Violent militant Islamic elements, often with the help of state sponsors, now operate worldwide and have a demonstrated global reach.

Local and regional conflicts, famine, economic disparity, mass movements of refugees, brutal and corrupt regimes, and the increasing porosity of national borders contribute to instability — fueling a frustration and desperation that increasingly finds expression in acts of terrorism. Ready access to information and information technologies, coupled with the ability to communicate globally via the Internet, fax, and other media, provides terrorists new tools for targeting, fundraising, propaganda dissemination, and operational communications. Just as the established political order is in a state of fundamental flux and transition, so is terrorism and the challenge it presents to the United States, its friends, and its allies.

The terrorist threat has changed markedly in recent years, due primarily to five factors: the disintegration of the Soviet Union; changing terrorist motivations; the proliferation of technologies of mass destruction; increased access to information and information technologies; and the accelerated centralization of vital components of the national infrastructure, which has increased their vulnerability to terrorist attack. DoD expects that the majority of terrorism directed against U.S. targets will be tied to ethnic and religious conflicts. It will be primarily urban in nature, often occurring in capital cities. Terrorism for the foreseeable future will remain a weapon of choice for governments, groups, and other parties to conflict.

Traditionally, terrorist movements that affected U.S. security interests were politically motivated, and even the most brutal groups usually refrained from mass casualty operations for fear of alienating their political constituencies and potential recruits. Today, religiously motivated terrorism is increasingly ascendant. Religious zealots, when members of a terrorist group or cult, usually exhibit few such constraints and actively seek to maximize carnage. An additional threat comes from religious cults that view the coming millennium in apocalyptic terms and seek through violence to hasten Armageddon. DoD anticipates that as the year 2000 approaches, such movements will become increasingly prevalent, prominent, and lethal.

The proliferation of weapons of mass destruction and the availability of individuals schooled in their design and construction represent another development that impacts fundamentally on the nature of terrorism. The fragmentation of the former Soviet Union and the lack of adequate controls on biological, chemical, and nuclear technologies have resulted in a flood of buyers eager to purchase lethal material from an expanding black market or from rogue states. Added to this volatile mix are scientists and technicians prepared to sell their skills to the highest bidder.

An emerging and significant threat is represented by improvised biological, chemical, and nuclear devices that exploit technologies that once were the sole preserve of world and regional powers. The potential to decimate large population centers and wreak havoc on an unprecedented scale has devolved from nation states to groups and even individuals. The possibility of a biological Unabomber and all that implies is a fast approaching reality. Proliferation enables those who were traditionally at the margins to play a major role on the world stage. Improvised weapons of mass destruction will likely prove to be the great equalizers of tomorrow, providing the means for the disaffected and deranged to directly impact on the core interests of world powers.

Religious zealotry creates the will to carry out mass casualty terrorist attacks; proliferation provides the means. It is this nexus of will and means that has forever changed the face of terrorism. Traditional forms of terrorism like car bombs, assassinations, suicide bombers, and aircraft downings will undoubtedly continue, but their impact will diminish as the public becomes increasingly inured to such operations. In a world of competing headlines, terrorists will find it necessary to escalate the carnage in order to maintain their ability to intimidate and terrorize. As a result, increased experimentation with improvised biological, chemical, and nuclear devices may be expected as a means to rivet public attention and thereby advance the terrorist agenda.

Paradoxically, progress has made key elements of the national infrastructure increasingly vulnerable. These elements include telecommunications, energy distribution, banking and securities, transportation, military/defense, water supply, emergency services, and public health.

As countries modernize, they become increasingly dependent on sophisticated technologies, with computers both running and linking vital, once disparate systems into a national infrastructure. Because of its complexity and interdependence, infrastructure presents unique targeting opportunities to a technologically sophisticated adversary. Complex national infrastructures are vulnerable because they all have critical nodes or choke points that, if properly attacked, will result in significant disruption or destruction. The attack may be computer generated or rely on more conventional assaults employing truck bombs, dynamite, or cable cutting to unleash a chain of events in which a service grid, pipeline, or air traffic control system collapses in a cascading effect.

Major power failures that black out large parts of the country, systemic problems with the air traffic control system, and breaks in highly vulnerable gas and oil pipeline systems are covered in detail by the press, discussed on radio talk shows, and dissected and analyzed on the Internet. Terrorists, as part of the attentive public, are increasingly aware that the national infrastructure represents a high value and vulnerable target.

Technological advances may have the unintended consequence of increasing system vulnerabilities. For example, fiber optic cables enable phone companies to use a single line to carry tens of thousands of conversations that not many years ago would have required thousands of separate copper cables.

The results have been greater efficiency, better service, and lower costs; however, there is a downside. Progress has heightened infrastructure efficiency, but the resultant reduction in redundancy has produced vulnerabilities that make U.S. infrastructure an increasingly attractive terrorist target. International banking and finance, transportation, the electric grid, the gas pipeline system, computer links and services, and more than 90 percent of all DoD communications are dependent on the telephone system. Major disruptions in service can be caused by an errant backhoe operator or an enterprising terrorist.

DoD divides its response to terrorism into two categories. Antiterrorism refers to defensive measures used to reduce the vulnerability of individuals and property to terrorist acts. Counterterrorism refers to offensive measures taken to prevent, deter, and respond to terrorism. Both fall under the rubric of Combating Terrorism. Force Protection is the umbrella security program involving the coordinated efforts of key U.S. departments and agencies designed to protect military and civilian personnel, their family members, and U.S. property from terrorist acts.

In response to the recent tragedies in Saudi Arabia, the Joint Staff established a Deputy Directorate for Combating Terrorism under the Director of Operations, Joint Staff. The Directorate is charged with the mission of supporting the Chairman and the Joint Chiefs of Staff in meeting the nation's security challenges as they relate to combating terrorism now and into the next century.

DoD also has been a leader in recognizing the vulnerability of the national infrastructure. To obtain a better understanding of the nature and extent of the problem, the Under Secretary of Defense for Policy on March 9, 1995, established the Infrastructure Policy Directorate. Its primary responsibilities relate to infrastructure warfare and information assurance. The Directorate has briefed senior government and cabinet officials and is conducting an in-depth examination of key infrastructure elements to determine how they interrelate and how best to protect them from attack. A series of working groups have been established to ensure continuity of effort.

To meet the challenge, the Deputy Secretary of Defense in August 1996 established the Critical Infrastructure Protection Working Group (CIPWG) to support actions directed in Executive Order 13010, Critical Infrastructure Protection, which was signed by the President on July 15, 1996. The CIPWG addresses issues related to threats and vulnerabilities of the defense infrastructure and information systems, develops recommendations for assurance technologies and procedures, and examines roles for DoD in infrastructure protection and assurance.

Antiterrorism

In recognition of the changing nature of the terrorist threat, DoD on August 27, 1996, established the Antiterrorism Coordinating Committee (ATCC). The committee meets monthly, as well as on an as needed basis. Its purpose is to identify issues that affect force protection, exchange ideas and information, and develop policy recommendations. It also serves a valuable function by providing a synergism that enhances the effectiveness of DoD's antiterrorism planning. The Assistant Secretary of Defense for Special Operations and Low-Intensity Conflict and the Joint Staff Director for Operations co-chair the ATCC Senior Steering Group. Meetings are attended by representatives from the Services; the Joint Staff; the Office of the Assistant Secretary of Defense for Command, Control, communications and Intelligence; the Defense Security Assistance Agency; the Defense Intelligence Agency (DIA); and other DoD elements as required.

To further the exchange of knowledge and experience, for the past seven years DoD has sponsored the Annual Worldwide Antiterrorism Conference. These conferences not only draw on the expertise of the U.S. antiterrorism community but on an international array of security, intelligence, and law enforcement specialists who offer new insights, perspectives, and recommendations for action.

Each conference focuses on a particular theme and specific force protection issues.

The 1996 theme was changing the terrorism mindset. Conference participants explored ways to make antiterrorism increasingly proactive rather than primarily defensive and reactive. They devoted considerable effort to the critical examination of terrorist attacks and the lessons learned. A conference report forwarded to Secretary Perry contains detailed recommendations for consideration and implementation.

To better prepare for the terrorist threats of the future and how they might impact on U.S. security interests, DoD in 1994 prepared a major study entitled, Terror-2000: The Future Face of Terrorism. The aim was to forecast the nature of the future terrorist threat, projecting significantly beyond the traditional one year timeframe. The study drew on the expertise and experience of American and foreign terrorism experts in an effort to anticipate changes in terrorist targeting, tactics, strategies, and capabilities. Many of the core predictions have come to pass and others appear increasingly likely. Central to the study were recommendations on how best to meet the future terrorist threat.

In response to the November 1995 bombing in Riyadh, Saudi Arabia, Secretary Perry established the Antiterrorism Task Force. The task force was directed to develop a plan of action to eliminate complacency and significantly enhance the security of DoD and DoD-associated facilities and personnel worldwide. The task force forwarded 22 major initiatives and recommendations to Secretary Perry, who approved an implementation plan on July 15, 1996. The more recent Downing Report, which examined the June 1996 bombing of Khobar Towers, produced a second set of recommendations. These have fundamentally changed the way DoD does business with regard to antiterrorism.

As a result of these two tragedies, a number of initiatives have been implemented. On September 16, 1996, Secretary Perry issued a revised Directive 2000.12, entitled DoD Combating Terrorism Program. This directive mandated Department-wide combating terrorism standards. In recognition that intelligence is the first line of defense, steps are being taken to improve its collection and use, and to get the intelligence product into the hands of the local commanders. DIA is engaged in an aggressive long-term collection and analytic effort designed to provide the type of information that can aid local commanders detect, deter, and prevent terrorist attack.

Close working relationships between DIA and other members of the national intelligence community are being made even stronger, and intelligence exchanges with U.S. friends and allies have been increased. To better protect the public and U.S. military forces from the consequences of a chemical or biological terrorist attack, the Commandant of the Marine Corps established a Chemical/Biological Incident Response Force (CBIRF). Formed in April 1996, the CBIRF is uniquely qualified to perform consequence management in an environment contaminated by chemical or biological agents.

In addition to DoD's accelerated focus on combating terrorism activities, steps are being taken to improve overall force protection. These include giving local commanders operational control over force protection; strengthening cooperation with host nations; raising funding levels of force protection programs, particularly in the area of antiterrorism; making the Chairman of the Joint Chiefs of Staff the focal point for force protection activities, including initiatives to standardize antiterrorism and force protection training for deploying forces; and realigning certain force protection responsibilities from the Department of State to the Department of Defense.

In addition, antiterrorism will be made a special interest item for inspectors general throughout the Department, and the Defense Federal Acquisitions Regulations will be changed to ensure antiterrorism readiness of DoD contractors.

Counterterrorism refers to DoD's offensive combating terrorism capabilities. These capabilities provide means to deter, defeat, and respond vigorously to all terrorist attacks against U.S. interests, wherever they may occur. Resources allocated to these sensitive activities have been significantly increased, and efforts are underway to maximize readiness so that U.S. counterterrorism forces are trained and equipped to meet any challenge posed by future forms of terrorism. U.S. counterterrorism forces receive the most advanced and diverse training available and continually exercise to maintain proficiency and to develop new skills. They regularly train with their foreign counterparts to maximize coordination and effectiveness. They also engage with counterpart organizations in a variety of exchange programs which not only hone their skills but also contribute to the development of mutual confidence and trust.

The war against terrorism will be a protracted conflict. It is war in which there are no front lines and in which terrorism's practitioners have intentionally blurred the distinction between combatants and noncombatants. Terrorism differs from traditional combat because it specifically targets the innocent and, as a result, is particularly repugnant.

Because each terrorist group and the challenge it represents are unique, DoD must work with the interagency counterterrorism community to develop a flexible response that is a mix of political, economic, military, and psycho-social capabilities, tailored to meet a broad range of challenges and threats. Terrorism is more than the bomb and the gun.

It is a struggle that ultimately is fought in the political arena and, as such, is also a war of ideas and ideologies. Combating terrorism requires patience, courage, imagination, and restraint. Perspective is essential. Overreaction and bombast play into terrorist hands. Good intelligence, a professional security force, and a measured response are necessary. Most important for any democracy in its struggle against terrorism is a public that is informed and engaged, and understands the nature of the threat, its potential cost, and why the fight against terrorism is its fight too. It is how well the United States meets this challenge that will determine the winners, the losers, and the price paid by each.

Terrorism In The Twenty-First Century

The Cold War is over but international terrorism remains a threat across the globe and especially to the United States and its allies. When looking at the future of international terrorism, several key questions need to be answered. They are: Why won't the terrorist threat go away? Is terrorism truly a serious threat or just Western paranoia to maintain military and police budgets? Where should terrorist actions be expected and for what reasons? What will be the impact of terrorism on individual nation states and overall global stability? And finally, will peaceful resolution and responses to terrorism be possible or will anti-terrorism efforts merely begin another version of arms escalation, punitive actions, and repressive governmental endeavors? This chapter will explore the global role of terrorism in the twenty-first century, including anti-terrorism responses and the possible consequences to nation states when they respond to terrorist acts.

Present and Future

Terrorism is defined in many ways and in its global context no one definition has gained universal acceptance.

However, for the purposes of this chapter, the definitions will be those contained in Title 22 of the United States Code, Section 2656(d). The US government has employed these definitions since 1983 and they are as follows:

The term "terrorism" means premeditated, politically motivated violence perpetrated against noncombatant (noncombatant is interpreted to include civilians and military personnel unarmed at the time of the incident) targets by subnational groups or clandestine agents, usually intended to influence an audience.

The term "international terrorism" means terrorism involving citizens or the territory of more than one country. The term "terrorist groups" means any group practicing, or that has significant subgroups that practice, international terrorism. What do these definitions tell us? First, international terrorism has not changed significantly in the past ten years despite radical changes in world politics. In fact, changes in the recent political balance of global power have generated increased terrorist activity. In 1982, Grant Wardlow, in Political Terrorism, stated, "Groups with little or no direct political power have demonstrated repeatedly in recent years that by employing certain tactics, central to which is the use of directed terror, they can achieve effects on a target community which are out of all proportion to their numerical or political power."

With reference to the Middle East, Mr. Wardlow's words are more true today than they were then. Despite the peace process and as a direct result of it, Middle Eastern terrorism in 1995 is being used to create unrest and widespread panic among the people of Israel, Egypt, Jordan, and apprehension for the people in the rest of the world. The world was psychologically ready to mark the end of the Cold War as the beginning of global peace.

The world community today is being subjected to the terrorism of the inclusive Middle East; to African terrorism in Angola, Ghana, Nigeria, Rwanda, and Somalia; to Asian terrorism in Afghanistan, India, Sri Lanka, Pakistan, Japan, the Philippines, and South Korea. What many had hoped would be the end of European terrorism is now marked by terrorist activities in Eastern Europe, France, Germany, Greece, Italy, Spain, Turkey, the United Kingdom, and the lands of the former Yugoslavia and the Soviet Union. Finally, Central and South American terrorism is waged in Chile, Columbia, Ecuador, Peru, and Nicaragua. Thus, the decline of animosity among traditional enemies, or the decline of traditional/conventional war as described by Van Creveld in his book, The Transformation of War, does not mean the end of organized violence or a decline in terrorist activity.

Historically, terrorist causes have been classified into two main types with numerous variations and some overlap between them. One broad type is called "nationalist-separatist" terrorism. This category is represented by members of "nations, national minorities, and ethnic or racial groups fighting for freedom from what they regard as foreign rule." Examples include the Irish Republican Army of Northern Ireland, the Spanish Basque ETA, the Palestine Liberation Organization HAMAS, several anti-Turkish Armenian groups, and the Puerto Rican FALN in the United States.

The second type of terrorism is the traditional group. This group bases its actions on political ideology, and is the most complicated. It represents organizations of both the political left and the right, and newly formed environmental groups with mixed ideological followers. Traditionally, these groups comprised Trotskyites, Maoists, Castroites, Che Guevara, Ho Chi Minh followers, West Germany's Baader-Meinhof Gang and its new United Germany offspring, and the Red Army Faction. Also included are Italy's Red Brigades, Argentina's ERP, the Japanese Red Army, and the Turkish People's Liberation Army. These examples of leftist terrorist groups have typically advocated some form of socialism to end "evil and oppression." But the reality of their actions has typically been contempt for authority and often a strong leaning toward anarchism.

The terrorist threat to democratic nation states is also represented by the "right" side of the political spectrum. Right-wing extremists, like the leftists, typically aspire for the violent overthrow of democratic governments in favour of ultra-nationalistic states. Jonathan Harris lists the following examples: The German Military Sports Group Hoffman; Italy's Black Order, Armed Revolutionary Nuclei; National Advanced Guard; Croatian Revolutionary Brotherhood; Spain's Youth Force; Warriors of Christ the King, America's Ku Klux Klan; and the American Nazi Party.

Within the political ideology type there exists a sub-category of terrorist whose ideology is religion-based and usually fundamentalist in nature. The oldest such group is the Muslim Brotherhood in the Middle East. Some new anti-abortion groups in North America responsible for bombings and assassinations, also fit into this category.

State support for terrorism such as that by Cuba, Iran, Libya, North Korea, Syria, South Yemen, and Iraq continues for many of these groups despite United Nations protests or sanctions and/or their political ideology. Terrorism is still a safe strategic weapon for countries, with little chance of punishment or reprisal for their sponsorship.

Additionally, the distinction between domestic and international terrorism is becoming a gray area as most terrorist organizations in pursuit of political change have expanded their operations beyond the borders of their own countries. By operating beyond their borders, terrorists add to the psychological fear equation by threatening to victimize citizens and interests of target countries anywhere in the world.

Terrorist organizations also resort to major criminal activity in addition to terrorist actions. Drug and arms trafficking is becoming a common method for raising money for terrorist activities. The recent alliance between drug traffickers in Peru and Columbia and terrorist organizations for mutual benefit, with added political impact with their own populations and governments, is an example of this new trend.

The number of terrorist incidents around the world continues to increase each year despite the best efforts of security forces. The United States, long considered invincible against terrorist attacks, has suffered more terrorist acts in the past two years than during the height of terrorist activity in 1983, and despite the massive counter-terrorism effort of the late eighties. The takeover of the Iranian Mission at the United Nations in New York in 1992 and the bombing of the World Trade Center in 1993 changed the face of terrorism for most Americans and the world. Not only was America no longer invincible, but small, loosely organized groups with radical agendas and insulated sponsorships, could act with basic immunity. The Oklahoma City bombing in 1995 only served to reinforce the severity of the problem.

While Americans could take some comfort that the rate of attacks against the United States interests and personnel fell in 1993, the salient point remains that one quarter of all attacks worldwide that year were directed at the United States. It is expected that Americans will continue to be targets because of their international presence and the worldwide media coverage experienced when Americans are targeted. These modern terrorists have changed their tactics as the world has changed. While revolutionary terrorism has prevailed for several decades, the current rise in ethnic and religious groups willing to use terrorist tactics to achieve their ends will cause major problems to global security and to individual nation states. The modern nation state, with its sophisticated infrastructure and its advanced technology systems, will find itself the most vulnerable to disruption and terrorist action.

Regardless of terrorist motivation, support, or organizational structure, terrorist behaviour should be understood for what it represents. Terrorist acts should be looked upon as "war." It is a war built on a strategy of intimidation and fear. Fear is a key to the strategy because it accomplishes the required dissemination of the terrorist's communication.

In its simplest form, the terrorist provides a "fear producing event" which is followed by media distribution of that event to the greatest extent possible. Manipulation of populations and media resources is crucial to the overall impact of the message. The reaction of the Japanese population to the 1995 subway chemical attack by a cult, with plans for additional nerve gas attacks, is a perfect example of the "war of fear" at work.

Future areas of concern

Terrorism in the future will be focused in four specific areas. Each area may impact others but, for the purposes of this paper, each should be considered self-contained and a primary focus for future terrorist acts. Additionally, most experts agree that no one "typical" terrorist threat will destroy a nation's sovereignty or destabilize the world. However, the extent or scope of individual terrorist acts is unlimited, and as shown in Japan, the self-imposed boundaries of terrorist groups can change overnight. The heretofore avoidance of chemical, biological, and nuclear terrorist acts has been broken. A violent act of mass destruction could, depending on the event, cause world reactions such as national boycotts, suspension of civil rights within a country, or international discrimination of a racial or ethnic group in a manner not previously considered by "the experts."

The first area of future terrorism is the economic sphere. As world nations become more interdependent in trade blocks, and multi-national corporate organizations increase the gap between prosperous versus non-prosperous nation-states, the opportunities for economic terrorism will expand. Groups using terrorist tactics can influence economics for either financial or political gain. The Chilean Grape Incident of 1989 is an excellent example.

In March 1989, at the waterfront in Philadelphia, inspectors of the US Food and Drug Administration, acting on an anonymous tip, examined crates of grapes arriving from Chile and discovered two cyanide-laced grapes. The evidence was the Chilean fruit had been poisoned. No citizen anywhere reported eating the tainted grapes. However, the world reacted. Chilean fruit was temporarily banned, triggering severe economic and political turmoil.

The Chilean grape incident is an example of traditional revolutionary terrorism, state-sponsored terrorism, or political terrorism. Yet the underlying motivation appears to have been economic. Trading between competing economies and nation states can include everything from protectionism, to dominating markets, to economic ruin. The rise of an insurgent Indian group within Mexico, just prior to the NAFTA agreement between Mexico and the United States, may be viewed as an issue of economic force and control. Some of the group's actions were called terrorist in nature. However, the group described itself as an economic insurgent movement.

The second area of future terrorism emanates from religious fundamentalism. The threat is worldwide, concentrated in the Muslim states, but by no means inclusive to those states. Much of the Muslim terrorist movement is supported and motivated by Iran. Along with Sudan and Syria, Iran considers terrorism to be a primary instrument of state policy. In addition, Iran's organizing struggle between its secular and religious factions has limited its interaction with other nation states and contributed to its isolation. The ascendancy of the religious extremists has expanded Iran's economic problems. Thus, it may appear logical for the leading mullahs to declare a Jihad against the West, (particularly the United States), the "Great Satan," as a means to shift away from internal problems, to support Islam in a growing secular world, and to restore the Islamic revolutionary spirit both at home and abroad.

Iran has led the world for the past four years as the most active state sponsor of terrorism. They have been implicated in terrorist attacks in Italy, Turkey, and Pakistan. Their intelligence services support terrorist acts, either directly or through extremist groups. Iranian intelligence agents are under arrest in Germany and France for their links to murders of Iranian dissidents. Iran is the preeminent sponsor of extremist Islamic and Palestinian groups. They provide funds, weapons, and training to Hizballah, the PIJ, the PLP-GC and HAMAS.

The premise of Iran leading a worldwide terrorist campaign against the West and the United States fulfills two major requirements for the leaders of Tehran. First, it provides both a moral and symbolic attack against those forces (US) that represent evil to Islam. Second, it provides the clear message of fear to both the Iranian people and neighboring nations that no individual or nation is above the wrath of Iran.

The Iranian leadership may feel confident in this behaviour based on earlier terrorist action. Bodansky in his work, TERROR illustrates the point:

Tehran has reason to be confident....two major terrorist strikes against the United States: the mid-air explosion of Pan Am flight 103 over Locherbie, Scotland on December, 1988, and, in San Diego, California, on March 10, 1989, the fire-bombing of a van driven by Sharon Lee Rodgers, wife of the captain of the USS Vincennes, who had mistakenly shot down the Iranian Airbus commercial flight in July 1988."

Additionally, Iran is the main source of support for the fundamentalist regime in Sudan, and for the Kurdistan Workers Party (PKK) which has been responsible for hundreds of terrorist acts in Turkey. The Iranian fundamentalists are currently the most active in terrorist activity around the world. Religious ideologies have long been associated with terrorism and the support of violence for religious purposes. The doctrines of Christian (Catholic and Protestant), Muslim (Shi'a and Sunni), Jewish, Hindu and Sikh religions have all been used to justify terrorism. Religious fundamentalism and dogma have provided individuals the support to carry out their fanatical or terrorist activities. However, it should be clearly understood that the vast majority of those who support fundamentalist movements do not become terrorists or even support violent activity.

The intensity of a fundamentalist terrorist differs little from a political, ethnic, or national terrorist. The added concept of having "God on your side" and promise of life after death adds a divine variable to the terrorist equation. These groups have recently been called "Superterrorists" because of their access to nuclear, chemical, biological, and conventional weapons, and computer technology. The true global threat from these terrorists is their willingness to use their new weapons. Since these terrorist targets represent "the unholy or unclean," the traditional terrorist objective of political control is substituted with destruction of "evil." As a result, the terrorists' use of nuclear, biological, and chemical weapons is considered ideal.

The terrorism of these fundamentalist groups is ideologically and religiously driven. It is critical for the leadership of these groups to present in a constant and conclusive way, the "rightness" of their views to their followers. The leaders of these organizations will take unilateral and arbitrary actions. However, these same leaders will attempt to legitimize their actions, their support, and the reactions of the world to them by addressing their own populations. The bombing of the World Trade Center should then be viewed as having a primary target audience made up of Islamic fundamentalists worldwide versus only Americans.

When non-traditional religious groups or cults are added to fundamentalist terrorist groups, the behaviours become even more confusing and unpredictable. An example of this is the Japanese subway cult attack which should be considered a peek into the future instead of a non-repeatable event. The third area of future terrorism will be "Technology Terror." The information and computer highway of our future also includes a fast lane for terrorists. Modern technology has made it possible for smaller, more radical groups to access sophisticated means of destruction without significant support systems or funding.

As computer systems become more powerful and cheaper, terrorists will develop greater ability to impact resources, intelligence, and terror operations with little or no risk, depending on advances "yet to be made" by the anti-terrorist forces. Using information warfare tools, terrorists will have access to the vast amounts of financial resources that travel the information highways. By using and attacking these financial conduits, terrorists can not only transfer funding from outside sponsors, but can illegally tap these vulnerable conduits to obtain the required informational resources to sustain their activities. They can cripple the financial markets by either direct attacks or by instilling a credibility gap in the electronic financial world.

As noted in the book, Information Warfare, "Money is the network that comprises hundreds of thousands of computers of every type, wired together in places as lofty as the Federal Reserve...and as mundane as the thousands of gas pumps around the world outfitted to take credit and debit cards." In addition to being a possible funding conduit, information warfare techniques can also provide the terrorist with an invaluable source of intelligence; from sharing information on bomb making with other organizations, to targeting individual travelers through the airline reservation system, to stealing military secrets through the ever expanding Internet presence by military organizations. Information warfare provides an invaluable aid to the intelligence-gathering ability of the modern, high-tech terrorist.

The information highway not only allows access to this vast wealth of information but allows access to this information from places safely within the borders of their safe havens. The use of the information highway can also provide the terrorist the ability to coordinate remote multiple-cell activity with very little possibility of discovery, and provide the terrorist a method for attracting worldwide attention to their acts of violence almost as the events are unfolding. This can make the command, control, and intelligence techniques used on the military battlefield available to terrorist groups worldwide.

Besides the support functions of managing resources, gathering intelligence, and disseminating information, the most obvious use of information warfare techniques is to create terror or chaos and wreak havoc against a target. When considering the use of information warfare techniques by terrorists, the first consideration is given to the most vulnerable target to information warfare attacks. By its very nature, information warfare attacks are most effective where the information highway has made the greatest inroads into people's everyday lives, business and governmental functions, and defense. Thus, the modern westernized societies are much more vulnerable to information warfare than are Third World nations. This vulnerability also corresponds to the nations most targeted by terrorists.

The types of terror that can be created by astute information warfare terrorists range from targeting key individuals to influencing decisions favourable to terrorist causes, to attacks that cause massive destruction and loss of life. A few examples follow for illustrative purposes. On the personal level, terrorists could use the information highway to gather incriminating information on key decision makers from cyberspace. Whether it is past bad check writing activity, subscribing to pornographic magazines, belonging to non-politically correct groups, or having a medical condition that has remained a secret, people in powerful positions of influence often have material in their past that might make them vulnerable to coercion.

However, if their past is not tainted, the terrorist could begin sowing the seeds of corruption along the electronic highway by altering credit history databases, banking records, mailing lists, medical records, etc. in enough detail to compromise the individuals despite their innocence. In the book, Information Warfare, Winn Schwartau recounts one incident about an individual being bombarded with hate mail and police inquiries because of a request for pedophilia information being sent by using their identification when in fact he sent no such request. Thus, information warfare tools in the hands of the terrorist have the potential to either influence or discredit influential individuals.

On the corporate level, terrorists could use information warfare techniques to cripple corporations physically or economically. Using techniques such as Trojan Horses, viruses, or spoofing, corporate information systems could be rendered inoperative by terrorist attacks. These attacks could bring systems such as corporate research and development, financial data management, personnel information, and shipping and receiving to a grinding halt.

The cost to corporations could be millions of dollars. Even without physically crippling these systems, enough doubt could be instilled in the operators of the systems to render the systems worthless. Examples include, faulty bookkeeping software, inventory control systems that generate random numbers, and shipping and invoicing systems that become so unreliable that they can no longer be trusted. With these unreliable systems, vast quantities of manpower have to be expended to ensure accuracy in the data that has become the life blood of the corporation.

Other examples of terrorism against corporations include: industrial espionage, modifying tests results in order to give inaccurate data, and release of data that would discredit the corporation or individuals within the corporation. Thus, besides being able to hold individuals hostage, terrorists could also hold corporations hostage through the use of their own information systems. On a more global level, nations become vulnerable to terrorist attacks through the use of information warfare techniques. National infrastructure such as banks, switched telephone systems, power grids, and air traffic control stations are but a few examples of targets that could cause massive disruption of life in a developed state if attacked. Nuclear power plants with bad controller chips, jamming of air craft transponders, and theft of national security information from military networks are other examples that could cause massive destruction and loss of life.

In addition to computers, terrorist groups have moved into the technology and missile age with hardware and human intelligence. For example, in 1973 it was rare for terrorists to use missile attacks. Today these missile attacks are common place. However, the future wave of technical terrorism will include more than missiles. These new technical terrorists will be intelligent, creative, and will have learned from past terrorist activities worldwide. In their book, Final Warning 1989, Kupperman and Kamen discuss a scenario where a Middle East terrorist group obtained nerve agents for a terrorist strike.

In 1995, a quasi-religious cult carried out a similar attack in Japan in a Tokyo subway; 16 people were killed and over 5,000 were injured. The police investigation revealed a terrorist plot of international mass destruction (for as yet undetermined religious reasons) by members of the Aum Shinri Kyo, or Supreme Truth Organization. Included among the cult membership are 30 cult chemists who worked for the cult's Science and Technology Ministry. According to police sources the 30 chemists are suspected of preparing the chemical, sarin, that was used in the subway attack. A terrorist organization with a Science and Technology Ministry may not be typical of past terrorist organizations; however, this high technology computer based organization is more mainstream than the world would expect.

The fourth area of future terrorism will be what Donald Hanle refers to as "apolitical terrorism," or terrorism for nonpolitical ends. There is some controversy with the apolitical category as some experts feels all terrorist acts have a political or social foundation, and, as such, should fall under the political umbrella. However, recent terrorist events around the world clearly indicate that some areas of terrorist activity do fall under the apolitical category. The apolitical terrorist should be considered the most dangerous type of terrorist. The availability of modern technology, nuclear, chemical, and biological weapons, combined with someone with a criminal or unbalanced psychological mindset, makes for an ominous concern.

An individual or small group of individuals with personal motives could carry out an event of mass destruction with relative ease and success. Additionally, such an individual or group will probably be available for hire on a national or global market. Modern technology, computers, and information resources all tend to facilitate the interaction and communication of both individuals and groups. The recent 19 April 1995 bombing in Oklahoma City of the federal building which left 167 people dead could be considered apolitical under certain conditions. If the two accused bombers, Terry Nichols and Timothy McVeigh, do not represent a particular group, organization, or movement, but rather were acting out their own anti-social and anti-government views, the terrorist act would not be exclusively politically motivated.

The act could then be described as the abnormal behaviour of two individuals based on either "psychotic" thinking in the grave sense and or criminal behaviour in the narrow sense. The psychotic thinking scenario is adequately describe by Hanle as, "...estranged and fragmented individuals...lose self identity and doomed by soulless bureaucracy..."

Another example of apolitical terrorism is the "Unibomber" in the United States. The Unibomber has attacked over a period of 17 years; his latest victim being a lobbyist for the timber industry. The victim was killed by a package bomb that went off in his Sacramento, California office. During the Unibomber's 17 year reign of terror, three victims have been killed and twenty-three have been injured. The Victims represent varied backgrounds and a particular motive or orientation to the terrorist is unknown. Both the FBI and local law enforcement agencies believe the Unibomber is brazen, typically cool, uncontrolled, and psychologically unstable. Unlike most political terrorist groups or state sponsored groups, the apolitical terrorist has little concern for political or economic repercussions.

As terrorism enters the twenty-first century and impacts the global community, a limited number of options will be available to counter the new threats. One option which received some success after the World Trade Center bombing is the economic incentive or bounty. After the

World Trade Center attack, the United States government offered a reward of several million dollars for the person or persons responsible for the attack. An informant in Pakistan provided the information that led to the arrest of Ramzi Yousef as the mastermind of the 1993 terrorist act. Yousef was arrested in Islamabad, Pakistan and immediately extradited to the United States (New York) where he awaits trial. An unfortunate follow-up to the arrest is the speculation that the subsequent killing in Pakistan of two American embassy personnel was revenge for the Yousef extradition.

The reward program is complicated because Pakistan is in the middle of sectarian violence between Sunni and Shiite Muslim groups. These groups not only engage fundamentalist terrorist activity, but overlap with the country's powerful drug Mafia and the Militant Muslim groups. This ongoing terrorist activity complicates the bounty program but does not negate it. Thus, the United States government, in an attempt repeats the success of its original "reward program," offered two million dollars in bounty for the killers of the two United States government workers.

A second option for Global Nation States against terrorism is "national resolve." It should be acknowledged that a foolproof system against terrorism in democratic societies does not exist. In the words of terrorism expert Stephen Sloan, "...there can never be a totally effective program to deter or prevent a determined adversary from seeking softer targets of opportunity in what he perceives to be a justified war against all." Simple procedures such as better intelligence and improved physical security of critical sites will, in most cases, deter a particular terrorist group. However, the overall result may be additional casualties, such as the revenge killings in Pakistan. A terrorist group deprived of a particular target will typically seek a more accessible alternative target.

The key point for the public of any nation attempting to combat terrorism, now as in the future, is that terrorist activity will take place and causalities will occur. As was evident after the Oklahoma City bombing, additional funding and legislation will result in the hardening of targets and drive some terrorist organizations underground. The realization for global society is that technology attacks, conventional or unconventional attacks, including hostage taking, will continue. The terrorist requirement for media coverage will typically exceed a democratic society's inclination to control the media or the public's demand for news. Thus, the future of our global society is more terrorism rather than less terrorism. Much of that terrorism will be religious and ethnic based. Economics, technology, and the whims of both criminal and psychotics will have ongoing and, at times, spectacular events. Additionally, terrorism has reached America both domestically and internationally. A result of terrorism in America will be more public and political efforts to counter terrorism by the West. Sadly, terrorism in the Third World and in developing countries will continue almost unabated.

Bibliography

Adams, James. *The Financing of Terror,* New York: Simon & Schuster, 1986.

Alexander, Yonah and Richard Latter, eds. *Terrorism and the Media: Dilemmas for Government, Journalists & the Public,* Washington, DC: Brassey's, 1990.

Andersan, Sean and Stephen Solan. *Historical Dictionary of Terrorism,* 2nd ed. Lanham, MD: Scarecrow, 2002.

Atkins, Stephen E. *Terrorism: A Reference Handbook,* Santa Barbara, CA: 1992.

Bell, J. Bower. *Transnational Terror, Washington,* DC: American Enterprise Institute, 1975.

Burton, Anthony. *Urban Terrorism: Theory, Practice, Response,* London: Cooper, 1975.

Chaliand, Gerald. *Terrorism: From Popular Struggle to Media Spectacle,* Atlantic Highlands, NJ: Saqi, 1987.

Comb, Cindy C. *Terrorism in Twenty-First Century,* 2nd ed. Upper Saddle River, NJ: Prentice Hall, 2002.

Crelinsten, Ronald D. and Denis Szabo. *Hostage- Taking,* Lexington, MA: Lexington Book, 1979.

Crenshaw, Martha. *Terrorism, Legitimacy, and Power,* Middletown, CT: Wesleyan University Press, 1983.

George, Alexander, ed. *Western State Terrorism,* New York: Routledge, 1991.

Gurr, Ted Robert. *Handbook of Political Conflict: Theory and Research,* New York: Free Press, 1980.

Harmon, Christopher C. *Terrorism Today,* London: Frank Cass, 2002.

Hoffman, Bruce. *Inside Terrorism,* New York: Columbia University Press, 1998.

Jenkins, Brian. *International Terrorism: The Other World War,* Santa Monica, CA: RAND, 1985.

Kushner, Harvey W. ed. *The Future of Terrorism: Violence in the New Millennium,* Thousand Oaks, CA: Sage, 1998.

Laqueur, Walter. *History of Terrorism,* New York: Transaction Publishers, 2001.

Lesser, Ian O. et al. *Countering the New Terrorism,* Santa Monica, CA: RAND, 1999.

Lewis Bernand. *The Political Language of Islam,* Chicago: University of Chicago Press, 1988.

Miller, Abraham H. *Terrorism and Hostage Negotiations,* Boulder, CO: Westview, 1980.

Moss, Robert. *Urban Guerrilla Warfare,* London: International Institute for Strategic Studies, 1971.

Netanyahu, Benzamin. *The Terrorism Reader,* New York: Meridian, 1986.

O'Neill, Bard E. *Insurgency and Terrorism: Inside Modern Revolutionary Warfare,* Washington, DC: Brassey's, 1990.

Peters, Rudolph. *Jihad in Classical and Modern Islam,* Princeton, NJ: Markus Wiener, 1996.

Picard, Robert G. *Media Portrayals of Terrorism: Functions and Meaning of News Coverage,* Ames: Iowa State University Press, 1993.

Pillar, Paul R. and Michael H. Armacost. *Terrorism and U.S. Foreign Policy, Washington,* DC: Brookings Institution, 2001.

Rashid, Ahmed. Jihad: *The Rise of Militant Islam I Central Asia,* New Haven, CT: Yale University Press, 2002.

Rosie, George. *The Dictionary of International Terrorism,* New York: Paragon House, 1987.

Schamis, Geraldo Jorge. *War and Terrorism in International Affairs,* New Brunswick, NJ: Transaction Publishers, 1980.

Segaller, Stephen. *Invisible Armies: Terrorism in the 1990s,* San Diego, CA: Harcourt Brace Jovanovich, 1987.

Sofaer, Abraham D. and Seymour E. Goodman. *The Transnational Dimension of Cyber Crime and Terrorism,* Stanford, CA: Hoover Institution, 2001.

Sonn, Richard D. *Anarchism,* New York: Twayne, 1992.

Stern, Jessia. *The Ultimate Terrorists,* Cambridge, MA: Harvard University Press, 1999.

Tanter, Raymond. *Rogue Regimes: Terrorism and Proliferation,* New York: St. Maytin's, 1998.

Tucker, Jonathan B. *Toxic Terror: Assessing Terrorist Use of Chemical and Biological Weapons,* Cambridge, MA: MIT Press, 2000.

U.S. Department of State, *Patterns of Global Terrorism,* Washington, DC [Annual].

Venzke, Ben N. *First Responder Chem- Bio Handbook,* Alexandria, VA: Tempest, 1998.

Wardlaw, Grant. *Political Terrorism: Theory, Tactics, and Counter-Measures,* New York: Cambridge University Press, 1989.

White, Jonathan R. *Terrorism: An Introduction,* 3rd ed. Belmont, CA: Wadsworth, 2001.

Whittaker, David J. *The Terrorism Reader,* London and New York: Routledge, 2001.

Zinn, Howard. *Terrorism and War*, New York: Seven Stories, 2002.

Index

A

American front 90
Anarchic areas 39, 52, 63
Areas of cooperation 120, 121
Assistance agreement 111, 112
Attribution error 297, 311, 313

B

Bilateral agreements 111

C

Chechen terrorism 129, 131
Combating terrorism 10, 28, 30, 32, 31, 51, 60, 124, 321, 323, 324, 325, 326, 331, 334, 335, 336
Commissioner 96
Cataclysmic nature 5
Communal roots 44
Counterterrorism 27, 31, 32, 37, 38, 39, 40, 41, 44, 51, 54, 58, 61, 83, 85, 89, 90, 91, 107, 119, 120, 121, 122, 133, 134, 135, 136, 232, 314, 335

D

Defeating new terrorist 127, 129, 131, 133, 135, 137, 139, 141, 143, 145, 147
Defending against terrorism 12
Diplomatic sanctions 53
Disagreements 91, 119, 124, 125, 135, 137
Dubious public perceptions 296
Developmental psychobiology 168
Diplomatic sanctions 53
Divine retribution 5
Dual-use goods 121
Dubious authenticity 121

E

Earthly peace 133, 134, 136, 141, 142, 144
Eastern terrorism 35, 37, 38, 50, 57, 64, 337
Economic sanctions 49, 54, 55, 56, 288
Economic terrorism 6, 342
Ethice of war 239
Exposure to terrorism 152
External affairs 96
Extradition agreement 111, 112

F

Fight against terrorism 32, 103, 109, 115, 118, 119, 121, 127, 180, 322, 323, 324, 336

Frightening prospect 319
Future battlefields 85
Fatwa 72
Foreign states 185
Future terrorism 25
Future threat 89
Future possible 283
Future terrorism 25, 342, 345

G

Governments to legislate 318

H

Hackers turned terrorist 211
History of tolerance 241
Horn of Africa 88

I

Improve security 321
Influence child 163, 165
Industrial laboratories 4
Institutional factor 300
Intelligence 29, 57, 59, 60, 189, 191, 295, 310, 332
Interfaith encounters 133, 142
Internal security 39, 58, 59, 62
International cooperation 57, 58, 133, 137, 145, 177, 289

J

Judicial cooperation 92, 107, 111, 122
Jihadists 86

L

Legitimate target 1
Liberal approach 115
Long-term ramifications 17
Living beyond fear 133, 140
Long-term prevention 146

M

Mobilize reluctant allies 38, 56
Moderated 161, 164
Mutant jihads 83
Millennial visions 65

N

Natural disasters 15, 149, 154, 157, 173
Neurotoxins 3
Non- proliferation 116
Non-military means 104

O

Oklahoma 17, 18, 19, 20, 22, 66, 74, 81, 161, 163, 166, 220, 245, 276, 277, 284, 288, 340, 350, 352
Organizational factors 75
Obscure target 18
Ominous trend 2

P

Pathological responses 167
Personal exposure 154, 155
Prayerful quest 144
Psychobiology 152, 168
Psychopathology 149, 150, 151, 155, 157, 158, 161, 296
Political constituencies 24
political endgame 49
Potential target 203
Pragmatic reservations 69

Preemptive war 95
Prime suspects 39
Public memory 33

R

Radical islamic 35, 36, 39, 40, 43, 44, 45, 47, 49, 56, 58, 59, 60
Regional conflicts 116
Religious agenda 73
Retro-fit building 21
Retaliate 11, 38, 58

S

School shootings 157, 159, 166
School systems 164
Suicide terrorism 293, 295, 297, 299, 301, 303, 305, 307, 309
Support and criticism 179
Security administrators 221
Sleeper cells 44
Sophisticated technologies 26
Store backup tapes 19
Systemic disruption 81

T

Techno terrorism 199
Threatened 9, 38, 49, 59, 60, 95, 104, 149, 162, 177, 178, 214
Transatlantic divergences 92, 106
Transition 13, 23, 24, 90, 272, 327, 328
Traumatic 148, 149, 150, 151, 152, 153, 155, 156, 157, 158, 160, 163, 164, 165, 166, 167

U

Unibomber 350
Unilaterally 38, 58, 92, 96, 101, 177, 250
Urban combat 100
Upgrade counterterrorism 39, 60

V

Virus library 190
Vulnerability 21, 24, 27, 28, 46, 52, 66, 82, 89, 133, 136, 140, 160, 162, 201, 206, 221, 226

W

War and terrorism 148, 149, 151, 153, 154, 155, 160, 173
Warfare 7, 8, 18, 28, 38, 52, 59
World trade center bombing 4, 17, 18, 35, 36, 229, 351
Worldwide war 86

Preemptive war 60
Prime suspects 59
Public memory 39

R

Radical Islamic [illegible] 80, 84
 [illegible] 43, 47, 49, 56, [illegible]
Regional conflicts 119
Reform agenda [illegible]
Retreat [illegible] 21
Retaliate 11, 38, [illegible]

S

School shooting 127, [illegible], 168
School systems 104
Suicide terrorism 273, [illegible], 297, 298, [illegible], 302, 305, [illegible], 309
Support and criticism 170
[illegible] 23
[illegible] 11
Sophisticated [illegible] technologies 26
[illegible] 29
Systemic disruption 33

T

Terror [illegible] 199
[illegible] 6, 38, 40, 79, 93, 99, [illegible] 177, 178, 234
Transnational divergences 92, 105
Transition 13, 24, 90, 272, 277, 278
Trauma [illegible] 148, 149, 150, 151, 152, 153, 155, 156, 157, 158, 160, 163, 164, 165, 166, 167

U

Unilateral [illegible]
Unilaterally 26, 58, 92, 96, 101, 172, 250
Union congress 100
Upgrade counterterrorism 34, 60

V

Virtual library 190
[illegible]

W

War and terrorism 148, 149, 151, [illegible]
[illegible]
World trade center bombing 5, [illegible]
Worldwide war 19